THE COMPLETE BOOK OF
MAIN COURSES

THE COMPLETE BOOK OF
MAIN COURSES

THE WORLD'S MOST POPULAR RECIPES: OVER 180 TIMELESS DISHES WITH
STEP-BY-STEP INSTRUCTIONS AND OVER 800 FABULOUS PHOTOGRAPHS

Jenni Fleetwood

HERMES
HOUSE

This edition is published by Hermes House an imprint of Anness Publishing Ltd
Hermes House, 88–89 Blackfriars Road, London SE1 8HA
tel. 020 7401 2077; fax 020 7633 9499; info@anness.com

www.hermeshouse.com; www.annesspublishing.com

If you like the images in this book and would like to investigate using them for publishing, promotions or advertising,
please visit our website www.practicalpictures.com for more information.

Publisher: Joanna Lorenz
Editorial Director: Helen Sudell
Editor: Joy Wotton
Production Controller: Pedro Nelson
Designers: Nigel Partridge, Steers McGillan Ltd and Sarah Williams
Recipes: Alex Barker, Carla Capalbo, Lesley Chamberlain, Jacqueline Clark, Roz Denny, Patrizia Diemling, Matthew Drennan,
Joanna Farrow, Valerie Ferguson, Jenni Fleetwood, Silvano Franco, Yasuko Fukuoka, Shirley Gill, Brian Glover, Nicola Graimes,
Juliet Harbutt, Deh-Ta Hsiung, Christine Ingram, Manisha Kanani, Emi Kasuko, Lucy Knox, Gilly Love, Lesley Mackley,
Norma MacMillan, Jane Milton, Sallie Morris, Keith Richmond, Anne Sheasby, Marlena Spieler, Linda Tubby,
Laura Washburn, Kate Whiteman
Photographers: Nicki Dowey, Michelle Garrett, Amanda Heywood, Janine Hosegood, David Jordan, Dave King, William Lingwood,
Thomas Odulate, Craig Robertson and Sam Stowell

ETHICAL TRADING POLICY
Because of our ongoing ecological investment programme, you, as our customer, can have the pleasure and reassurance of knowing
that a tree is being cultivated on your behalf to naturally replace the materials used to make the book you are holding.
For further information about this scheme, go to www.annesspublishing.com/trees

© Anness Publishing Ltd 2005, 2007

Previously published as part of a larger compendium, *The Ultimate Book of Main Course Dishes*

NOTES
All nutritional information is given per portion unless otherwise stated.
Bracketed terms are intended for American readers.
For all recipes, quantities are given in both metric and imperial measures and, where appropriate, measures are also given in standard
cups and spoons. Follow one set, but not a mixture, because they are not interchangeable.
Standard spoon and cup measures are level.
1 tsp = 5ml, 1 tbsp = 15ml, 1 cup = 250ml/8fl oz
Australian standard tablespoons are 20ml. Australian readers should use 3 tsp in place of 1 tbsp for measuring small quantities of
flour, salt etc.
Medium (US large) eggs are used unless otherwise stated.

CONTENTS

INTRODUCTION

Fifty years ago, main dishes were just that – the most important part of any meal and the course around which all others revolved. Most cookbooks of that era focused on the roast, the casserole or the mixed grill, paying scant attention to any other dishes. Then came the food revolution. People started eating out more and, as they dwelt on the delights of appetizers and desserts, main dishes started to take second place. In some restaurants, main courses disappeared entirely. Now it appears as though the pendulum has swung again. Nostalgia, coupled with nutritional advice that stresses the importance of eating small amounts of protein with plenty of vegetables, has put the main course back where it rightfully belongs – as the pivotal part of every meal.

However, the main course still has something of an image problem. Appetizers and desserts are seen as enticing and exciting, but main courses seem to have earned adjectives like "comforting", "robust", "satisfying" and "rib-sticking". When it comes to planning a special occasion meal, most of us have no difficulty in deciding what to serve for the first and final courses – it's what comes between the first and the last that proves to be the most problematic.

That's where this book comes in. With over 185 recipes you need never struggle for inspiration again. In fact, the difficulty will lie in deciding what to choose from this superb collection, whether it be a colourful healthy salad, a stunning soufflé, a pasta dish or the full works in the form of a meat or chicken roast or a hearty casserole.

BREAKING THE RULES

The days of the marathon meal – with an appetizer or soup leading to the fish course, followed by a main dish, a sorbet (sherbet), dessert, crackers and cheese and, finally, coffee – have largely disappeared. And today it is perfectly acceptable simply to serve guests a satisfying stew with lots of deliciously crusty bread for mopping up the juices, a beautiful baked fish with a pile of buttery new potatoes or a home-baked pie with a crisp salad. The rule is that there are virtually no rules, so that when you are entertaining at home, you can dispense with soups and appetizers altogether, if you like, or you can simply offer guests canapés with their drinks as they arrive.

The classic meat-and-two-veg theme has also vanished as more people have either become vegetarians or simply chosen to limit the amount of meat they eat. Today, a main course can be a roulade, a pie, a risotto, a substantial soup – or anything else you choose to serve. A curry with a cooling raita and plump Peshwari naan would go down well, as would a home-made pizza with a stylish marinara topping. It is even perfectly acceptable to serve sausages and mash and, if you prop the sausages on a mound of spicy mashed sweet potato and surround them with caramelized onions, you'll be recreating a fashionable restaurant dish that will delight your guests.

You don't necessarily have to serve vegetables alongside your chosen main dish either. Instead, they can star in the appetizer or appear in a salad, served French-style as a separate course. When serving vegetables, consider a fresh medley of steamed batons of carrots, leeks and celery, for instance, or a mixture of roast vegetables. That way you cut down on last-minute cooking, and avoid the flurry in the kitchen when your guests have just arrived. You'll have time to make them welcome.

Although the rules may have been relaxed somewhat, some of the old suggestions remain intact, simply because they make good sense. Whatever you choose to serve, the

Left: A filling risotto made with fresh seafood is an elegant and delicious alternative to a traditional meat-and-three-vegetable main meal.

meal should always be balanced in terms of flavours, colours and textures. For example, it wouldn't be a good idea to serve a creamy mousse as a main course then follow it with a silky-smooth dessert, or to serve a juicy Thai stew or curry after a soup. If the main course is quite dry, for example a

country meat loaf, it should be accompanied by a succulent side dish, such as creamed leeks or mushrooms. It also makes good sense to try and avoid using the same ingredients in successive courses as repeatedly encountering the same flavours and textures can be boring.

THE FINER DETAILS

The appearance of the food on the plate has become just as important as the actual dish itself, so do give some thought to the colours and shapes of the ingredients used in the dish. Although the ubiquitous sprig of parsley seems to have been consigned to the great herb garden in the sky, more interesting garnishes, such as tiny bunches of redcurrants, braided chives or cucumber ribbons can add colour and shape to any plate. Just make sure

Left: Casseroles and curries are best served as a main course when they are not preceded by soups.

Above: Beautifully presented and elegantly garnished food will create a sophisticated look.

the garnish is appropriate – try lemon wedges with a fish dish, a fresh sprig of herbs on a vegetable stew, or spring onion curls with an Asian curry.

STRESS-FREE COOKING

When planning any meal, make life easy for yourself by preparing or cooking as much as possible ahead of time. Ease a heavy workload by using kitchen appliances such as the microwave oven, food processor and any other time-saving appliances you may have. Make use of your fridge and freezer – many dishes are even better when made ahead of time and reheated.

Most importantly, enjoy yourself – cooking and sharing good food with friends and family is one of life's greatest pleasures, so master these main dishes and you'll have many wonderful meals in store.

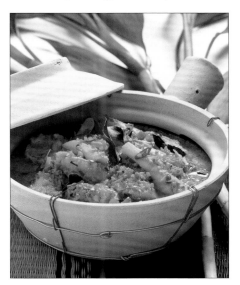

PREPARING AND COOKING AHEAD

The marvellous thing about many main dishes is that they can be prepared in advance and cooked when required. Not only does this keep stress levels low but it also ensures that success levels remain high. Slow-cooked dishes, such as casseroles and stews, are also a boon as they need little attention and reward the cook by quietly gaining in flavour as they simmer in the oven. At the other end of the spectrum are dishes such as stir-fries and salads, which need little or no cooking. This time, careful preparation is the key. Salad leaves can be washed and dried, then bagged and put in the refrigerator. Not only will they be ready to toss together at the last minute, but they will also become crisper on standing. Stir-fry vegetables should all be cut to a similar size. Although it is not a good idea to do this too far ahead, because valuable nutrients will be lost, such advance preparation is helpful when you know you will be in a hurry later.

COOKING IN ADVANCE

Dishes such as stews, curries and casseroles often benefit from being made the day before they are to be served. This allows time for the flavours of the different ingredients to meld. If it is more convenient, you can cook dishes like this even further ahead,

Right: The components of a salad can be prepared in advance, ready for last-minute assembly when required.

freeze them and defrost them when you need to. The food must be cold before being placed in the freezer. Let it cool for a little, then place the dish or pot in a sink of very cold or iced water to accelerate the chilling process. Some china is designed to withstand extremes of temperature and can be used in both the oven and the freezer, but it is not recommended that you switch between the two without either allowing the hot food to cool, or the frozen food to thaw completely. It is best to thaw dishes overnight in the refrigerator. If you use a microwave for thawing, always follow the instructions in your handbook, and stir the stew or casserole frequently as it thaws, to make sure the item thaws evenly. When thawing a large block of frozen food in the microwave, it is a good idea to defrost it in short bursts, with a resting time between each, so that the heat that is generated spreads throughout the defrosting food and is not concentrated only in certain areas.

Rather than tie up a favourite straight-sided casserole or gratin dish by transferring it to the freezer for several weeks, tip the contents into a pan or dish, then wash the casserole or

dish and line it with microwave-proof film (wrap). Return the casserole or stew to the dish, and place it in the freezer. Lift out the contents when frozen, then double wrap and label the block and return it to the freezer. When you want to serve the food, just unwrap the block and return it to the original dish for thawing and reheating.

LEFTOVERS

As with freshly cooked food intended for the freezer, leftovers should be cooled quickly if they are to be kept for another meal. Leaving leftovers in their original dishes to cool slowly in a warm kitchen could encourage harmful bacteria to multiply in the food, causing illness. So transfer leftovers to clean, cold dishes and as soon as they have cooled, cover them and place them in the refrigerator. Use the next day and reheat thoroughly.

Leftovers can also be recycled, and the remains of dishes such as chicken, game or meat casseroles, can be used as a filling for a pie. A simple fish pie, topped with mashed potato, can easily be transformed into hot, crisp fish cakes. However, you should not rework ingredients more than once.

Left: Cooking casseroles and stews a day ahead is not only convenient, but also improves the flavour of the dish.

FREEZING TIPS AND TECHNIQUES

• Cool food rapidly, then wrap securely and label – with a description, the date and number of servings. If you are freezing several items at the same time, use the fast-freeze facility on your freezer.

• Hearty soups and stews freeze well, unless they contain chopped potatoes, rice, barley or pasta, which lose texture and become mushy on freezing. If these ingredients are included in the recipe, add them after thawing, then simmer the soup or stew until these ingredients are fully cooked.

• Stews and casseroles freeze well, but leave a little head room in the container to allow the liquid to expand during the freezing process.

• Blot the surface of a stew to remove surplus fat before freezing or chill so that fat solidifies and can be lifted off. Fat can become rancid, especially if a dish is frozen for a long time. Omit bacon unless you are freezing a composite dish for just a few weeks.

• Make sure that any pieces of meat or poultry in a dish that includes a sauce or gravy are fully submerged in the liquid, to reduce the risk of their drying out in the freezer.

• Although fish in sauce can be frozen, the thawed and reheated dish will not taste so good as when it was originally made, so it is better to cook such dishes on the day you serve them.

• Small items, such as meatballs, burgers and fish cakes, freeze well. Open-freeze them on trays, then wrap individually so that you can remove just as many as you need at any time.

Rice advice

Although rice can be cooked ahead of time and frozen or chilled for reheating, it is essential that it is cooled quickly and thoroughly before being stored. It should be reheated until it is very hot and served immediately. Never keep cooked rice warm for long periods. These precautions are necessary to avoid food poisoning.

STORAGE TIMES

• Meat casseroles and stews improve in taste if they are cooked ahead, but they should not be kept in the refrigerator for more than 2 days before being reheated and served.

• Soups can be frozen for a period of up to 3 months. Leave adequate space when wrapping the container to allow for expansion on freezing.

• Casseroles or stews containing bacon, pork or ham should not be frozen for more than 6 weeks. If these ingredients are not present, optimum freezing time is 2 months.

• Minced (ground) beef dishes, such as chilli con carne, freeze well. These can be stored for up to 2 months.

• Curries freeze well for up to 3 months, but the flavour of the spices deteriorates after this.

• Cooked pasta dishes, such as lasagne and cannelloni, can be frozen for up to 3 months.

• Cooked fish dishes in sauce can be frozen for up to 1 month only. Frozen fish cakes should be used within 2 months.

Above: Make the most of your freezer by batch-cooking suitable dishes, such as stews, casseroles and chilli con carne.

REHEATING

It is important always to make sure that a dish has thawed completely before reheating. Food should be piping hot all the way through before being served, especially if it contains meat on the bone. Timing will depend on the specific ingredients and the quantities being used, but as a guide, a chicken casserole that has been thawed to room temperature should be reheated for 45–60 minutes in an oven preheated to 200°C/400°F/Gas 6. Stir the casserole and check its temperature occasionally. Such delicate foods as fish should not be reheated for so long that their flavour and texture is spoiled. If you reheat foods in a pan on top of the stove, stir them frequently to prevent them from sticking to the base of the pan. If you use the microwave to reheat food, then follow the instructions in your handbook for the precise cooking time.

CHOOSING ACCOMPANIMENTS

The decision about what side-dishes to serve with your chosen main dish will depend very much on whatever else is on the menu. You don't have to serve a vast array of vegetable accompaniments, especially if you've started the meal with a salad or a fruit appetizer, such as grapefruit cocktail or a slice of melon. It is, however, traditional (and sound nutritional sense) to offer a carbohydrate of some sort alongside the main dish. Obvious choices would be rice, potatoes, pasta and bread, but you could also choose grains such as couscous, polenta and lentils or even quinoa (pronounced keen-wa), an extremely nutritious and tasty South American grain, that is cooked in a similar way to rice.

RICE

If you choose rice, make sure that it complements the main course. Basmati rice, with its slightly nutty flavour, is perfect for Indian dishes, whereas Thai fragrant rice is the first choice for a green or red curry from that country. Try to experiment with the more unusual rices, too, such as the red rice from the Camargue and California. Brown rice makes a good accompaniment to vegetable casseroles and stews, or it can be cooked, cooled and made into a salad to serve with kebabs and grilled meat.

POTATOES

Mashed or creamed potato tastes great with creamy fish dishes, fried liver and sausages and pork casserole. The modern trend is to flavour the mash with garlic, mustard or herbs. You could try a mixture of mashed potato and celeriac, or mashed potato and swede (rutabaga). Sweet potato mash tastes great, too – for extra interest, stir in a few spoonfuls of a hot Mexican tomato salsa. For smooth results, use a ricer, potato masher or fork.

Roast potatoes and baked layered potatoes are great served with roasts, baked fish or pot roasts, while potato chips (French fries) or fried potatoes are often partnered with steak.

Baked potatoes, split and topped with butter, cream cheese, Stilton or crème fraîche are delicious with grills (broils). When the first new potatoes arrive in the shops, they are a special treat, especially if you toss the boiled or steamed potatoes with butter and chopped fresh parsley or finely grated lemon rind. For flap-free main courses, consider potato dishes that don't require any last-minute attention.

GRAINS AND PULSES

Couscous is an excellent partner for Moroccan tagines and similar dishes that have quite a lot of liquid. It is readily available from supermarkets and the latest pre-cooked forms of couscous are exceptionally quick and easy to prepare. Polenta is an Italian staple and is a very good alternative to mashed potato. Soft polenta can be served with stews and casseroles and when polenta is grilled, it is an excellent alternative to bread. Quinoa, which is available from health food stores, is a nutty-flavoured grain that goes well with vegetable stews, such as ratatouille, and bean pots. Although lentils are usually included as an ingredient in a recipe, Puy lentils are a classic French accompaniment. Serve them hot with braised meat and game.

Left: Mashed potato is a versatile accompaniment, whether served plain or flavoured with herbs or mustard.

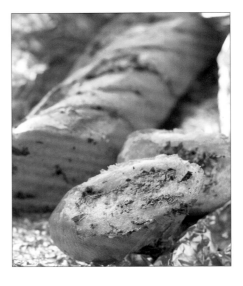

Above: Serve piping-hot garlic bread with baked pasta dishes.

PASTA

There are many different forms of pasta, from Italian spaghetti and tagliatelle to the wide range of Asian egg and rice noodles. Choose the type that suits your dish, not just in terms of its origin, but also to reap maximum value from the shape. Slim or flat noodles are not only great with thin, creamy sauces, they also go well with stir-fried vegetables, while penne and rigatoni are sturdy enough for chunky sauces.

BREAD

If you are serving a rich casserole or stew that has plenty of gravy or sauce, a rustic loaf or a supply of freshly baked wholemeal (whole-wheat) rolls will not only suit the mood of the meal, but also give guests an excuse to mop up every last drop of gravy. There are dozens of delicious loaves available, so try some unusual varieties. Soda bread is perfect with an Irish stew, while lavash, a large flat bread that is torn into pieces at the table, is great with Middle Eastern dishes. Italian breads, such as focaccia, are ideal with hearty casseroles such as osso bucco. Garlic bread is delicious with fish brochettes, grilled (broiled) pork chops or lamb steaks cooked on the barbecue. For a change, make your own garlic butter and transform rolls into individual garlic and herb breads.

SALADS

Although substantial salads, such as Insalata di Mare or Salad Niçoise, make perfect main course dishes in their own right, those salads that are less elaborate and substantial are better served as accompaniments to main meals. Use really fresh ingredients as these have a far superior flavour and crisp texture.

Salads don't work particularly well with meat or chicken stews or very creamy dishes, but they are perfect partners for pizzas, cold pies, baked pasta dishes such as lasagne, roulades, fajitas and grilled (broiled) fish and meat dishes. A simple green salad tossed with fresh herbs picked from the garden or window box is ideal and not overly time-consuming to make. Salads based on tomatoes, with added ingredients such as red onion or orange segments, are not only versatile but also simple to prepare.

Salad dressings should be kept simple so as not to compete with the other flavours in the bowl. A mixture of lemon juice, olive oil, fresh herbs, salt and freshly ground black pepper proves ideal for most salads and takes minutes to prepare, and any dressing that you don't use can be stored in the refrigerator until needed.

Below: A crisp salad is easy to prepare and goes well with main courses that don't contain a lot of sauce.

VEGETABLES

The choice of which vegetables to serve as accompaniments depends on what is part of the main dish. A main dish that includes a selection of vegetables, such as escalopes of chicken with baby vegetables, would be good on its own, or with potatoes or a similar starch vegetable. However, you might wish to offer a selection of three or four different vegetables with roast lamb or pork. Try to balance crisp vegetables such as roast potatoes, lightly cooked broccoli and crunchy cabbage with creamy offerings such as puréed celeriac, carrot or parsnip.

Always imagine what the food will look like on the plate and aim to have a mixture of colours and textures. For example, baby carrots, puréed spinach and fried potatoes would add colour as well as texture to a main course, whereas mashed potato, cauliflower and braised celery would look – and taste – rather plain and dreary.

CONDIMENTS AND SAUCES

Many dishes are enhanced if they are served with a complementary relish or sauce. Roasts are traditionally served with rich-flavoured sauces: cranberry sauce with turkey, mint sauce with lamb and horseradish cream with beef. Spicy

Below: Braised leeks make a wonderful accompaniment when teamed with sweet carrots.

food is best with a cooling condiment. Curry, for instance, is complemented by a cucumber raita. When serving chilli dishes, piquant relishes and tomato salsas are perfect, adding colour and texture to the meal. Classic Italian salsa verde is a natural partner for sautéed fish or grilled steak, while a rich onion gravy goes well with sausages, liver, pork chops or toad-in-the-hole. Dark rich gravies are also good with mounds of creamy mashed potato.

Classic vegetable companions

Some vegetables seem to go particularly well with specific meat, poultry or fish dishes.
• The slightly tart flavour of braised red cabbage with apples is excellent with roast pork or baked ham.
• Fennel, with its delicate, almost aniseedy flavour, is the perfect partner for fish or chicken.
• Sweet-tasting corn and smoked haddock go well together, but it is better to use naturally-coloured haddock to avoid overdoing the yellow theme.
• Mashed swede (rutabaga) is the classic accompaniment for haggis, but also tastes great with herbed sausages or spicy minced (ground) beef patties.
• Spinach is classically served with veal dishes and it also goes well with fish dishes.
• Sweet potatoes, especially when candied, are simply superb with baked ham. They are also the classic accompaniment for Thanksgiving turkey.
• Green beans frequently partner tomato-based stews, but they are also very good with grilled meats and fish.
• Roast vegetables, such as aubergines (eggplant), red onion, courgettes (zucchini) and celery, make a colourful bed for baked chicken breast portions or pork chops, and are also excellent with roast meats of all types.

HEARTY SOUPS

Whether you're cooking for the family, or having friends around for a casual supper, nothing beats a bowl of steaming soup on a chilly day. Soup spells comfort as well as flavour, and when the soup is a substantial one, such as Clam Chowder or Chunky Lamb and Chickpea Broth, there's no need for elaborate accompaniments. A little freshly grated Parmesan, if appropriate, some warm bread rolls, the salt cellar and pepper mill — and the meal is served. For a sophisticated occasion, serve Seafood Laksa or Bouillabaisse. The preparation may take a little longer, but the ease of serving will be just the same.

SPINACH AND RICE SOUP

USE VERY YOUNG SPINACH LEAVES TO PREPARE THIS LIGHT AND FRESH-TASTING SOUP.

SERVES FOUR

INGREDIENTS

675g/1½lb fresh spinach
  leaves, washed
45ml/3 tbsp extra virgin olive oil
1 small onion, finely chopped
2 garlic cloves, finely chopped
1 small fresh red chilli, seeded and
  finely chopped
225g/8oz/generous 1 cup risotto rice
1.2 litres/2 pints/5 cups
  vegetable stock
salt and freshly ground black pepper
shavings of pared Parmesan or
  Pecorino cheese, to serve

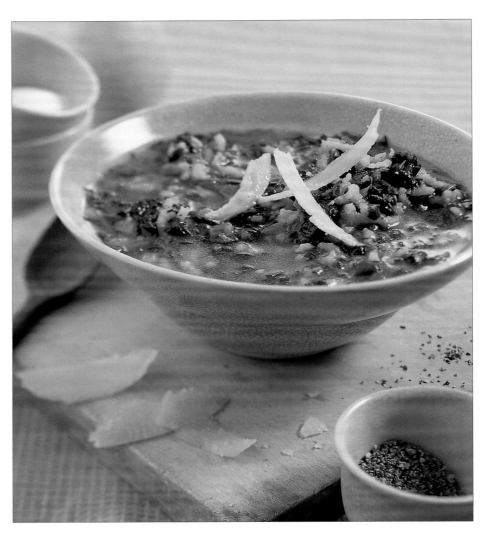

1 Place the spinach in a large pan with just the water that clings to its leaves after washing. Add a large pinch of salt. Heat gently until the spinach has wilted, then remove from the heat and drain, reserving any liquid.

2 Either chop the spinach finely using a large kitchen knife or place in a food processor and process the leaves to a fairly coarse purée.

VARIATION
You can substitute Swiss chard for the spinach, if you like.

COOK'S TIP
Buy Parmesan or Pecorino cheese in the piece from a reputable supplier, and it will be full of flavour and easy to grate or shave with a vegetable peeler.

3 Heat the oil in a large pan. Add the onion, garlic and chilli and cook gently for 4–5 minutes, until softened. Stir in the rice until well coated, then pour in the stock and reserved spinach liquid. Bring to the boil, lower the heat and simmer for 10 minutes.

4 Add the spinach and season with salt and pepper to taste. Cook the soup for a further 5–7 minutes, until the rice is tender. Taste and adjust the seasoning, if necessary. Ladle into heated bowls, top with the shavings of Parmesan or Pecorino and serve immediately.

Per portion: Energy 340Kcal/1431kJ; Protein 9.2g; Carbohydrate 52.3g, of which sugars 3.4g; Fat 11.9g, of which saturates 1.9g; Cholesterol 0mg; Calcium 320mg; Fibre 4g; Sodium 449mg.

LOBSTER BISQUE

BISQUE IS A LUXURIOUS, VELVETY SOUP, WHICH CAN BE MADE WITH ANY CRUSTACEANS.

SERVES SIX

INGREDIENTS
- 500g/1¼lb fresh lobster
- 75g/3oz/6 tbsp butter
- 1 onion, chopped
- 1 carrot, diced
- 1 celery stick, diced
- 45ml/3 tbsp brandy, plus extra for serving (optional)
- 250ml/8fl oz/1 cup dry white wine
- 1 litre/1¾ pints/4 cups fish stock
- 15ml/1 tbsp tomato purée (paste)
- 75g/3oz/scant ½ cup long grain rice
- 1 fresh bouquet garni
- 150ml/¼ pint/⅔ cup double (heavy) cream, plus extra to garnish
- salt, ground white pepper and cayenne pepper

1 Cut the lobster into pieces. Melt half the butter in a large pan, add the vegetables and cook over a low heat until soft. Put in the lobster and stir until the shell on each piece turns red.

2 Pour over the brandy and set it alight. When the flames die down, add the wine and boil until reduced by half. Pour in the fish stock and simmer for 2–3 minutes. Remove the lobster.

3 Stir in the tomato purée and rice, add the bouquet garni and cook until the rice is tender. Meanwhile, remove the lobster meat from the shell and return the shells to the pan. Dice the lobster meat and set it aside.

COOK'S TIP
It is best to buy a live lobster, chilling it in the freezer until it is comatose and then killing it just before cooking. If you can't face the procedure, use a cooked lobster; take care not to over-cook the flesh. Stir for only 30–60 seconds.

4 When the rice is cooked, discard all the larger pieces of shell. Tip the mixture into a blender or food processor and process to a purée. Press the purée through a fine sieve placed over the clean pan. Stir the mixture, then heat until almost boiling. Season with salt, pepper and cayenne, then lower the heat and stir in the cream. Dice the remaining butter and whisk it into the bisque. Add the diced lobster meat and serve immediately. If you like, pour a small spoonful of brandy into each soup bowl and swirl in a little extra cream.

Per portion: Energy 406Kcal/1684kJ; Protein 20.3g; Carbohydrate 13.7g, of which sugars 3.1g; Fat 25.2g, of which saturates 15g; Cholesterol 153mg; Calcium 84mg; Fibre 0.7g; Sodium 365mg.

CLAM CHOWDER

If fresh clams are hard to find, use frozen or canned clams for this classic recipe from New England. Large clams should be cut into chunky pieces. Reserve a few clams in their shells for garnish, if you like. Traditionally, the soup is served with savoury biscuits called saltine crackers. You should be able to find these in any good delicatessen.

SERVES FOUR

INGREDIENTS

100g/3¾oz salt pork or thinly sliced
  unsmoked bacon, diced
1 large onion, chopped
2 potatoes, peeled and cut into
  1cm/½in cubes
1 bay leaf
1 fresh thyme sprig
300ml/½ pint/1¼ cups milk
400g/14oz cooked clams, cooking
  liquid reserved
150ml/¼ pint/⅔ cup double
  (heavy) cream
salt, ground white pepper and
  cayenne pepper
finely chopped fresh parsley, to garnish

1 Put the salt pork or unsmoked bacon in a pan, and heat gently, stirring frequently, until the fat runs and the meat is starting to brown. Add the chopped onion and cook over a low heat, stirring occasionally, until softened but not browned.

2 Add the cubed potatoes, the bay leaf and thyme sprig, stir well to coat with fat, then pour in the milk and reserved clam liquid and bring to the boil. Lower the heat and simmer for about 10 minutes, until the potatoes are tender but still firm. Lift out the bay leaf and thyme sprig and discard.

3 Remove the shells from most of the clams. Add all the clams to the pan and season to taste with salt, pepper and cayenne. Simmer gently for 5 minutes more, then stir in the cream. Heat until the soup is very hot, but do not allow it to boil. Pour into a warmed tureen, garnish with the chopped fresh parsley and serve immediately.

CHINESE CRAB AND CORN SOUP

Frozen white crab meat works as well as fresh in this delicately flavoured soup.

SERVES FOUR

INGREDIENTS

600ml/1 pint/2½ cups fish or
  chicken stock
2.5cm/1in fresh root ginger, very
  thinly sliced
400g/14oz can creamed corn
150g/5oz cooked white crab meat
15ml/1 tbsp arrowroot or
  cornflour (cornstarch)
15ml/1 tbsp Chinese rice wine or
  dry sherry
15–30ml/1–2 tbsp light soy sauce
1 egg white
salt and ground white pepper
shredded spring onions (scallions),
  to garnish

COOK'S TIP

This soup is sometimes made with whole kernel corn, but creamed corn gives a better texture. If you can't find it in a can, use thawed frozen creamed corn instead; the result will be just as good.

1 Put the stock and ginger in a large, heavy pan and bring to the boil over a medium heat. Stir in the creamed corn and bring back to the boil.

2 Turn off the heat and add the crab meat. Put the arrowroot or cornflour in a cup and stir in the rice wine or sherry to make a smooth paste, then stir this into the soup. Cook over a low heat for about 3 minutes, until the soup has thickened and is slightly glutinous in consistency. Add light soy sauce, salt and white pepper to taste.

3 In a bowl, whisk the egg white to a stiff foam. Gradually fold it into the soup. Ladle the soup into heated bowls, garnish each portion with spring onions and serve immediately.

VARIATION

To make prawn (shrimp) and corn soup, substitute 150g/5oz cooked peeled and deveined prawns for the crab meat. Chop the peeled prawns coarsely and add to the soup at the beginning of step 2.

Top per portion: Energy 439Kcal/1829kJ; Protein 25.6g; Carbohydrate 25.9g, of which sugars 8.8g; Fat 26.6g, of which saturates 15.2g; Cholesterol 136mg; Calcium 204mg; Fibre 1.8g; Sodium 1638mg.
Below per portion: Energy 201Kcal/852kJ; Protein 11.3g; Carbohydrate 33.8g, of which sugars 9.9g; Fat 3.2g, of which saturates 0.5g; Cholesterol 27mg; Calcium 17mg; Fibre 1.4g; Sodium 695mg.

MATELOTE

Traditionally this fishermen's soup is made from freshwater fish, including eel, although in Normandy, they use sea fish and conger eel. Any firm fish can be used, but try to include at least some eel, and use a robust dry white or red wine for extra flavour.

SERVES SIX

INGREDIENTS

   1kg/2¼lb mixed fish, including
      450g/1lb conger eel if possible
   50g/2oz/¼ cup butter
   1 onion, thickly sliced
   2 celery sticks, thickly sliced
   2 carrots, thickly sliced
   1 bottle dry white or red wine
   1 fresh bouquet garni containing
      parsley, bay leaf and chervil
   2 cloves
   6 black peppercorns
   beurre manié for thickening
      (see Cook's Tip)
   salt and cayenne pepper
For the garnish
   25g/1oz/2 tbsp butter
   12 baby (pearl) onions, peeled
   12 button (white) mushrooms
   chopped flat leaf parsley

1 Cut all the fish into thick slices, removing any obvious bones. Melt the butter in a large pan, add the fish and sliced vegetables and stir over a medium heat until lightly browned. Pour in the wine and enough cold water to cover. Add the bouquet garni and spices and season. Bring to the boil, lower the heat and simmer gently for 20–30 minutes, until the fish is tender, skimming the surface occasionally.

2 Meanwhile, prepare the garnish. Heat the butter in a deep frying pan and sauté the baby onions until golden and tender. Add the mushrooms and cook until golden. Season and keep hot.

3 Strain the soup through a large sieve placed over a clean pan. Discard the herbs and spices in the sieve, then divide the fish among deep soup plates (you can skin the fish if you wish, but this is not essential) and keep hot.

4 Reheat the soup until it boils. Lower the heat and whisk in the *beurre manié* little by little until the soup thickens. Season to taste with salt and pepper and pour over the fish. Garnish each portion with the sautéed baby onions and mushrooms and sprinkle with chopped parsley. Serve immediately.

COOK'S TIP
To make the *beurre manié* for thickening, mix 15g/½oz/1 tbsp softened butter with 15ml/1 tbsp plain (all-purpose) flour. Add to the boiling soup, a pinch at a time, whisking constantly.

Per portion: Energy 305Kcal/1275kJ; Protein 32.1g; Carbohydrate 5.7g, of which sugars 4.6g; Fat 8.4g, of which saturates 4.6g; Cholesterol 94mg; Calcium 49mg; Fibre 1.6g; Sodium 169mg.

PROVENÇAL FISH SOUP

THE RICE MAKES THIS A SUBSTANTIAL MAIN MEAL SOUP. BASMATI OR THAI RICE HAS THE BEST FLAVOUR, BUT ANY LONG GRAIN RICE COULD BE USED. IF USING A QUICK-COOK RICE, COOK THE VEGETABLES FOR LONGER BEFORE ADDING THE RICE.

SERVES FOUR TO SIX

INGREDIENTS

450g/1lb fresh mussels
about 250ml/8fl oz/1 cup white wine
675–900g/1½–2lb mixed white fish
  fillets such as monkfish, plaice,
  flounder, cod or haddock
6 large scallops
30ml/2 tbsp olive oil
3 leeks, chopped
1 garlic clove, crushed
1 red (bell) pepper, seeded and cut
  into 2.5cm/1in pieces
1 yellow (bell) pepper, seeded and
  cut into 2.5cm/1in pieces
175g/6oz fennel, cut into
  4cm/1½in pieces
400g/14oz can chopped tomatoes
about 1.2 litres/2 pints/5 cups
  well-flavoured fish stock
generous pinch of saffron threads,
  soaked in 15ml/1 tbsp hot water
175g/6oz/scant 1 cup basmati
  rice, soaked
8 large raw prawns (shrimp), peeled
  and deveined
salt and ground black pepper
30–45ml/2–3 tbsp fresh dill,
  to garnish
crusty bread, to serve (optional)

1 Scrub the mussels and pull off the beards, discarding any shellfish that do not close when tapped with a knife. Place them in a heavy pan. Add 90ml/ 6 tbsp of the wine, cover tightly, bring to the boil over a high heat and cook, shaking the pan occasionally, for about 3 minutes or until all the mussels have opened. Strain, reserving the liquid. Set aside half the mussels in their shells for the garnish; shell the rest and put them in a bowl. Discard any mussels that have not opened.

2 Cut the fish into 2.5cm/1in cubes. Detach the corals from the scallops and slice the white flesh into three or four pieces. Add the scallops to the fish and the corals to the mussels.

3 Heat the olive oil in a pan and cook the leeks and garlic for 3–4 minutes, until softened. Add the peppers and fennel and cook for 2 minutes more.

4 Add the tomatoes, stock, saffron water, reserved mussel liquid and the remaining wine. Season well and cook for 5 minutes. Drain the rice, stir it into the mixture, cover and simmer for 10 minutes, until it is just tender.

5 Carefully stir in the white fish and cook over a low heat for 5 minutes. Add the prawns and cook for a further 2 minutes, then add the scallop corals and mussels and cook for 2–3 minutes more, until all the fish is tender. If the soup seems dry, add a little extra white wine or stock, or a little of both. Spoon into warmed soup dishes, top with the mussels in their shells and sprinkle with the dill. Serve with fresh crusty bread, if you like.

COOK'S TIP

To make your own fish stock, place about 450g/1lb white fish trimmings – bones, heads, but not gills – in a large pan. Add a chopped onion, carrot, bay leaf, fresh parsley sprig, 6 peppercorns and a 5cm/ 2in piece of pared lemon rind. Pour in 1.2 litres/2 pints/5 cups water, bring to the boil and simmer for 25–30 minutes. Strain through muslin (cheesecloth).

Per portion: Energy 544Kcal/2283kJ; Protein 55.9g; Carbohydrate 49.2g, of which sugars 11.7g; Fat 9.3g, of which saturates 1.4g; Cholesterol 143mg; Calcium 177mg; Fibre 5.6g; Sodium 325mg.

SEAFOOD LAKSA

A LAKSA IS A MALAYSIAN STEW OF FISH, POULTRY, MEAT OR VEGETABLES WITH NOODLES. AUTHENTIC LAKSAS ARE OFTEN VERY HOT, AND COOLED BY THE COCONUT MILK AND THE NOODLES. IF YOU WOULD PREFER A SPICY VERSION, ADD A LITTLE CHILLI POWDER INSTEAD OF SOME OF THE PAPRIKA.

SERVES FOUR TO FIVE

INGREDIENTS

    3 medium-hot fresh red
      chillies, seeded
    4–5 garlic cloves
    5ml/1 tsp mild paprika
    10ml/2 tsp fermented shrimp paste
    25ml/1½ tbsp chopped fresh root
      ginger or galangal
    250g/9oz small red shallots
    25g/1oz fresh coriander (cilantro),
      preferably with roots
    45ml/3 tbsp groundnut (peanut) oil
    5ml/1 tsp fennel seeds, crushed
    2 fennel bulbs, cut into thin wedges
    600ml/1 pint/2½ cups fish stock
    300g/11oz thin vermicelli
      rice noodles
    450ml/¾ pint/scant 2 cups
      coconut milk
    juice of 1–2 limes
    30–45ml/2–3 tbsp Thai fish sauce
    450g/1lb firm white fish fillet, such
      as monkfish, halibut or snapper
    450g/1lb large raw prawns (shrimp)
      (about 20), peeled and deveined
    small bunch of fresh holy basil or
      ordinary basil
    2 spring onions (scallions),
      thinly sliced

1 Put the chillies, garlic, paprika, shrimp paste, ginger or galangal and 2 shallots in a food processor, blender or spice grinder and process to a paste. Remove the roots and stems from the coriander and add them to the paste; chop and reserve the coriander leaves. Add 15ml/1 tbsp of the oil to the paste and process again until fairly smooth.

2 Heat the remaining oil in a large pan. Add the remaining shallots, the fennel seeds and fennel wedges. Cook over a medium heat, stirring occasionally, until lightly browned, then add 45ml/3 tbsp of the spice paste and stir-fry for about 1–2 minutes. Pour in the fish stock and bring to the boil. Reduce the heat and simmer for 8–10 minutes.

3 Meanwhile, cook the vermicelli rice noodles according to the packet instructions. Drain and set aside.

4 Add the coconut milk and the juice of 1 lime to the pan of shallots. Stir in 30ml/2 tbsp of the fish sauce. Bring to a simmer and taste, adding a little more spice paste, lime juice or fish sauce as necessary.

5 Cut the fish into chunks and add to the pan. Cook for 2–3 minutes, then add the prawns and cook until they turn pink. Chop most of the basil and add to the pan with the reserved coriander.

6 Divide the noodles among wide bowls, then ladle in the soup. Sprinkle with spring onions and the remaining whole basil leaves. Serve immediately.

Per portion: Energy 524Kcal/2199kJ; Protein 43.1g; Carbohydrate 65.1g, of which sugars 6.3g; Fat 10.1g, of which saturates 2g; Cholesterol 233mg; Calcium 162mg; Fibre 1.9g; Sodium 356mg.

BOUILLABAISSE

AUTHENTIC BOUILLABAISSE COMES FROM THE SOUTH OF FRANCE AND INCLUDES RASCASSE (SCORPION FISH) AS AN ESSENTIAL INGREDIENT. IT IS, HOWEVER, PERFECTLY POSSIBLE TO MAKE THIS WONDERFUL MAIN-COURSE SOUP WITHOUT IT. USE AS LARGE A VARIETY OF FISH AS YOU CAN.

SERVES FOUR

INGREDIENTS

45ml/3 tbsp olive oil
2 onions, chopped
2 leeks, white parts only, chopped
4 garlic cloves, chopped
450g/1lb ripe tomatoes, peeled
   and chopped
3 litres/5 pints/12 cups boiling fish
   stock or water
15ml/1 tbsp tomato purée (paste)
large pinch of saffron threads
1 fresh bouquet garni, containing
   2 thyme sprigs, 2 bay leaves and
   2 fennel sprigs
3kg/6½lb mixed fish, cleaned and
   cut into large chunks
4 potatoes, peeled and
   thickly sliced
salt, pepper and cayenne pepper
a bowl of Rouille and a bowl of
   Aioli, to serve
For the garnish
16 slices of French bread, toasted
   and rubbed with garlic
30ml/2 tbsp chopped fresh parsley

1 Heat the oil in a large pan. Add the onions, leeks, garlic and tomatoes. Cook until slightly softened. Stir in the stock or water, tomato purée and saffron. Add the bouquet garni and boil until the oil is amalgamated. Lower the heat; add the fish and potatoes.

COOK'S TIP
Suitable fish for Bouillabaisse include rascasse, conger eel, monkfish, red gurnard and John Dory.

2 Simmer the soup for 5–8 minutes, removing each type of fish as it becomes cooked. Continue to cook until the potatoes are very tender. Season well with salt, pepper and cayenne.

3 Divide the fish and potatoes among individual soup plates. Strain the soup and ladle it over the fish. Garnish with toasted French bread and parsley. Serve with rouille and aioli.

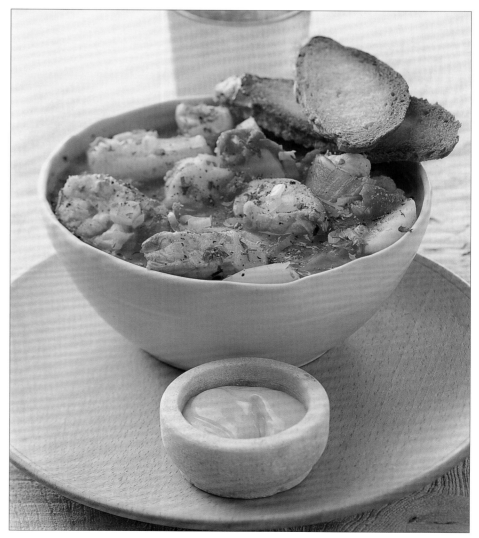

Per portion: Energy 814Kcal/3426kJ; Protein 142.3g; Carbohydrate 28.1g, of which sugars 10.8g; Fat 15.1g, of which saturates 2.2g; Cholesterol 345mg; Calcium 121mg; Fibre 4.9g; Sodium 895mg.

MEDITERRANEAN LEEK <u>AND</u> FISH SOUP <u>WITH</u> TOMATOES

THIS CHUNKY SOUP, WHICH IS ALMOST A STEW, MAKES A ROBUST AND WONDERFULLY AROMATIC MEAL IN A BOWL. SERVE IT WITH CRISP-BAKED CROÛTES SPREAD WITH A SPICY GARLIC MAYONNAISE.

SERVES FOUR

INGREDIENTS
 30ml/2 tbsp olive oil
 2 large thick leeks, white and green
   parts separated, both thinly sliced
 5ml/1 tsp crushed coriander seeds
 good pinch of dried red chilli flakes
 300g/11oz salad potatoes, sliced
 200g/7oz can Italian peeled
   chopped plum tomatoes
 600ml/1 pint/2½ cups fish stock
 150ml/¼ pint/⅔ cup fruity white wine
 1 fresh bay leaf
 1 star anise
 strip of pared orange rind
 good pinch of saffron threads
 450g/1lb white fish fillets, such as
   monkfish, sea bass, cod or haddock
 450g/1lb small squid, cleaned
 250g/9oz uncooked peeled
   prawns (shrimp)
 30–45ml/2–3 tbsp chopped parsley
 salt and ground black pepper
To serve
 1 short French loaf, sliced and toasted
 spicy garlic mayonnaise

1 Gently heat the oil in a pan, then add the green part of the leeks, the coriander and chilli and cook for 5 minutes.

2 Add the potatoes and tomatoes and pour in the stock and wine. Add the bay leaf, star anise, orange rind and saffron.

3 Bring to the boil, reduce the heat and part-cover the pan. Simmer for 20 minutes, or until the potatoes are tender. Taste and adjust the seasoning.

4 Cut the fish into chunks. Cut the squid sacs into rectangles and score a criss-cross pattern into them without cutting right through.

5 Add the fish to the soup and cook gently for 4 minutes. Add the prawns and cook for 1 minute. Add the squid and the shredded white part of the leek and cook, stirring occasionally, for 2 minutes.

6 Stir in the chopped parsley and serve with toasted French bread and spicy garlic mayonnaise.

Per portion: Energy 326Kcal/1379kJ; Protein 49.7g; Carbohydrate 17.5g, of which sugars 4.4g; Fat 4.2g, of which saturates 0.9g; Cholesterol 421mg; Calcium 106mg; Fibre 2.9g; Sodium 333mg.

FISH SOUP WITH ROUILLE

MAKING THIS SOUP IS SIMPLICITY ITSELF, ALTHOUGH THE EXQUISITE FLAVOUR SUGGESTS IT IS THE PRODUCT OF PAINSTAKING PREPARATION AND COOKING.

SERVES SIX

INGREDIENTS
  1kg/2¼lb mixed fish
  30ml/2 tbsp olive oil
  1 onion, chopped
  1 carrot, chopped
  1 leek, chopped
  2 large ripe tomatoes, chopped
  1 red (bell) pepper, seeded
    and chopped
  2 garlic cloves, peeled
  150g/5oz/⅔ cup tomato
    purée (paste)
  1 large fresh bouquet garni,
    containing 3 parsley sprigs, 3 celery
    sticks and 3 bay leaves
  300ml/½ pint/1¼ cups white wine
  salt and ground black pepper
For the rouille
  2 garlic cloves, coarsely chopped
  5ml/1 tsp coarse salt
  1 thick slice of white bread, crust
    removed, soaked in water and
    squeezed dry
  1 fresh red chilli, seeded and
    coarsely chopped
  45ml/3 tbsp olive oil
  salt and cayenne pepper
For the garnish
  12 slices of baguette, toasted in
    the oven
  50g/2oz/½ cup grated Gruyère cheese

1 Cut the fish into 7.5cm/3in chunks, removing any obvious bones. Heat the oil in a large, heavy pan, then add the fish, onion, carrot, leek, tomatoes and red pepper. Cook over a medium heat, stirring occasionally, until the vegetables begin to colour.

2 Add all the other soup ingredients, then pour in just enough cold water to cover the mixture. Season well and bring to just below boiling point, then lower the heat to a bare simmer, cover and cook for 1 hour.

3 Meanwhile, make the rouille. Put the garlic and coarse salt in a mortar and crush to a paste with a pestle. Add the soaked bread and chilli and pound until smooth, or purée in a food processor. Whisk in the olive oil, a drop at a time, to make a smooth, shiny sauce that resembles mayonnaise. Season with salt and add a pinch of cayenne if you like a fiery taste. Set the rouille aside.

4 Lift out and discard the bouquet garni from the soup. Purée the soup in batches in a food processor, then strain through a fine sieve placed over a clean pan, pushing the solids through with the back of a ladle.

5 Reheat the soup without letting it boil. Check the seasoning and ladle into individual bowls. Top each serving with two slices of toasted baguette, a spoonful of rouille and some grated Gruyère.

COOK'S TIP
Any firm fish can be used for this recipe. If you use whole fish, include the heads, which enhance the flavour of the soup.

Per portion: Energy 513Kcal/2159kJ; Protein 41.3g; Carbohydrate 48.2g, of which sugars 11.7g; Fat 14.8g, of which saturates 3.6g; Cholesterol 85mg; Calcium 192mg; Fibre 4.4g; Sodium 642mg.

PUMPKIN, RICE AND CHICKEN SOUP

THIS IS A WARM, COMFORTING CHICKEN SOUP WHOSE SPICE AND ORANGE RIND GARNISH WILL BRIGHTEN THE DULLEST WINTER DAY. FOR AN EVEN MORE SUBSTANTIAL MEAL, ADD A LITTLE MORE RICE AND MAKE SURE YOU USE ALL THE CHICKEN FROM THE STOCK.

SERVES FOUR

INGREDIENTS

1 wedge of pumpkin, about 450g/1lb
15ml/1 tbsp sunflower oil
25g/1oz/2 tbsp butter
6 green cardamom pods
2 leeks, chopped
115g/4oz/generous ½ cup basmati
  rice, soaked
350ml/12fl oz/1½ cups milk
salt and freshly ground black pepper
generous strips of pared orange rind,
  to garnish
For the chicken stock
  2 chicken quarters
  1 onion, quartered
  2 carrots, chopped
  1 celery stalk, chopped
  6–8 peppercorns
  900ml/1½ pints/3¾ cups water

1 First make the chicken stock. Place the chicken quarters, onion, carrots, celery and peppercorns in a large, heavy pan. Pour in the water and bring to the boil over a low heat. Skim off any scum on the surface if necessary, then lower the heat, cover and simmer gently for 1 hour.

2 Strain the chicken stock into a clean, large bowl, discarding the vegetables. Skin and bone one or both chicken pieces and cut the flesh into strips. (If not using both chicken pieces for the soup, reserve the other piece for another recipe.)

3 Peel the pumpkin and remove all the seeds and pith, so that you have about 350g/12oz flesh. Cut the flesh into 2.5cm/1in cubes.

4 Heat the oil and butter in a pan, add the cardamom pods and cook for about 2–3 minutes, until slightly swollen. Add the leeks and pumpkin. Cook, stirring, for 3–4 minutes over a medium heat, then lower the heat, cover and sweat for 5 minutes more, or until the pumpkin is quite soft, stirring once or twice.

5 Measure out 600ml/1 pint/2½ cups of the stock and add to the pumpkin mixture. Bring to the boil, then lower the heat, cover and simmer gently for 10–15 minutes, until the pumpkin is soft.

6 Pour the remaining stock into a measuring jug (cup) and make up with water to 300ml/½ pint/1¼ cups. Drain the rice and put it into a pan. Pour in the stock, bring to the boil, then simmer for about 10 minutes, until the rice is tender. Add seasoning to taste.

7 Remove and discard the cardamom pods, then process the soup in a blender or food processor until smooth. Pour it back into a clean saucepan and stir in the milk, chicken and rice (with any stock that has not been absorbed). Heat until simmering. Ladle into warm bowls, garnish with the strips of pared orange rind and freshly ground black pepper and serve immediately with wholemeal (whole-wheat) bread.

Per portion: Energy 336Kcal/1406kJ; Protein 25.4g; Carbohydrate 33.9g, of which sugars 7.8g; Fat 11g, of which saturates 5g; Cholesterol 71mg; Calcium 168mg; Fibre 2.9g; Sodium 122mg.

CHICKEN AND LEEK SOUP
WITH PRUNES AND BARLEY

THIS RECIPE IS BASED ON THE TRADITIONAL SCOTTISH SOUP, COCK-A-LEEKIE. THE UNUSUAL COMBINATION OF LEEKS AND PRUNES IS SURPRISINGLY DELICIOUS.

SERVES SIX

INGREDIENTS

1 chicken, weighing about 2kg/4¼lb
900g/2lb leeks
1 fresh bay leaf
a few each fresh parsley stalks and
  thyme sprigs
1 large carrot, thickly sliced
2.4 litres/4 pints/10 cups chicken or
  beef stock
115g/4oz/generous ½ cup
  pearl barley
400g/14oz ready-to-eat prunes
salt and ground black pepper
chopped fresh parsley, to garnish

1 Cut the breast portions off the chicken and set aside. Place the remaining carcass in a large pan. Cut half the leeks into 5cm/2in lengths and add them to the pan. Tie the bay leaf, parsley and thyme into a bouquet garni and add to the pan with the carrot and the stock. Bring to the boil, then reduce the heat and cover. Simmer gently for 1 hour. Skim off any scum when the water first boils and during simmering.

2 Add the chicken breast portions and cook for another 30 minutes, until they are just cooked. Leave until cool enough to handle, then strain the stock into a bowl. Reserve all the chicken meat. Discard all the skin, bones, cooked vegetables and herbs. Skim as much fat as you can from the stock, then return it to the pan.

3 Meanwhile, rinse the pearl barley thoroughly in a sieve under cold running water, then cook it in a large pan of boiling water over a medium heat for about 10 minutes. Drain, rinse well again and drain thoroughly.

4 Add the pearl barley to the stock. Bring to the boil over a medium heat, then lower the heat and cook very gently for 15–20 minutes, until the barley is just cooked and tender. Season the soup with 5ml/1 tsp salt and black pepper to taste.

5 Add the prunes. Slice the remaining leeks and add them to the pan. Bring to the boil, then simmer for 10 minutes, or until the leeks are just cooked.

6 Slice the chicken breast portions and add them to the soup with the remaining chicken meat, sliced or cut into neat pieces. Reheat if necessary, then ladle the soup into deep plates and sprinkle with chopped parsley.

Per portion: Energy 606Kcal/2533kJ; Protein 44.9g; Carbohydrate 40g, of which sugars 23.9g; Fat 30.8g, of which saturates 8.4g; Cholesterol 220mg; Calcium 45mg; Fibre 4.2g; Sodium 405mg.

POT-COOKED UDON IN MISO SOUP

Udon is a white wheat noodle, more popular in the south and west of Japan than the north. It is eaten with various hot and cold sauces and soups. Here, in this dish known as Miso Nikomi Udon, the noodles are cooked in a clay pot with a rich miso soup.

SERVES FOUR

INGREDIENTS
  200g/7oz skinless, boneless chicken
    breast portions
  10ml/2 tsp sake
  2 abura-age (thin deep fried tofu)
  900ml/1½ pints/3¾ cups dashi
    stock, or the same amount
    of water and 7.5ml/1½ tsp
    dashi-no-moto
  6 large fresh shiitake mushrooms,
    stalks removed, quartered
  4 spring onions (scallions), trimmed
    and chopped into 3mm/⅛in lengths
  30ml/2 tbsp mirin
  about 90g/3½oz aka miso or
    hatcho miso
  300g/11oz dried udon noodles
  4 eggs
  seven spice powder (optional)

4 Put the mirin and miso paste into a small bowl. Scoop 30ml/2 tbsp soup from the pan and mix this in well.

5 To cook the udon, boil at least 2 litres/3½ pints/9 cups water in a large pan. The water should not come higher than two-thirds the depth of the pan. Cook the udon for 6 minutes and drain.

6 Put the udon in one large flameproof clay pot or casserole (or divide among four small pots). Mix the miso paste into the soup and check the taste. Add more miso if required. Ladle in enough soup to cover the udon, and arrange the soup ingredients on top of the udon.

7 Put the soup on a medium heat and break the eggs on top. When the soup bubbles, wait for 1 minute, then cover and remove from the heat. Leave to stand for 2 minutes. Serve with seven spice powder, if you like.

1 Cut the chicken into bitesize pieces and place in a shallow dish. Sprinkle with sake and leave to marinate in a cool place for 15 minutes.

2 Put the abura-age in a sieve and thoroughly rinse with hot water from the kettle to wash off the oil. Drain on kitchen paper and cut each abura-age into four squares.

3 To make the soup, heat the dashi stock in a large pan. When it has come to the boil, add the chicken pieces, shiitake mushrooms and abura-age and cook for 5 minutes over a medium heat. Remove the pan from the heat and add the spring onions.

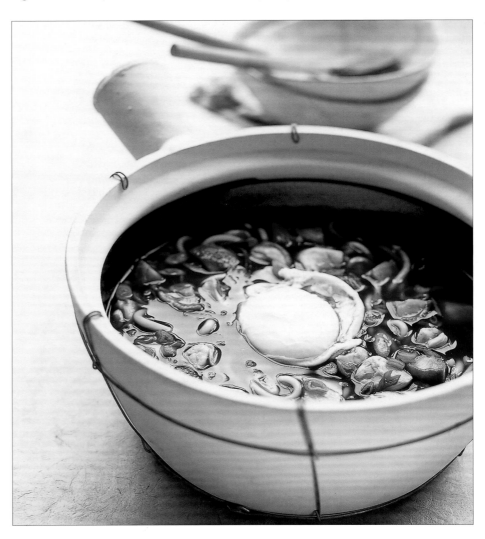

Per portion: Energy 666Kcal/2781kJ; Protein 49.6g; Carbohydrate 61.9g, of which sugars 1.8g; Fat 24.4g, of which saturates 1.8g; Cholesterol 225mg; Calcium 1536mg; Fibre 0.7g; Sodium 655mg.

HOT AND SOUR SOUP

ONE OF CHINA'S MOST POPULAR SOUPS, THIS IS FAMED FOR ITS CLEVER BALANCE OF FLAVOURS. THE "HOT" COMES FROM PEPPER; THE "SOUR" FROM VINEGAR. SIMILAR SOUPS ARE FOUND THROUGHOUT ASIA, SOME RELYING ON CHILLIES AND LIME JUICE TO PROVIDE THE ESSENTIAL FLAVOUR CONTRAST.

SERVES SIX

INGREDIENTS
 4–6 dried shiitake mushrooms
 2–3 small pieces of wood ear (dried
  Chinese mushroom) and a few
  golden needles (lily buds) (optional)
 115g/4oz pork fillet (tenderloin), cut
  into fine strips
 45ml/3 tbsp cornflour (cornstarch)
 150ml/¼ pint/⅔ cup water
 15–30ml/1–2 tbsp sunflower oil
 1 small onion, finely chopped
 1.5 litres/2½ pints/6¼ cups beef or
  chicken stock, or 2 × 300g/11oz
  cans consommé made up to the full
  quantity with water
 150g/5oz drained fresh firm
  tofu, diced
 60ml/4 tbsp rice vinegar
 15ml/1 tbsp light soy sauce
 1 egg, beaten
 5 ml/1 tsp sesame oil
 salt and ground white or black pepper
 2–3 spring onions (scallions),
  shredded, to garnish

1 Place the shiitake mushrooms in a bowl, with the pieces of wood ear and the golden needles, if using. Add sufficient warm water to cover and leave to soak for about 30 minutes. Drain the mushrooms, reserving the soaking water. Cut off and discard the mushroom stems and slice the caps finely. Trim away any tough stem from the wood ears, then chop them finely. Using kitchen string, tie the golden needles into a bundle.

2 Lightly dust the strips of pork fillet with some of the cornflour. Mix the remaining cornflour to a smooth paste with the measured water.

3 Heat the oil in a wok or pan and cook the onion until soft. Increase the heat and cook the pork until it changes colour. Add the stock or consommé, mushrooms, soaking water, and wood ears and golden needles, if using. Bring to the boil, then simmer for 15 minutes.

4 Discard the golden needles, lower the heat and stir in the cornflour paste to thicken. Add the tofu, vinegar, soy sauce, and salt and pepper.

5 Bring the soup to just below boiling point, then drizzle in the beaten egg by letting it drop from a whisk (or to be authentic, the fingertips) so that it forms threads in the soup. Stir in the sesame oil and serve at once, garnished with spring onion shreds.

Per portion: Energy 169Kcal/709kJ; Protein 7.6g; Carbohydrate 19.7g, of which sugars 0.8g; Fat 7.2g, of which saturates 1.2g; Cholesterol 44mg; Calcium 141mg; Fibre 0.2g; Sodium 351mg.

MISO SOUP WITH PORK AND VEGETABLES

THIS IS QUITE A RICH AND FILLING SOUP. ITS JAPANESE NAME, TANUKI JIRU, MEANS RACCOON SOUP FOR HUNTERS, BUT AS RACCOONS ARE NOT EATEN NOWADAYS, PORK IS NOW USED.

SERVES FOUR

INGREDIENTS
    200g/7oz lean boneless pork
    15cm/6in piece gobo or 1 parsnip
    50g/2oz mooli (daikon)
    4 fresh shiitake mushrooms
    ½ konnyaku or ½ × 225–285g/
      8–10¼oz packet tofu
    a little sesame oil, for stir-frying
    600ml/1 pint/2½ cups dashi stock, or
      the same amount of water and
      10ml/2 tsp dashi-no-moto
    70ml/4½ tbsp miso
    2 spring onions (scallions), chopped
    5ml/1 tsp sesame seeds

1 Press the meat down on a chopping board using the palm of your hand and slice horizontally into very thin long strips, then cut the strips crossways into small pieces. Set the pork aside.

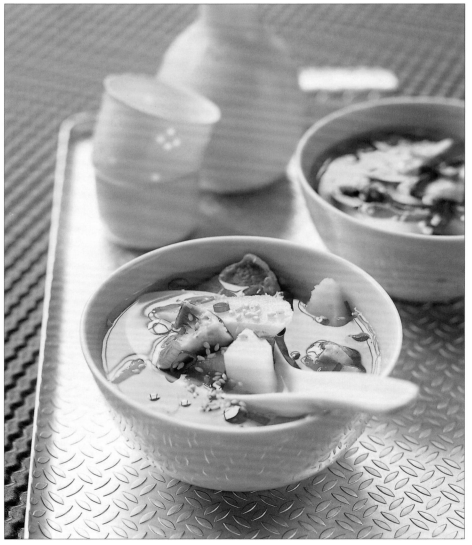

2 Peel the gobo using a potato peeler, then cut diagonally into 1cm/½in thick slices. Quickly plunge the slices into a bowl of cold water to stop them discolouring. If you are using parsnip, peel, cut it in half lengthways, then cut it into 1cm/½in thick half-moon-shaped slices.

3 Peel and slice the mooli into 1.5cm/ ⅔in thick discs. Cut the discs into 1.5cm/⅔in cubes. Remove the shiitake stalks and cut the caps into quarters.

4 Place the konnyaku in a pan of boiling water and cook for 1 minute. Drain and cool. Cut in quarters lengthways, then crossways into 3mm/ ⅛in thick pieces.

5 Heat a little sesame oil in a heavy cast-iron or enamelled pan until purple smoke rises. Stir-fry the pork, then add the tofu, if using, the konnyaku and all the vegetables except for the spring onions. When the colour of the meat has changed, add the stock.

6 Bring to the boil over a medium heat, and skim off the foam until the soup looks fairly clear. Reduce the heat, cover, and simmer for 15 minutes.

7 Put the miso in a small bowl, and mix with 60ml/4 tbsp hot stock to make a smooth paste. Stir one-third of the miso into the soup. Taste and add a little more miso if required. Add the spring onion and remove from the heat. Serve very hot in individual soup bowls and sprinkle with sesame seeds.

Per portion: Energy 114Kcal/475kJ; Protein 15.8g; Carbohydrate 1g, of which sugars 0.8g; Fat 5.2g, of which saturates 1.1g; Cholesterol 32mg; Calcium 306mg; Fibre 0.4g; Sodium 41mg.

CHUNKY LAMB AND CHICKPEA BROTH

THIS JEWISH DISH OF SAVOURY MEATS AND BEANS IS BAKED IN A VERY LOW OVEN FOR SEVERAL HOURS. A PARCEL OF RICE IS OFTEN ADDED TO THE BROTH PART-WAY THROUGH COOKING, WHICH PRODUCES A LIGHTLY PRESSED RICE WITH A SLIGHTLY CHEWY TEXTURE.

SERVES EIGHT

INGREDIENTS

250g/9oz/1 cup chickpeas, soaked overnight
45ml/3 tbsp olive oil
1 onion, chopped
10 garlic cloves, chopped
1 parsnip, sliced
3 carrots, sliced
5–10ml/1–2 tsp ground cumin
2.5ml/½ tsp ground turmeric
15ml/1 tbsp chopped fresh root ginger
2 litres/3½ pints/8 cups beef stock
1 potato, peeled and cut into chunks
½ marrow (large zucchini), sliced or cut into chunks
400g/14oz fresh or canned tomatoes, diced
45–60ml/3–4 tbsp brown or green lentils
2 bay leaves
250g/9oz salted meat such as salt (corned) beef (or double the quantity of lamb)
250g/9oz piece of lamb
½ large bunch fresh coriander (cilantro), chopped
200g/7oz/1 cup long grain rice
1 lemon, cut into wedges and a spicy sauce or fresh chillies, finely chopped, to serve

1 Preheat the oven to 120°C/250°F/ Gas ½. Drain the chickpeas.

2 Heat the oil in a large flameproof casserole, add the onion, garlic, parsnip, carrots, cumin, turmeric and ginger and cook for 2–3 minutes. Add the chickpeas, stock, potato, marrow, tomatoes, lentils, bay leaves, salted meat, lamb and coriander. Cover and cook in the oven for about 3 hours.

COOK'S TIP
Add 1–2 pinches of bicarbonate of soda (baking soda) to the soaking chickpeas to make them tender, but do not add too much as it can make them mushy.

3 Put the rice on a double thickness of muslin (cheesecloth) and tie together at the corners, leaving enough room for the rice to expand while it is cooking.

4 Two hours before the end of cooking, remove the casserole from the oven. Place the rice parcel in the casserole, anchoring the edge of the muslin parcel under the lid so that the parcel is held above the soup and allowed to steam. Return the casserole to the oven and continue cooking for a further 2 hours.

5 Carefully remove the lid and the rice. Skim any fat off the top of the soup and ladle the soup into warm bowls with a scoop of the rice and one or two pieces of meat. Serve with lemon wedges and a spoonful of hot sauce or chopped fresh chillies.

Per portion: Energy 384Kcal/1619kJ; Protein 22.1g; Carbohydrate 46.8g, of which sugars 5.6g; Fat 13.4g, of which saturates 3.9g; Cholesterol 43mg; Calcium 95mg; Fibre 5.4g; Sodium 88mg.

FRAGRANT BEETROOT AND VEGETABLE SOUP WITH SPICED LAMB KUBBEH

THE JEWISH COMMUNITY FROM COCHIN IN INDIA IS SCATTERED NOW BUT THEY ARE STILL FAMOUS FOR THEIR CUISINE. THIS TANGY SOUP IS SERVED WITH DUMPLINGS MADE OF BRIGHT YELLOW PASTA WRAPPED AROUND A SPICY LAMB FILLING AND A SPOONFUL OF FRAGRANT GREEN HERB PASTE.

SERVES SIX TO EIGHT

INGREDIENTS
    15ml/1 tbsp vegetable oil
    ½ onion, finely chopped
    6 garlic cloves
    1 carrot, diced
    1 courgette (zucchini), diced
    ½ celery stick, diced (optional)
    4–5 cardamom pods
    2.5ml/½ tsp curry powder
    4 vacuum-packed beetroot (beets)
      (cooked not pickled), finely diced
      and juice reserved
    1 litre/1¾ pints/4 cups
      vegetable stock
    400g/14oz can chopped tomatoes
    45–60ml/3–4 tbsp chopped fresh
      coriander (cilantro) leaves
    2 bay leaves
    15ml/1 tbsp sugar
    salt and ground black pepper
    15–30ml/1–2 tbsp white wine
      vinegar, to serve
For the kubbeh
    2 large pinches of saffron threads
    15ml/1 tbsp hot water
    15ml/1 tbsp vegetable oil
    1 large onion, chopped
    250g/9oz lean minced (ground) lamb
    5ml/1 tsp vinegar
    ½ bunch fresh mint, chopped
    115g/4oz/1 cup plain (all-purpose) flour
    2–3 pinches of salt
    2.5–5ml/½–1 tsp ground turmeric
    45–60ml/3–4 tbsp cold water
For the ginger and coriander paste
    4 garlic cloves, chopped
    15–25ml/1–1½ tbsp chopped
      fresh root ginger
    ½–4 fresh mild chillies
    ½ large bunch of fresh
      coriander (cilantro)
    30ml/2 tbsp white wine vinegar
    extra virgin olive oil

COOK'S TIP
Serve any leftover paste with meatballs or spread on sandwiches.

1 To make the paste, put the garlic, ginger and chillies in a food processor and process. Add the coriander, vinegar, oil and salt and process to a purée. Set aside.

2 To make the kubbeh filling, place the saffron and hot water in a small bowl and leave to infuse (steep). Meanwhile, heat the oil in a pan and cook the onion until softened. Put the onion and saffron water in a food processor and blend. Add the lamb, season and blend. Add the vinegar and mint, then chill.

3 To make the kubbeh dough, put the flour, salt and ground turmeric in a food processor, then gradually add the water, processing until it forms a sticky dough. Knead on a floured surface for 5 minutes, wrap in a plastic bag and leave to stand for 30 minutes.

4 Divide the dough into 10–15 pieces. Roll each into a ball, then, using a pasta machine, roll into very thin rounds.

5 Lay the rounds on a well-floured surface. Place a spoonful of filling in the middle of each. Dampen the edges of the dough, then bring them together and seal. Set aside on a floured surface.

6 To make the soup, heat the oil in a pan, add the onion and cook for about 10 minutes, or until softened but not browned. Add half the garlic, the carrot, courgette, celery, if using, cardamom pods and curry powder and cook for 2–3 minutes.

7 Add three of the diced beetroot, the stock, tomatoes, coriander, bay leaves and sugar to the pan. Bring to the boil, then reduce the heat and simmer for about 20 minutes.

8 Add the remaining beetroot, beetroot juice and garlic to the soup. Season with salt and pepper to taste and set aside until ready to serve.

9 To serve, reheat the soup and poach the dumplings in a large pan of salted boiling water for about 4 minutes. Using a slotted spoon, remove the dumplings from the water as they are cooked and place on a plate to keep warm.

10 Ladle the soup into bowls, adding a dash of vinegar to each bowl, then add two or three dumplings and a small spoonful of the ginger and coriander paste to each. Serve immediately.

Per portion: Energy 253Kcal/1061kJ; Protein 12.2g; Carbohydrate 26.6g, of which sugars 10.8g; Fat 11.6g, of which saturates 3.4g; Cholesterol 32mg; Calcium 73mg; Fibre 2.8g; Sodium 90mg.

Egg and Cheese Dishes

Although eggs and cheese feature in every one of the recipes that follow, they are not always principal ingredients. In this eclectic collection, Sea Trout Mousse rubs shoulders with Classic Cheese Soufflé and a very up-market omelette that was invented in honour of the novelist Arnold Bennett. Roulades make very good main courses, and this chapter includes a delectable combination of leek roulade with cheese walnut and sweet pepper filling. Many recipes are ideal for vegetarians — if cheese is included, choose a variety made without rennet.

POTATO AND RED PEPPER FRITTATA

A FRITTATA IS LIKE A LARGE OMELETTE. THIS TASTY VERSION IS FILLED WITH POTATOES AND PLENTY OF HERBS. DO USE FRESH MINT IN PREFERENCE TO DRIED IF YOU CAN FIND IT.

2 Whisk together the eggs, mint and seasoning in a bowl, then set aside. Heat the oil in a large frying pan.

3 Add the onion, garlic, peppers and potatoes to the pan and cook, stirring occasionally, for 5 minutes.

4 Pour the egg mixture over the vegetables in the frying pan and stir gently over a low heat.

5 Push the mixture towards the centre of the pan as it cooks to allow the liquid egg to run on to the base. Meanwhile preheat the grill (broiler).

6 When the frittata is lightly set, place the pan under the hot grill for 2–3 minutes until the top is a light golden brown colour.

7 Serve hot or cold, cut into wedges piled high on a serving dish and garnished with sprigs of mint.

SERVES THREE TO FOUR

INGREDIENTS
  450g/1lb small new or
    salad potatoes
  6 eggs
  30ml/2 tbsp chopped
    fresh mint
  30ml/2 tbsp olive oil
  1 onion, chopped
  2 garlic cloves, crushed
  2 red (bell) peppers, seeded and
    coarsely chopped
  salt and ground black pepper
  fresh mint sprigs,
    to garnish

1 Cook the potatoes in their skins in lightly salted, boiling water until just tender. Drain and leave to cool slightly, then cut into thick slices.

Per portion: Energy 374Kcal/1563kJ; Protein 16.7g; Carbohydrate 34.9g, of which sugars 11.3g; Fat 19.4g, of which saturates 4.5g; Cholesterol 381mg; Calcium 87mg; Fibre 3.9g; Sodium 162mg.

FRITTATA WITH LEEK, RED PEPPER AND SPINACH

ALTHOUGH ITALIAN FRITTATA IS GENERALLY SLIGHTLY SOFTER IN TEXTURE, IT IS NOT HUGELY DIFFERENT FROM SPANISH TORTILLA. THIS COMBINATION OF SWEET LEEK, RED PEPPER AND SPINACH IS WONDERFULLY DELICIOUS WITH THE EGG.

SERVES THREE TO FOUR

INGREDIENTS

   30ml/2 tbsp olive oil
   1 red (bell) pepper, seeded and diced
   2.5–5ml/½–1 tsp ground
     toasted cumin
   3 leeks (about 450g/1lb),
     thinly sliced
   150g/5oz small spinach leaves
   45ml/3 tbsp pine nuts, toasted
   5 large (US extra large) eggs
   15ml/1 tbsp chopped fresh basil
   15ml/1 tbsp chopped fresh flat
     leaf parsley
   salt and ground black pepper
   watercress, to garnish
   50g/2oz/⅔ cup grated Parmesan
     cheese, to serve (optional)

1 Heat a frying pan and add the oil. Add the red pepper and cook over a medium heat, stirring occasionally, for 6–8 minutes, until soft and beginning to brown. Add 2.5ml/½ tsp of the cumin and cook for another 1–2 minutes.

2 Stir in the leeks, then part-cover the pan and cook gently for about 5 minutes, until the leeks have softened and collapsed. Season with salt and ground black pepper.

3 Add the spinach and cover. Leave the spinach to wilt in the steam for 3–4 minutes, then stir to mix it into the vegetables, adding the pine nuts.

4 Beat the eggs with salt, pepper, the remaining cumin, basil and parsley. Add to the pan and cook over a gentle heat until the bottom of the omelette sets and turns golden brown. Pull the edges of the omelette away from the sides of the pan as it cooks and tilt the pan so that the uncooked egg runs underneath.

5 Preheat the grill (broiler). Flash the frittata under the hot grill to set the egg on top, but do not let it become too brown. Cut the frittata into wedges and serve warm, garnished with watercress and sprinkled with Parmesan, if using.

VARIATION

A delicious way to serve frittata is to pack it into a slightly hollowed-out crusty loaf and then drizzle it with a little extra virgin olive oil. Wrap tightly in clear film (plastic wrap) and leave to stand for 1–2 hours before cutting into thick slices. It is ideal picnic fare.

Per portion: Energy 268Kcal/1115kJ; Protein 15.5g; Carbohydrate 9.3g, of which sugars 8g; Fat 19g, of which saturates 2g; Cholesterol 0mg; Calcium 132mg; Fibre 5.5g; Sodium 265mg.

LEEK ROULADE WITH CHEESE, WALNUT AND SWEET PEPPER FILLING

THIS ROULADE IS SURPRISINGLY EASY TO PREPARE, AND IT MAKES A GOOD MAIN COURSE WHEN SERVED WITH HOME-MADE TOMATO SAUCE. IT IS ALSO EXCELLENT AS PART OF A BUFFET.

SERVES FOUR TO SIX

INGREDIENTS
    butter or oil, for greasing
    30ml/2 tbsp fine dry
      white breadcrumbs
    75g/3oz/1 cup finely grated
      Parmesan cheese
    50g/2oz/¼ cup butter
    2 leeks, thinly sliced
    40g/1½oz/⅓ cup plain (all-
      purpose) flour
    250ml/8fl oz/1 cup milk
    5ml/1 tsp Dijon mustard
    1.5ml/¼ tsp freshly grated nutmeg
    2 large (US extra large) eggs,
      separated, plus 1 egg white
    2.5ml/½ tsp cream of tartar
    salt and ground black pepper
    rocket (arugula) and balsamic
      dressing, to serve
For the filling
    2 large red (bell) peppers
    350g/12oz/1½ cups ricotta cheese,
    90g/3½oz/scant 1 cup
      chopped walnuts
    4 spring onions (scallions), chopped
    15g/½oz/½ cup fresh basil leaves

1 Grease and line a 30 × 23cm/ 12 × 9in Swiss roll tin (jelly roll pan) with baking parchment, then sprinkle with the breadcrumbs and 30ml/2 tbsp of the grated Parmesan. Preheat the oven to 190°C/375°F/Gas 5.

2 Melt the butter in a pan and cook the leeks for 5 minutes, until softened.

3 Stir in the flour and cook over a low heat, stirring constantly, for 2 minutes, then gradually stir in the milk. Cook for 3–4 minutes, stirring constantly to make a thick sauce.

4 Stir in the mustard and nutmeg and season with salt and plenty of pepper. Reserve 30–45ml/2–3 tbsp of the remaining Parmesan, then stir the rest into the sauce. Cool slightly.

5 Beat the egg yolks into the sauce. In a scrupulously clean bowl, whisk the egg whites and cream of tartar until stiff. Stir 2–3 spoonfuls of the egg white into the leek mixture, then carefully fold in the remaining egg white.

6 Pour the mixture into the tin and gently level it out using a spatula. Bake for 15–18 minutes, until risen and just firm to a light touch in the centre. If the roulade is to be served hot, increase the oven temperature to 200°C/400°F/Gas 6 after removing the roulade.

7 Meanwhile, heat the grill (broiler). Halve and seed the peppers, then grill (broil) them, skin sides uppermost, until black. Place in a bowl, cover and leave for 10 minutes. Peel and cut into strips.

8 Beat the cheese with the walnuts and spring onions. Chop half the basil and beat it into the mixture. Season to taste.

9 Place a large sheet of baking parchment on the work surface and sprinkle with the remaining Parmesan. Turn out the roulade on to it. Strip off the lining paper and allow the roulade to cool slightly. Spread the cheese mixture over it and top with the red pepper strips. Tear the remaining basil leaves and sprinkle them over the top.

10 Using the parchment as a guide, roll up the roulade and roll it on to a serving platter. If serving hot, roll the roulade on to a baking sheet, cover with a tent of foil and bake for 15–20 minutes. Serve with rocket and drizzle with dressing.

Per portion: Energy 602Kcal/2500kJ; Protein 32.9g; Carbohydrate 22.3g, of which sugars 13.7g; Fat 44.1g, of which saturates 18g; Cholesterol 184mg; Calcium 486mg; Fibre 4.3g; Sodium 740mg.

SOFT TACOS WITH SPICED OMELETTE

SERVED HOT, WARM OR COLD, THESE TACOS MAKE EASY FOOD ON THE MOVE FOR YOUNGER MEMBERS OF THE FAMILY, WHEN THEY NEED SOMETHING NOURISHING TO TAKE ON A PICNIC, HIKE OR CYCLE RIDE.

SERVES FOUR

INGREDIENTS
    30ml/2 tbsp sunflower oil
    50g/2oz/1 cup beansprouts
    50g/2oz carrots, cut into
      thin sticks
    25g/1oz Chinese cabbage, chopped
    15ml/1 tbsp light soy sauce
    4 eggs
    1 small spring onion (scallion),
      thinly sliced
    5ml/1 tsp Cajun seasoning
    25g/1oz/2 tbsp butter
    4 soft flour tortillas, warmed in
      the oven or microwave
    salt and ground black pepper

COOK'S TIP
You can buy fresh soft tortillas in large supermarkets. They freeze well, so keep a packet or two in the freezer.

1 Heat the oil in a small frying pan and stir-fry the beansprouts, carrot sticks and chopped cabbage until they begin to soften. Add the soy sauce, stir to combine and set aside.

2 Place the eggs, sliced spring onion, Cajun seasoning, salt and ground black pepper in a bowl, and beat together. Melt the butter in a small pan until it sizzles. Add the beaten eggs and cook over a gentle heat, stirring constantly, until almost firm.

3 Divide the vegetables and scrambled egg evenly among the tortillas, fold up into cones or parcels and serve. For travelling, the tacos can be wrapped in kitchen paper and foil.

VARIATION
Fill warm pitta breads with this spicy omelette mixture. Mini pitta breads are perfect for younger children who may find the folded tacos difficult to handle.

FRENCH COUNTRY-STYLE EGGS

THIS VARIATION ON AN OMELETTE COOKS THE "FILLING" IN THE OMELETTE MIXTURE ITSELF. YOU CAN INCORPORATE LOTS OF DIFFERENT INGREDIENTS, SUCH AS LEFTOVER VEGETABLES.

SERVES TWO

INGREDIENTS
    45–75ml/3–5 tbsp sunflower oil
    50g/2oz thick bacon rashers (strips)
      or pieces, rinds removed
      and chopped
    2 thick slices of bread,
      cut into small cubes
    1 small onion, chopped
    1–2 celery sticks, thinly sliced
    115g/4oz cooked potato, diced
    5 eggs, beaten
    2 garlic cloves, crushed
    handful of young spinach or sorrel
      leaves, stalks removed,
      torn into pieces
    few fresh parsley sprigs, chopped
    salt and ground black pepper

1 Heat the oil in a large heavy frying pan, and cook the bacon and bread cubes until they are crisp and turning golden. Add the chopped onion, celery and diced potato, and continue cooking over a low heat, stirring frequently until all the vegetables have softened and are beginning to turn golden brown.

2 Beat the eggs with the garlic and seasoning, and pour over the vegetables. When the underside is beginning to set, add the spinach or sorrel. Cook until they have wilted and the omelette is only just soft in the middle. Fold the omelette in half and slide it out of the pan. Serve topped with the parsley, if you like.

Top per portion: Energy 280Kcal/1168kJ; Protein 9.5g; Carbohydrate 24.2g, of which sugars 2g; Fat 16.7g, of which saturates 5.5g; Cholesterol 204mg; Calcium 80mg; Fibre 1.5g; Sodium 217mg.
Below per portion: Energy 488Kcal/2034kJ; Protein 23.7g; Carbohydrate 26.2g, of which sugars 3.4g; Fat 32.7g, of which saturates 6.7g; Cholesterol 483mg; Calcium 130mg; Fibre 2.1g; Sodium 649mg.

CLASSIC CHEESE SOUFFLÉ

A LIGHT, DELICATE, MELT-IN-THE-MOUTH CHEESE SOUFFLÉ MAKES ONE OF THE MOST DELIGHTFUL BRUNCHES IMAGINABLE. ALL YOU NEED TO GO WITH IT IS SALAD, A GLASS OF GOOD WINE AND PLENTY OF TIME TO RELAX AND ENJOY A LAZY WEEKEND.

SERVES TWO TO THREE

INGREDIENTS
- 50g/2oz/¼ cup butter
- 30–45ml/2–3 tbsp dried breadcrumbs
- 200ml/7fl oz/scant 1 cup milk
- 30g/1¼oz/3 tbsp plain (all-purpose) flour
- pinch of cayenne pepper
- 2.5ml/½ tsp mustard powder
- 50g/2oz/½ cup mature (sharp) grated Cheddar cheese
- 25g/1oz/⅓ cup freshly grated Parmesan cheese
- 4 eggs, separated, plus 1 egg white
- salt and ground black pepper

2 Heat the milk in a large pan. Add the remaining butter, flour and cayenne, with the mustard powder. Bring to the boil over a low heat, whisking steadily until the mixture thickens to a smooth sauce.

5 Add a few spoonfuls of the beaten egg whites to the sauce to lighten it. Beat well, then tip the rest of the whites into the pan and, with a large metal spoon, gently fold in the egg whites, using a figure-of-eight movement to combine the mixtures.

1 Preheat the oven to 190°C/375°F/Gas 5. Melt 15ml/1 tbsp of the butter and use to grease a 1.2 litre/2 pint/5 cup soufflé dish thoroughly. Coat the inside of the dish with breadcrumbs. Shake out any excess.

3 Simmer the sauce for a minute or two, then turn off the heat and whisk in all the Cheddar and half the Parmesan. Cool a little, then beat in the egg yolks. Check the seasoning; the mixture should be well seasoned. Set aside.

6 Pour the mixture into the prepared soufflé dish, level the top and, to help the soufflé rise evenly, run your finger around the inside rim of the dish.

7 Place the dish on a baking sheet. Sprinkle the remaining Parmesan over the top of the soufflé mixture and bake for about 25 minutes, until risen and golden brown. Serve immediately.

VARIATIONS
- Crumbled blue cheese, such as Stilton, Shropshire Blue or Fourme d'Ambert, will produce a soufflé with a much stronger, sharper flavour.
- This soufflé can also be served as a more substantial main meal by adding a few extra ingredients. Try putting a layer of chopped vegetables, such as ratatouille or sautéed mushrooms, at the base of the dish before adding the cheese mixture. Bake as above.

4 Whisk the egg whites in a large grease-free bowl until they form soft, glossy peaks. Do not overbeat or the whites will become grainy and difficult to fold in.

COOK'S TIP
It is important to serve soufflé the moment it is cooked and taken from the oven. Otherwise, the wonderful puffed top may sink before it reaches the expectantly waiting diners.

Per portion: Energy 654Kcal/2721kJ; Protein 31.9g; Carbohydrate 28.2g, of which sugars 5.5g; Fat 46.1g, of which saturates 25.3g; Cholesterol 476mg; Calcium 558mg; Fibre 0.8g; Sodium 797mg.

SOUFFLÉ OMELETTE WITH MUSHROOMS

A LIGHT-AS-AIR OMELETTE MAKES AN IDEAL MEAL FOR ONE, ESPECIALLY WITH THIS DELICIOUS FILLING. USE A COMBINATION OF DIFFERENT MUSHROOMS IF YOU LIKE.

SERVES ONE

INGREDIENTS
    2 eggs, separated
    15g/½oz/1 tbsp butter
    flat leaf parsley or coriander
       (cilantro) leaves, to garnish
For the mushroom sauce
    15g/½oz/1 tbsp butter
    75g/3oz/generous 1 cup button
       (white) mushrooms, thinly sliced
    15ml/1 tbsp plain (all-purpose) flour
    85–120ml/3–4fl oz/⅓–½ cup milk
    5ml/1 tsp chopped fresh
       parsley (optional)
    salt and ground black pepper

1 To make the mushroom sauce, melt the butter in a pan or frying pan and add the sliced mushrooms. Cook gently for 4–5 minutes, stirring occasionally, until tender and golden.

2 Stir in the flour, then gradually add the milk, stirring constantly. Cook until boiling and thickened. Add the parsley, if using, and season to taste with salt and pepper. Keep warm.

3 Beat the egg yolks with 15ml/1 tbsp water and season with a little salt and pepper. Whisk the egg whites until stiff, then fold into the egg yolks using a metal spoon. Preheat the grill (broiler).

4 Melt the butter in a large frying pan and pour the egg mixture into the pan. Cook over a gentle heat for 2–4 minutes. Place the frying pan under the grill and cook for a further 3–4 minutes until the top is golden brown.

5 Slide the omelette on to a warmed serving plate, pour the mushroom sauce over the top and fold the omelette in half. Serve, garnished with parsley or coriander leaves.

COOK'S TIP
For extra flavour, add a few drops of Worcestershire sauce to the mushrooms as they are cooking.

Per portion: Energy 566Kcal/2348kJ; Protein 18.9g; Carbohydrate 20.1g, of which sugars 4.7g; Fat 46.1g, of which saturates 25g; Cholesterol 471mg; Calcium 199mg; Fibre 1.4g; Sodium 423mg.

OMELETTE ARNOLD BENNETT

CREATED FOR THE AUTHOR ARNOLD BENNETT, WHO FREQUENTLY DINED AT THE SAVOY HOTEL IN LONDON, THIS CREAMY, SMOKED HADDOCK SOUFFLÉ OMELETTE IS NOW SERVED ALL OVER THE WORLD.

SERVES TWO

INGREDIENTS

175g/6oz smoked haddock fillet,
  poached and drained
50g/2oz/4 tbsp butter, diced
175ml/6fl oz/¾ cup whipping or
  double (heavy) cream
4 eggs, separated
40g/1½oz/⅓ cup grated mature
  (sharp) Cheddar cheese
ground black pepper
watercress, to garnish

COOK'S TIP

Try to buy traditional cold-smoked haddock that does not contain artificial colouring for this recipe. Besides being better for you, it gives the omelette a lighter, more attractive colour.

1 Remove the skin and any bones from the haddock fillet and discard. Carefully flake the flesh using a fork.

2 Melt half the butter with 60ml/4 tbsp of the cream in a fairly small non-stick pan, then add the flaked fish and stir together gently. Cover the pan with a lid, remove it from the heat and set aside to cool completely.

3 Mix the egg yolks with 15ml/1 tbsp cream. Add pepper, then stir into the fish. In a separate bowl, mix the cheese and the remaining cream. Stiffly whisk the egg whites, then fold into the fish mixture. Heat the remaining butter in an omelette pan, add the fish mixture and cook until browned underneath. Pour the cheese mixture over and grill (broil) until bubbling. Garnish and serve.

Per portion: Energy 821Kcal/3396kJ; Protein 36.1g; Carbohydrate 2.6g, of which sugars 2.6g; Fat 74g, of which saturates 42.6g; Cholesterol 577mg; Calcium 280mg; Fibre 0g; Sodium 1123mg.

PRAWN, EGG AND AVOCADO MOUSSES

LIGHT AND CREAMY, WITH LOTS OF TEXTURE AND A DELICIOUS COMBINATION OF FLAVOURS, THESE LITTLE MOUSSES ARE BEST SERVED AS A LIGHT LUNCH ON THE DAY YOU MAKE THEM.

SERVES SIX

INGREDIENTS

olive oil, for greasing
11g/¼oz sachet (envelope) gelatine
juice and rind of 1 lemon
60ml/4 tbsp good mayonnaise
60ml/4 tbsp chopped fresh dill
5ml/1 tsp anchovy essence (extract)
5ml/1 tsp Worcestershire sauce
4 eggs, hard-boiled, shelled
  and chopped
175g/6oz/1 cup cooked, peeled
  prawns (shrimp), chopped if large
1 large ripe but just firm avocado,
  peeled, stoned (pitted) and diced
250ml/8fl oz/1 cup double (heavy) or
  whipping cream, lightly whipped
2 egg whites
salt and ground black pepper
fresh dill sprigs, to garnish
hot bread or toast, to serve

1 Lightly grease six small ramekins, then wrap a piece of greaseproof (waxed) paper tightly around each of the dishes to form a collar. Make sure that the paper comes well above the top of the dish, allowing plenty of room for the mousse to stand above the top of the dish. Secure firmly with tape so that the paper will support the mousse as it sets. If you prefer, prepare one small soufflé dish rather than individual ramekins.

2 Place the gelatine, lemon juice and 15ml/1 tbsp hot water in a small bowl, and place over a pan of hot water. Stir until the mixture becomes clear. Cool slightly, then blend in the lemon rind, mayonnaise, dill and sauces.

3 Mix the chopped hard-boiled eggs, prawns and avocado in a medium bowl. Stir in the gelatine mixture, then fold in the whipped cream.Whisk the egg whites until holding soft peaks and fold into the mixture with seasoning to taste. Spoon into the ramekins and chill for about 4 hours. Garnish with dill and serve with hot bread or toast.

COOK'S TIP
Other fish or shellfish can make a good alternative to prawns. Try substituting the same quantity of smoked trout or cooked crab meat.

Per portion: Energy 431Kcal/1778kJ; Protein 7.5g; Carbohydrate 1.7g, of which sugars 1.2g; Fat 43.9g, of which saturates 17.5g; Cholesterol 131mg; Calcium 50mg; Fibre 0.8g; Sodium 195mg.

SMOKED FISH AND ASPARAGUS MOUSSE

THIS ELEGANT MOUSSE LOOKS VERY SPECIAL WITH ITS STUDDING OF ASPARAGUS AND SMOKED SALMON. SERVE A MUSTARD AND DILL DRESSING SEPARATELY IF YOU LIKE.

SERVES EIGHT

INGREDIENTS
  15ml/1 tbsp powdered gelatine
  juice of 1 lemon
  105ml/7 tbsp fish stock
  50g/2oz/¼ cup butter, plus extra
    for greasing
  2 shallots, finely chopped
  225g/8oz smoked trout fillets
  105ml/7 tbsp sour cream
  225g/8oz/1 cup low-fat cream cheese
    or cottage cheese
  1 egg white
  12 spinach leaves, blanched
  12 fresh asparagus spears,
    lightly cooked
  115g/4oz smoked salmon, cut into
    long strips
  salt
  shredded beetroot (beet) and leaves,
    to garnish

4 Grease a 1 litre/1¾ pint/4 cup loaf tin (pan) or terrine with butter, then line it with the spinach leaves. Carefully spread half the trout mousse over the spinach-covered base, arrange the asparagus spears on top, then cover with the remaining trout mousse.

5 Arrange the smoked salmon strips lengthways on the mousse and fold over the overhanging spinach leaves. Cover with clear film (plastic wrap) and chill for 4 hours, until set. To serve, remove the clear film, turn out on to a serving dish and garnish.

1 Sprinkle the gelatine over the lemon juice and leave until spongy. In a small pan, heat the fish stock, then add the soaked gelatine and stir to dissolve completely. Set aside. Melt the butter in a small pan, add the shallots and cook gently until softened but not coloured.

2 Break up the smoked trout fillets and put them in a food processor with the shallots, sour cream, stock mixture and cream or cottage cheese. Process until smooth, then spoon into a bowl.

3 In a clean bowl, beat the egg white with a pinch of salt to soft peaks. Fold into the fish. Cover the bowl and chill for 30 minutes, or until starting to set.

Per portion: Energy 174Kcal/723kJ; Protein 15.8g; Carbohydrate 2.8g, of which sugars 2.6g; Fat 11g, of which saturates 6g; Cholesterol 58mg; Calcium 75mg; Fibre 0.8g; Sodium 432mg.

STRIPED FISH TERRINE

SERVE THIS ATTRACTIVE TERRINE COLD OR JUST WARM, WITH A HOLLANDAISE SAUCE IF YOU LIKE. IT IS IDEAL FOR A SUMMER LUNCHEON OR BUFFET.

SERVES EIGHT

INGREDIENTS
15ml/1 tbsp sunflower oil
450g/1lb salmon fillet, skinned
450g/1lb sole fillets, skinned
3 egg whites
105ml/7 tbsp double (heavy) cream
15ml/1 tbsp finely chopped
  fresh chives
juice of 1 lemon
115g/4oz/1 cup fresh or frozen
  peas, cooked
5ml/1 tsp chopped fresh mint leaves
salt, ground white pepper and
  grated nutmeg
thinly sliced cucumber, salad cress
  and chives, to garnish

1 Grease a 1 litre/1¾ pint/4 cup loaf tin (pan) or terrine with the oil. Slice the salmon thinly, then cut it and the sole into long strips, 2.5cm/1in wide. Preheat the oven to 200°C/400°F/Gas 6.

2 Line the terrine neatly with alternate slices of salmon and sole, leaving the ends overhanging the edge. You should be left with about a third of the salmon and half the sole.

3 In a grease-free bowl, beat the egg whites with a pinch of salt until they form soft peaks. Purée the remaining sole in a food processor. Spoon into a mixing bowl, season, then fold in two-thirds of the egg whites, followed by two-thirds of the cream. Put half the mixture into a second bowl; stir in the chives. Add nutmeg to the first bowl.

4 Purée the remaining salmon, scrape it into a bowl; add the lemon juice. Fold in the remaining whites, then the cream.

5 Process the peas and mint. Season the mixture and spread it over the base of the terrine, smoothing the surface with a spatula. Spoon over the sole with chives mixture and spread evenly.

6 Add the salmon mixture, then finish with the plain sole mixture. Cover with the overhanging fish fillets and make a lid of oiled foil. Stand the terrine in a roasting pan and pour in enough boiling water to come halfway up the sides.

7 Bake for 15–20 minutes, until the top fillets are just cooked and the mousse feels springy. Remove the foil, lay a wire rack over the top of the terrine and invert both rack and terrine on to a lipped baking sheet to catch the cooking juices that drain out. Keep these to make fish stock or soup.

8 Leaving the tin in place, let the terrine stand for about 15 minutes, then turn the terrine over again. Invert it on to a serving dish and lift off the tin carefully. Serve warm, or chill in the refrigerator first and serve cold. Garnish with thinly sliced cucumber, salad cress and chives before serving.

COOK'S TIPS
• Pop the salmon into the freezer about an hour before slicing it. If it is almost frozen, it will be much easier to slice.
• You can line the tin or terrine with oven-safe clear film (plastic wrap) after greasing and before adding the salmon and sole strips. This makes it a little easier to turn out the terrine but is not strictly necessary.

Per portion: Energy 245Kcal/1019kJ; Protein 23.8g; Carbohydrate 1.9g, of which sugars 0.6g; Fat 15.8g, of which saturates 5.7g; Cholesterol 74mg; Calcium 38mg; Fibre 0.7g; Sodium 107mg.

QUENELLES OF SOLE

TRADITIONALLY, THESE LIGHT FISH "DUMPLINGS" ARE MADE WITH PIKE, BUT THEY ARE EVEN BETTER MADE WITH SOLE OR OTHER WHITE FISH. IF YOU ARE FEELING EXTRAVAGANT, SERVE THEM WITH A CREAMY SHELLFISH SAUCE STUDDED WITH CRAYFISH TAILS OR PRAWNS.

SERVES SIX

INGREDIENTS
   450g/1lb sole fillets, skinned and cut
     into large pieces
   4 egg whites
   600ml/1 pint/2½ cups double
     (heavy) cream
   salt, ground white pepper and
     grated nutmeg
For the sauce
   1 small shallot, finely chopped
   60ml/4 tbsp dry vermouth
   120ml/4fl oz/½ cup fish stock
   150ml/¼ pint/⅔ cup double
     (heavy) cream
   50g/2oz/¼ cup butter, diced
   chopped fresh parsley, to garnish

1 Check the sole for stray bones, then put the pieces in a blender or food processor. Add a generous pinch of salt and a grinding of pepper. Switch on and, with the motor running, add the egg whites one at a time through the feeder tube to make a smooth purée. Press the purée through a metal sieve placed over a bowl. Stand the bowl of purée in a larger bowl and surround it with plenty of crushed ice or ice cubes.

2 Whip the cream until very thick and floppy, but not stiff. Gradually fold it into the fish mousse, making sure each spoonful has been absorbed completely before adding the next. Season with salt and pepper, then stir in nutmeg to taste. Cover the bowl of mousse and transfer it, still in its bowl of ice, to the refrigerator. Chill for several hours.

3 To make the sauce, combine the shallot, vermouth and fish stock in a small pan. Bring to the boil and cook until reduced by half. Add the cream and boil again until the sauce has the consistency of single (light) cream. Strain, return to the pan and whisk in the butter, one piece at a time, until the sauce is very creamy. Season and keep hot, but do not let it boil.

4 Bring a wide shallow pan of lightly salted water to the boil, then reduce the heat so that the water surface barely trembles. Using two tablespoons dipped in hot water, shape the fish mousse into ovals. As each quenelle is shaped, slip it into the simmering water.

5 Poach the quenelles, in batches, for 8–10 minutes, until they feel just firm to the touch, but are still slightly creamy inside. As each is cooked, lift it out on a slotted spoon, drain on kitchen paper and keep hot. When all the quenelles are cooked, arrange them on heated plates. Pour the sauce around. Serve garnished with parsley.

COOK'S TIP
Keep the heat low when poaching, as quenelles disintegrate in boiling water.

Per portion: Energy 767Kcal/3165kJ; Protein 17.6g; Carbohydrate 2.5g, of which sugars 2.5g; Fat 75.3g, of which saturates 46.1g; Cholesterol 227mg; Calcium 86mg; Fibre 0g; Sodium 195mg.

SEA TROUT MOUSSE

THIS DELICIOUSLY CREAMY MOUSSE MAKES A LITTLE SEA TROUT GO A LONG WAY. IT IS EQUALLY GOOD MADE WITH FRESH SALMON FILLETS IF SEA TROUT IS UNAVAILABLE.

SERVES SIX

INGREDIENTS
    250g/9oz sea trout fillet
    120ml/4fl oz/½ cup fish stock
    2 gelatine leaves, or 15ml/1 tbsp
      powdered gelatine
    juice of ½ lemon
    30ml/2 tbsp dry sherry or
      dry vermouth
    30ml/2 tbsp freshly grated Parmesan
    300ml/½ pint/1¼ cups
      whipping cream
    2 egg whites
    15ml/1 tbsp sunflower oil
    salt and ground white pepper
For the garnish
    5cm/2in piece of cucumber, with
      peel, thinly sliced and halved
    fresh dill or chervil

3 When the trout is cool enough to handle, remove the skin and flake the flesh. Pour the stock into a food processor or blender. Process briefly, then gradually add the flaked trout, lemon juice, sherry or vermouth and Parmesan through the feeder tube, continuing to process the mixture until it is smooth. Scrape into a large bowl and leave to cool completely.

4 Lightly whip the cream in a bowl; fold it into the cold trout mixture. Season to taste, then cover with clear film (plastic wrap) and chill until the mousse is just beginning to set. It should have the consistency of mayonnaise.

5 In a grease-free bowl, beat the egg whites with a pinch of salt until softly peaking. Using a large metal spoon, stir one-third into the trout mixture to slacken it, then fold in the rest.

6 Lightly grease six ramekins with the sunflower oil. Divide the mousse among the ramekins and level the surface. Place in the refrigerator for 2–3 hours, until set. Just before serving, arrange a few slices of cucumber and a small herb sprig on each mousse and add a little chopped dill or chervil.

1 Put the sea trout in a shallow pan. Pour in the fish stock and heat to simmering point. Poach the fish for 3–4 minutes, until it is lightly cooked. Strain the stock into a jug (pitcher) and leave the trout to cool slightly.

2 Add the gelatine to the hot stock and stir until it has dissolved completely. Set aside until required.

COOK'S TIP
Serve the mousse with Melba toast, if you like. Toast thin slices of bread on both sides under the grill (broiler), then cut off the crusts and carefully slice each piece of toast in half horizontally. Return to the grill pan, untoasted sides up, and grill (broil) again. The thin slices will swiftly brown and curl.

Per portion: Energy 286Kcal/1181kJ; Protein 12g; Carbohydrate 1.5g, of which sugars 1.5g; Fat 25.2g, of which saturates 13.9g; Cholesterol 58mg; Calcium 94mg; Fibre 0g; Sodium 111mg.

SALADS

These are salads in a starring role — main course dishes that can be served solo or used as the main attractions on a buffet table. For a summer lunch, Chicken and Mango Salad would be an excellent choice, or you might like to celebrate a special occasion with a magnificent Insalata di Mare. As the weather cools, introduce a hint of warmth with a Warm Dressed Salad with Poached Eggs or Seared Swordfish with Citrus Dressing. For a picnic or packed lunch, Bean Salad with Tuna and Red Onion would be the ideal choice. Pack the dressing separately and add it about half an hour before serving.

PERUVIAN SALAD

THIS REALLY IS A SPECTACULAR-LOOKING SALAD. IT COULD BE SERVED AS A SIDE DISH OR WOULD MAKE A DELICIOUS LIGHT LUNCH. IN PERU, WHITE RICE WOULD BE USED, BUT BROWN RICE ADDS AN INTERESTING TEXTURE AND FLAVOUR.

SERVES FOUR

INGREDIENTS
225g/8oz/2 cups cooked long grain brown or white rice
15ml/1 tbsp chopped fresh parsley
1 red (bell) pepper
1 small onion, sliced
olive oil, for sprinkling
115g/4oz green beans, halved
50g/2oz/½ cup baby corn
4 quail's eggs, hard-boiled
25–50g/1–2oz Spanish ham, cut into thin slices (optional)
1 small avocado
lemon juice, for sprinkling
75g/3oz mixed salad leaves
15ml/1 tbsp capers
about 10 stuffed olives, halved

For the dressing
1 garlic clove, crushed
60ml/4 tbsp olive oil
45ml/3 tbsp sunflower oil
30ml/2 tbsp lemon juice
45ml/3 tbsp natural (plain) yogurt
2.5ml/½ tsp mustard
2.5ml/½ tsp sugar
salt and freshly ground black pepper

1 Make the dressing by placing all the ingredients in a bowl and whisking with a fork until smooth. Alternatively, shake the ingredients together in a jam jar.

2 Put the cooked rice into a large, glass salad bowl and spoon in about half the dressing. Add the chopped parsley, stir well to mix and set aside in a cool place.

3 Cut the pepper in half, remove the seeds and pith, then place the halves, cut side down, in a small roasting pan. Add the onion rings. Sprinkle the onion with a little olive oil, place the pan under a hot grill (broiler) and cook for 5–6 minutes, until the pepper blackens and blisters and the onion turns golden. You may need to stir the onion once or twice so that it grills (broils) evenly.

4 Stir the onion in with the rice. Put the pepper in a plastic bag and knot the bag. When the steam has loosened the skin on the pepper halves and they are cool enough to handle, peel them and cut the flesh into thin strips.

COOK'S TIP
This dish looks particularly attractive if served in a deep, glass salad bowl. Guests can then see the various layers, starting with the white rice, then the green salad leaves, topped by the bright colours of peppers, corn, eggs and olives.

5 Cook the green beans in boiling water for 2 minutes, then add the corn and cook for 1–2 minutes more, until tender. Drain both vegetables, refresh them under cold water, then drain again. Place in a large mixing bowl and add the red pepper strips, quails' eggs and ham, if using.

6 Peel the avocado, remove the stone (pit), and cut the flesh into slices or chunks. Sprinkle with the lemon juice to prevent discoloration. Put the salad leaves in a separate mixing bowl, add the avocado and mix lightly. Arrange the salad on top of the rice.

7 Stir about 45ml/3 tbsp of the remaining dressing into the green bean and pepper mixture. Pile this on top of the salad.

8 Sprinkle the capers and stuffed olives on top and serve the salad with the remaining dressing.

Per portion: Energy 404Kcal/1675kJ; Protein 6.3g; Carbohydrate 25.6g, of which sugars 6.9g; Fat 31.3g, of which saturates 5.2g; Cholesterol 58mg; Calcium 75mg; Fibre 3.7g; Sodium 598mg.

CAESAR SALAD

THIS MUCH-ENJOYED SALAD WAS CREATED BY CAESAR CORDONI IN TIJUANA IN 1924. BE SURE TO USE CRISP LETTUCE AND ADD THE SOFT EGGS AND GARLIC CROÛTONS AT THE LAST MINUTE.

3 Add the remaining olive oil to the salad leaves and season with salt and pepper. Toss to coat well.

4 Break the soft-boiled eggs on top. Sprinkle with the lemon juice and toss to combine the ingredients.

5 Add the grated Parmesan cheese and anchovies, if using, then toss again.

6 Sprinkle the croûtons on top of the salad and serve immediately.

COOK'S TIPS
To make a tangier dressing, mix the olive oil with 30ml/2 tbsp white wine vinegar, 2.5ml/½ tsp mustard, 5ml/1 tsp sugar, and salt and pepper.

SERVES SIX

INGREDIENTS
175ml/6fl oz/¾ cup salad oil,
   preferably olive oil
115g/4oz/2 cups French or
   Italian bread, cut in 2.5cm/
   1in cubes
1 large garlic clove, crushed with
   the flat side of a knife
1 cos or romaine lettuce
2 eggs, boiled for 1 minute
120ml/4fl oz/½ cup
   lemon juice
50g/2oz/⅔ cup freshly grated
   Parmesan cheese
6 anchovy fillets, drained and
   finely chopped (optional)
salt and ground black pepper

1 Heat 50ml/2fl oz/¼ cup of the oil in a frying pan. Add the bread and garlic and cook, stirring constantly, until the cubes are golden brown. Drain on kitchen paper and discard the garlic.

2 Tear large lettuce leaves into smaller pieces. Put all the lettuce in a bowl.

Per portion: Energy 307Kcal/1272kJ; Protein 8g; Carbohydrate 11.7g, of which sugars 1.4g; Fat 25.7g, of which saturates 5.4g; Cholesterol 84mg; Calcium 149mg; Fibre 0.7g; Sodium 230mg.

WARM DRESSED SALAD <u>WITH</u> POACHED EGGS

SOFT POACHED EGGS, CHILLI, HOT CROÛTONS AND COOL, CRISP SALAD LEAVES MAKE A LIVELY AND UNUSUAL COMBINATION. THIS DELICIOUS SALAD IS PERFECT FOR A SUMMER LUNCH.

SERVES TWO

INGREDIENTS
- ½ small loaf Granary (whole-wheat) bread
- 45ml/3 tbsp chilli oil
- 2 eggs
- 115g/4oz mixed salad leaves
- 45ml/3 tbsp extra virgin olive oil
- 2 garlic cloves, crushed
- 15ml/1 tbsp balsamic vinegar
- 50g/2oz Parmesan cheese, shaved
- ground black pepper (optional)

1 Carefully cut the crust from the Granary loaf and discard. Cut the bread into 2.5cm/1in cubes.

2 Heat the chilli oil in a large frying pan. Add the bread cubes and cook for about 5 minutes, tossing the cubes occasionally, until they are crisp and golden brown all over.

COOK'S TIP
If you are very sensitive to spicy flavours, cook the croûtons in olive oil or a nut oil, such as walnut or hazelnut, rather than using chilli oil.

3 Meanwhile, bring a pan of water to the boil. Break each egg into a jug (pitcher) and carefully slide into the water, one at a time. Gently poach the eggs for about 4 minutes until cooked.

4 Divide the salad leaves between two plates. Remove the croûtons from the pan and arrange them over the leaves.

5 Wipe the pan clean with kitchen paper. Then heat the olive oil in the pan, add the garlic and vinegar and cook over high heat for 1 minute. Pour the warm dressing over the salads.

6 Place a poached egg on each salad. Top with thin Parmesan shavings and a little ground black pepper, if you like.

Per portion: Energy 730Kcal/3042kJ; Protein 26.2g; Carbohydrate 48.4g, of which sugars 3.9g; Fat 49.3g, of which saturates 12.1g; Cholesterol 215mg; Calcium 556mg; Fibre 3.8g; Sodium 890mg.

THAI PRAWN SALAD WITH GARLIC DRESSING AND FRIZZLED SHALLOTS

IN THIS INTENSELY FLAVOURED SALAD, PRAWNS AND MANGO ARE PARTNERED WITH A SWEET-SOUR GARLIC DRESSING HEIGHTENED WITH THE HOT TASTE OF CHILLI. THE CRISP FRIZZLED SHALLOTS ARE A TRADITIONAL ADDITION TO THAI SALADS.

SERVES FOUR TO SIX

INGREDIENTS
675g/1½lb raw prawns (shrimp), peeled and deveined with tails on
finely shredded rind of 1 lime
½ fresh red chilli, seeded and finely chopped
30ml/2 tbsp olive oil, plus extra for brushing
1 ripe but firm mango
2 carrots, cut into long thin shreds
10cm/4in piece cucumber, sliced
1 small red onion, halved and thinly sliced
a few fresh coriander (cilantro) sprigs
a few fresh mint sprigs
45ml/3 tbsp roasted peanuts, coarsely chopped
4 large shallots, thinly sliced and fried until crisp in 30ml/2 tbsp groundnut (peanut) oil
salt and ground black pepper
For the dressing
1 large garlic clove, chopped
10–15ml/2–3 tsp caster (superfine) sugar
juice of 2 limes
15–30ml/1–2 tbsp Thai fish sauce
1 fresh red chilli, seeded
5–10ml/1–2 tsp light rice vinegar

1 Place the prawns in a glass or china dish and add the lime rind and chilli. Season with salt and pepper and spoon the oil over them. Toss to mix and leave to marinate for 30–40 minutes.

2 For the dressing, place the garlic in a mortar with 10ml/2 tsp caster sugar and pound until smooth, then work in the juice of 1½ limes and 15ml/1 tbsp of the Thai fish sauce.

3 Transfer the dressing to a jug (pitcher). Finely chop half the chilli. and add it to the dressing. Taste and add more sugar, lime juice, fish sauce and the rice vinegar to taste.

COOK'S TIP
To devein prawns, make a shallow cut down the back of the prawn using a small, sharp knife. Using the tip of the knife, lift out the thin, black vein, then rinse the prawn thoroughly under cold, running water.

4 Peel and stone (pit) the mango, then cut it into very fine strips.

5 Toss together the mango, carrots, cucumber and onion, and half the dressing. Arrange the salad on individual plates or in bowls.

6 Heat a ridged, cast-iron griddle pan or heavy frying pan until very hot. Brush with a little olive oil, then sear the prawns for 2–3 minutes on each side, until they turn pink and are patched with brown on the outside. Arrange the prawns on the salads.

7 Sprinkle the remaining dressing over the salads and top with the sprigs of coriander and mint. Finely shred the remaining chilli and sprinkle it over the salads with the peanuts and crisp-fried shallots. Serve immediately.

Per portion: Energy 349Kcal/1458kJ; Protein 33.5g; Carbohydrate 15.4g, of which sugars 13.7g; Fat 17.4g, of which saturates 3g; Cholesterol 329mg; Calcium 162mg; Fibre 2.8g; Sodium 596mg.

PRAWN SALAD

IN MEXICO, THIS SALAD WOULD FORM THE FISH COURSE IN A FORMAL MEAL, BUT IT IS SO GOOD THAT YOU'LL WANT TO SERVE IT ON ALL SORTS OF OCCASIONS. IT IS PERFECT FOR A BUFFET LUNCH.

SERVES FOUR

INGREDIENTS
    450g/1lb cooked peeled
      prawns (shrimp)
    juice of 1 lime
    3 tomatoes
    1 ripe but firm avocado
    30ml/2 tbsp hot chilli sauce
    5ml/1 tsp sugar
    150ml/¼ pint/⅔ cup sour cream
    2 Little Gem (Bibb) lettuces
    salt and ground black pepper
    fresh basil leaves and strips of green
      (bell) pepper to garnish

1 Put the prawns in a large bowl, add the lime juice and salt and pepper. Toss lightly, then leave to marinate.

2 Cut a cross in the base of each tomato. Place them in a heatproof bowl and pour over boiling water to cover.

3 After 3 minutes, lift the tomatoes out on a slotted spoon and plunge them into a bowl of cold water. Drain. The skins will have begun to peel back easily from the crosses.

4 Peel the tomatoes completely, then cut them in half and squeeze out the seeds. Chop the flesh into 1cm/½in cubes and add it to the prawns.

5 Cut the avocado in half, remove the skin and stone (pit), then slice the flesh into 1cm/½in chunks. Add it to the prawn and tomato mixture.

6 Mix the hot chilli sauce, sugar and sour cream in a bowl. Fold into the prawn mixture. Line a bowl with the lettuce leaves, then top with the prawn mixture. Cover and chill for at least 1 hour, then garnish with fresh basil and strips of green pepper. Crusty bread makes a perfect accompaniment.

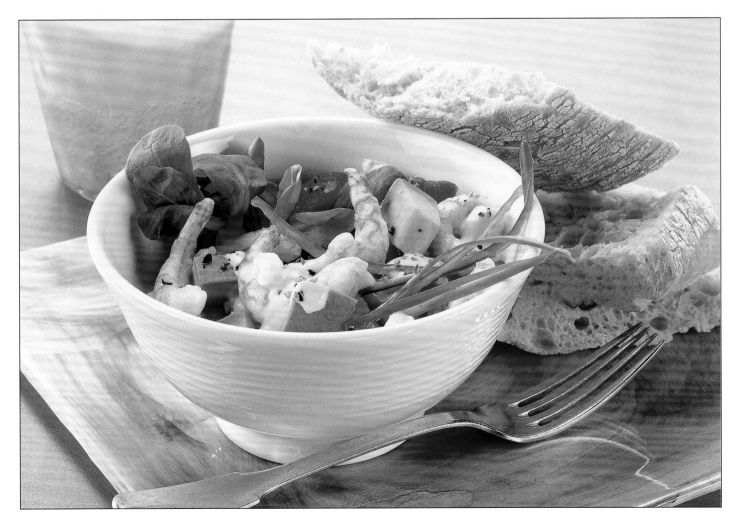

Per portion: Energy 284Kcal/1185kJ; Protein 28.1g; Carbohydrate 5g, of which sugars 4.4g; Fat 16.9g, of which saturates 6.7g; Cholesterol 114mg; Calcium 226mg; Fibre 2.3g; Sodium 1814mg.

INSALATA DI MARE

YOU CAN VARY THE SEAFOOD IN THIS ITALIAN SALAD ACCORDING TO WHAT IS AVAILABLE, BUT TRY TO INCLUDE AT LEAST TWO KINDS OF SHELLFISH AND SOME SQUID. THE SALAD IS GOOD WARM OR COLD.

SERVES FOUR

INGREDIENTS
- 450g/1lb live mussels, scrubbed and bearded
- 450g/1lb small clams, scrubbed
- 105ml/7 tbsp dry white wine
- 225g/8oz squid, cleaned
- 4 large scallops, with their corals
- 30ml/2 tbsp olive oil
- 2 garlic cloves, finely chopped
- 1 small dried red chilli, crumbled
- 225g/8oz whole cooked prawns (shrimp), in the shell
- 6–8 large chicory (Belgian endive) leaves
- 6–8 radicchio leaves
- 15ml/1 tbsp chopped fresh flat leaf parsley, to garnish

For the dressing
- 5ml/1 tsp Dijon mustard
- 30ml/2 tbsp white wine vinegar
- 5ml/1 tsp lemon juice
- 120ml/4fl oz/½ cup extra virgin olive oil
- salt and ground black pepper

1 Put the mussels and clams in a large pan with the white wine. Cover and cook over a high heat, shaking the pan occasionally, for about 4 minutes, until they have opened. Discard any that remain closed. Use a slotted spoon to transfer the shellfish to a bowl, then strain and reserve the cooking liquid and set it aside.

2 Cut the squid into thin rings; chop the tentacles. Leave small squid whole. Halve the scallops horizontally.

3 Heat the oil in a frying pan, add the garlic, chilli, squid, scallops and corals, and sauté for about 2 minutes, until just cooked and tender. Lift the squid and scallops out of the pan; reserve the oil.

4 When the shellfish are cool enough to handle, shell them, keeping a dozen of each in the shell. Peel all but 6–8 of the prawns. Pour the shellfish cooking liquid into a small pan, set over a high heat and reduce by half. Mix all the shelled and unshelled mussels and clams with the squid and scallops, then add the prawns.

5 To make the dressing, whisk the mustard with the vinegar and lemon juice together and season to taste. Add the olive oil, whisk vigorously, then whisk in the reserved cooking liquid and the oil from the frying pan. Pour the dressing over the seafood mixture and toss lightly to coat well.

6 Arrange the chicory and radicchio leaves around the edge of a large serving dish and pile the mixed seafood salad into the centre. Sprinkle with the chopped flat leaf parsley and serve immediately or chill first.

Per portion: Energy 445Kcal/1861kJ; Protein 41.1g; Carbohydrate 3.8g, of which sugars 1g; Fat 27.9g, of which saturates 4.3g; Cholesterol 241mg; Calcium 219mg; Fibre 0.5g; Sodium 585mg.

WHITEFISH SALAD

Smoked whitefish is one of the glories of deli food and, made into a salad with mayonnaise and sour cream, it becomes indispensable as a brunch dish. Eat it with a stack of bagels, pumpernickel or rye bread. If you can't find smoked whitefish, use any other smoked firm white fish, such as halibut or cod.

SERVES FOUR TO SIX

INGREDIENTS

1 smoked whitefish, skinned
  and boned
2 celery sticks, chopped
½ red, white or yellow onion
  or 3–5 spring onions
  (scallions), chopped
45ml/3 tbsp mayonnaise
45ml/3 tbsp sour cream or Greek
  (US strained plain) yogurt
juice of ½–1 lemon
1 round lettuce
ground black pepper
5–10ml/1–2 tsp chopped fresh
  parsley, to garnish

1 Break the smoked fish into bitesize pieces. In a bowl, combine the chopped celery, onion or spring onion, mayonnaise, and sour cream or yogurt, and add lemon juice to taste.

2 Fold the fish into the mixture and season with pepper. Arrange the lettuce leaves on serving plates, then spoon the whitefish salad on top. Serve chilled, sprinkled with parsley.

Per portion: Energy 172Kcal/719kJ; Protein 16g; Carbohydrate 4.3g, of which sugars 3.4g; Fat 10.4g, of which saturates 2g; Cholesterol 35mg; Calcium 62mg; Fibre 1.1g; Sodium 640mg.

SALAD NIÇOISE

MADE WITH THE FRESHEST OF INGREDIENTS, THIS CLASSIC PROVENÇAL SALAD MAKES A SIMPLE YET UNBEATABLE SUMMER DISH. SERVE WITH COUNTRY-STYLE BREAD AND CHILLED WHITE WINE.

SERVES FOUR

INGREDIENTS

    115g/4oz green beans, trimmed
      and cut in half
    115g/4oz mixed salad leaves
    ½ small cucumber, thinly sliced
    4 ripe tomatoes, quartered
    50g/2oz can anchovies, drained
    4 eggs, hard-boiled
    1 tuna steak, about 175g/6oz
    olive oil, for brushing
    ½ bunch of small radishes, trimmed
    50g/2oz/½ cup small
      black olives
    salt and ground black pepper
For the dressing
    90ml/6 tbsp extra virgin olive oil
    2 garlic cloves, crushed
    15ml/1 tbsp white wine vinegar

1 To make the dressing, whisk together the oil, garlic and vinegar in a bowl and season to taste with salt and pepper. Alternatively, shake together in a screw-top jar. Set aside.

2 Cook the green beans in a pan of boiling water for 2 minutes, until just tender, then drain.

3 Mix together the salad leaves, sliced cucumber, tomatoes and green beans in a large, shallow bowl. Halve the anchovies lengthways and shell and quarter the eggs.

VARIATION

Opinions vary on whether Salad Niçoise should include potatoes but, if you like, include a few small cooked new potatoes.

4 Preheat the grill (broiler). Brush the tuna with olive oil and sprinkle with salt and black pepper. Grill (broil) for 3–4 minutes on each side until cooked through. Cool, then flake with a fork.

5 Sprinkle the flaked tuna, sliced anchovies, quartered eggs, radishes and olives over the salad. Pour over the dressing and toss together lightly to combine. Serve immediately.

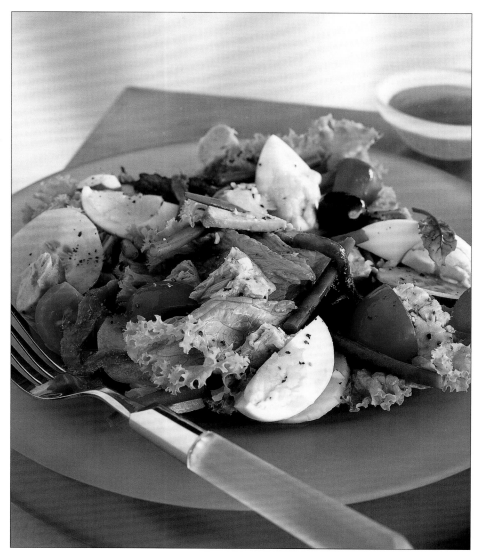

Per portion: Energy 378Kcal/1569kJ; Protein 23g; Carbohydrate 5.1g, of which sugars 4.7g; Fat 29.6g, of which saturates 5.2g; Cholesterol 241mg; Calcium 122mg; Fibre 2.5g; Sodium 889mg.

BEAN SALAD WITH TUNA AND RED ONION

THIS MAKES A GREAT, SUMMERY MAIN MEAL IF SERVED WITH A GREEN SALAD, SOME GARLIC MAYONNAISE AND PLENTY OF WARM, CRUSTY BREAD.

SERVES FOUR

INGREDIENTS
   250g/9oz/1⅓ cups dried haricot
      (navy) or cannellini beans, soaked
      overnight in cold water
   1 bay leaf
   200–250g/7–9oz fine green
      beans, trimmed
   1 large red onion, very thinly sliced
   45ml/3 tbsp chopped fresh flat
      leaf parsley
   200–250g/7–9oz good-quality canned
      tuna in olive oil, drained
   200g/7oz cherry tomatoes, halved
   salt and ground black pepper
   a few onion rings, to garnish
For the dressing
   90ml/6 tbsp extra virgin olive oil
   15ml/1 tbsp tarragon vinegar
   5ml/1 tsp tarragon mustard
   1 garlic clove, finely chopped
   5ml/1 tsp grated lemon rind
   a little lemon juice
   pinch of caster (superfine)
      sugar (optional)

1 Drain the beans and bring them to the boil in fresh water with the bay leaf added. Boil rapidly for 10 minutes, then reduce the heat and boil steadily for 1–1½ hours, until tender. Drain well. Discard the bay leaf.

3 Blanch the green beans in plenty of boiling water for 3–4 minutes. Drain, refresh under cold water and drain thoroughly again.

5 Flake the tuna into large chunks with a knife and toss it into the beans with the tomato halves.

2 Meanwhile, place all the dressing ingredients apart from the lemon juice and sugar in a jug (pitcher) and whisk until mixed. Season to taste with salt, pepper, lemon juice and a pinch of caster sugar, if you like. Leave to stand.

4 Place both types of beans in a bowl. Add half the dressing and toss to mix. Stir in the onion and half the chopped parsley, then season to taste with salt and pepper.

6 Arrange the salad on four individual plates. Drizzle the remaining dressing over the salad and sprinkle the remaining chopped parsley on top. Garnish with a few onion rings and serve immediately, at room temperature.

Per portion: Energy 443Kcal/1857kJ; Protein 29.1g; Carbohydrate 33.7g, of which sugars 6.4g; Fat 22.3g, of which saturates 3.3g; Cholesterol 25mg; Calcium 100mg; Fibre 12g; Sodium 162mg.

SEARED SWORDFISH WITH CITRUS DRESSING

THIS CONTEMPORARY JAPANESE DISH TAKES CONVENTIONAL SALAD INGREDIENTS AND MIXES THEM WITH SHOYU, DASHI AND SESAME OIL FOR A BRIGHT, NEW TASTE. FRESH FISH IS SLICED THINLY AND SEARED OR MARINATED, THEN SERVED WITH SALAD LEAVES AND VEGETABLES.

SERVES FOUR

INGREDIENTS
    75g/3oz mooli (daikon), peeled
    50g/2oz carrot, peeled
    1 Japanese or salad cucumber
    10ml/2 tsp vegetable oil
    300g/11oz skinned fresh swordfish
      steak, cut against the grain
    2 cartons salad cress
    15ml/1 tbsp toasted
      sesame seeds
For the dressing
    105ml/7 tbsp shoyu
    105ml/7 tbsp second dashi stock,
      or the same amount of water and
      5ml/1 tsp dashi-no-moto
    30ml/2 tbsp toasted sesame oil
    juice of ½ lime
    rind of ½ lime, shredded into
      thin strips

1 Make the vegetable garnishes first. Use a very sharp knife, mandolin or vegetable slicer with a julienne blade to make very thin (about 4cm/1½in long) strands of mooli, carrot and cucumber. Soak the mooli and carrot in ice-cold water for 5 minutes, then drain well and keep in the refrigerator.

2 Mix together all the ingredients for the dressing and stir well, then chill.

3 Heat the oil in a small frying pan until smoking hot. Sear the fish for 30 seconds on all sides. Plunge it into cold water in a bowl to stop the cooking. Dry on kitchen paper and wipe off as much oil as possible.

4 Cut the swordfish steak in half lengthways before slicing it into 5mm/¼in thick pieces in the other direction, against the grain.

5 Arrange the fish slices in a ring on individual plates. Mix the vegetable strands, salad cress and sesame seeds. Fluff up with your hands, then shape them into a sphere. Gently place it in the centre of the plate, on the swordfish. Pour the dressing around the plate's edge and serve immediately.

COOK'S TIP
This dish is traditionally made with fillet cut with the grain. To prepare, cut it in half lengthways, then slice against the grain by holding a knife horizontally to the chopping board.

Per portion: Energy 192Kcal/799kJ; Protein 15.6g; Carbohydrate 4.1g, of which sugars 3.7g; Fat 12.7g, of which saturates 2g; Cholesterol 31mg; Calcium 53mg; Fibre 1.1g; Sodium 1887mg.

WARM CHICKEN AND TOMATO SALAD WITH HAZELNUT DRESSING

THIS SIMPLE, WARM SALAD COMBINES PAN-FRIED CHICKEN AND SPINACH WITH A LIGHT, NUTTY DRESSING. SERVE IT FOR LUNCH ON AN AUTUMN DAY.

SERVES FOUR

INGREDIENTS
45ml/3 tbsp olive oil
30ml/2 tbsp hazelnut oil
15ml/1 tbsp white wine vinegar
1 garlic clove, crushed
15ml/1 tbsp chopped fresh mixed herbs
225g/8oz baby spinach leaves
250g/9oz cherry tomatoes, halved
1 bunch of spring onions
   (scallions), chopped
2 skinless, chicken breast fillets, cut
   into thin strips
salt and ground black pepper

VARIATIONS
• Use other meat or fish, such as steak, pork fillet (tenderloin) or salmon fillet, in place of the chicken.
• Any salad leaves can be used instead of the baby spinach.

1 First make the dressing: place 30ml/ 2 tbsp of the olive oil, the hazelnut oil, vinegar, garlic and chopped herbs in a small bowl or jug (pitcher) and whisk together until mixed. Set aside.

2 Trim any long stalks from the spinach leaves, then place in a large serving bowl with the tomatoes and spring onions, and toss together to mix.

3 Heat the remaining olive oil in a frying pan, and stir-fry the chicken over a high heat for 7–10 minutes, until it is cooked, tender and lightly browned.

4 Arrange the cooked chicken pieces over the salad. Give the dressing a quick whisk to blend, then drizzle it over the salad. Add salt and pepper to taste, toss lightly and serve immediately.

Per portion: Energy 234Kcal/973kJ; Protein 20.5g; Carbohydrate 3.6g, of which sugars 3.5g; Fat 15.3g, of which saturates 2.4g; Cholesterol 53mg; Calcium 114mg; Fibre 2.2g; Sodium 131mg.

CHICKEN AND MANGO SALAD WITH ORANGE RICE

THIS FRESH AND DELICIOUS RECIPE DRAWS ITS INSPIRATION FROM ALL OVER THE WORLD.

SERVES FOUR

INGREDIENTS
  15ml/1 tbsp sunflower oil
  1 onion, chopped
  1 garlic clove, crushed
  30ml/2 tbsp red curry paste
  10ml/2 tsp apricot jam
  30ml/2 tbsp chicken stock
  about 450g/1lb cooked chicken, cut
    into small pieces
  150ml/¼ pint/⅔ cup natural
    (plain) yogurt
  60–75ml/4–5 tbsp mayonnaise
  1 large mango, peeled, stoned
    (pitted) and cut into 1cm/½in dice
  fresh flat leaf parsley sprigs,
    to garnish
  poppadums, to serve
For the orange rice
  175g/6oz/scant 1 cup white long
    grain rice
  225g/8oz carrots, grated
    (about 1⅓ cups)
  1 large orange, cut
    into segments
  40g/1½oz/⅓ cup roasted flaked
    (sliced) almonds
For the dressing
  45ml/3 tbsp olive oil
  60ml/4 tbsp sunflower oil
  45ml/3 tbsp lemon juice
  1 garlic clove, crushed
  15ml/1 tbsp chopped mixed fresh
    herbs, such as tarragon, parsley,
    chives
  salt and freshly ground black pepper

1 Heat the oil in a frying pan. Add the onion and garlic and cook over a medium heat, stirring occasionally, for 3–4 minutes, until soft.

2 Stir in the curry paste and cook for about 1 minute, stirring constantly, then lower the heat and stir in the apricot jam and chicken stock. Mix well, then add the chopped chicken and stir until it is thoroughly coated in the paste. Spoon into a bowl, cover with clear film (plastic wrap) and leave to cool.

3 Meanwhile, boil the rice in plenty of lightly salted water until just tender. Drain, rinse under cold water and drain again. When cool, stir into the grated carrots and add the orange segments and flaked almonds.

4 Make the dressing by whisking all the ingredients together in a bowl.

5 When the chicken mixture is cool, stir in the yogurt and mayonnaise, then add the mango, stirring it in carefully so as not to break the flesh. Chill for about 30 minutes.

6 When ready to serve, pour the dressing into the rice salad and mix well. Spoon on to a platter and mound the cold curried chicken on top. Garnish with flat leaf parsley and serve with poppadums.

COOK'S TIP
A simple way of dicing a mango is to take two thick slices from either side of the large flat stone (pit) without peeling the fruit. Make criss-cross cuts in the flesh on each slice and then turn inside out. The cubes of flesh will stand proud of the skin and can be easily cut off.

Per portion: Energy 776Kcal/3245kJ; Protein 35.9g; Carbohydrate 60.2g, of which sugars 21.1g; Fat 45.3g, of which saturates 6.4g; Cholesterol 93mg; Calcium 172mg; Fibre 4.5g; Sodium 206mg.

WARM SALAD OF BAYONNE HAM AND NEW POTATOES

WITH A LIGHTLY SPICED NUTTY DRESSING, THIS WARM SALAD IS AS DELICIOUS AS IT IS FASHIONABLE, AND AN EXCELLENT CHOICE FOR INFORMAL ENTERTAINING.

SERVES FOUR

INGREDIENTS
    225g/8oz new potatoes, halved
        if large
    50g/2oz green beans
    115g/4oz young spinach leaves
    2 spring onions (scallions), sliced
    4 eggs, hard-boiled and quartered
    50g/2oz Bayonne ham, cut
        into strips
    juice of ½ lemon
    salt and ground black pepper
For the dressing
    60ml/4 tbsp olive oil
    5ml/1 tsp ground turmeric
    5ml/1 tsp ground cumin
    50g/2oz/½ cup shelled hazelnuts

1 Cook the potatoes in salted, boiling water for 10–15 minutes, or until tender, then drain. Cook the beans in salted, boiling water for 2 minutes, then drain.

2 Toss the potatoes and beans with the spinach and spring onions in a bowl.

3 Arrange the hard-boiled egg quarters on the salad and sprinkle the strips of ham over the top. Sprinkle with the lemon juice and season with plenty of salt and pepper.

4 Heat the dressing ingredients in a large frying pan and continue to cook, stirring frequently, until the nuts turn golden. Pour the hot, nutty dressing over the salad and serve immediately.

VARIATION
Replace the potatoes with a 400g/14oz can mixed beans and pulses. Drain and rinse the beans and pulses, then drain again. Toss lightly with the green beans and spring onions.

Per portion: Energy 323Kcal/1341kJ; Protein 12.4g; Carbohydrate 10.9g, of which sugars 2.2g; Fat 25.8g, of which saturates 4.2g; Cholesterol 199mg; Calcium 105mg; Fibre 2.3g; Sodium 270mg.

WARM SALAD WITH HAM, EGG AND ASPARAGUS

WHEN YOU THINK IT'S TOO HOT FOR PASTA, TRY SERVING IT IN A WARM SALAD. HERE IT IS COMBINED WITH HAM, EGGS AND ASPARAGUS. A MUSTARD DRESSING MADE FROM THE ASPARAGUS STEMS CREATES A RICH AND TANGY ACCOMPANIMENT.

SERVES FOUR

INGREDIENTS
   450g/1lb asparagus
   450g/1lb dried tagliatelle
   225g/8oz cooked ham, in 5mm/¼in
      thick slices, cut into sticks
   2 eggs, hard-boiled and sliced
   50g/2oz Parmesan cheese, shaved
   salt and ground black pepper
For the dressing
   50g/2oz cooked potato
   75ml/5 tbsp olive oil, preferably Sicilian
   15ml/1 tbsp lemon juice
   10ml/2 tsp Dijon mustard
   120ml/4fl oz/½ cup vegetable stock

VARIATIONS
Use sliced chicken instead of the ham or thin slices of softer Italian cheese, such as Fontina or asiago.

1 Trim and discard the tough woody part of the asparagus. Cut the spears in half and cook the thicker halves in boiling salted water for 12 minutes. After 6 minutes add the tips. Drain, then refresh under cold water until warm.

2 Finely chop 150g/5oz of the thick asparagus pieces. Place in a food processor with the dressing ingredients and process until smooth.

3 Cook the pasta in a large pan of salted water according to the packet instructions, until tender. Refresh under cold water until warm, and drain.

4 To serve, toss the pasta with the asparagus sauce and divide among four plates. Top with the ham, hard-boiled eggs and asparagus tips. Serve immediately with a sprinkling of Parmesan cheese shavings.

Per portion: Energy 707Kcal/2975kJ; Protein 36g; Carbohydrate 88.4g, of which sugars 6.6g; Fat 25.8g, of which saturates 6.4g; Cholesterol 159mg; Calcium 230mg; Fibre 5.3g; Sodium 859mg.

BEEF AND GRILLED SWEET POTATO SALAD WITH SHALLOT AND HERB DRESSING

THIS SALAD MAKES A GOOD MAIN DISH FOR A SUMMER BUFFET, ESPECIALLY IF THE BEEF HAS BEEN CUT INTO FORK-SIZE STRIPS. IT IS ABSOLUTELY DELICIOUS WITH A SIMPLE POTATO SALAD AND SOME PEPPERY LEAVES, SUCH AS WATERCRESS, MIZUNA OR ROCKET.

SERVES SIX TO EIGHT

INGREDIENTS
  800g/1¾lb fillet (tenderloin) of beef
  5ml/1 tsp black peppercorns, crushed
  10ml/2 tsp chopped fresh thyme
  60ml/4 tbsp olive oil
  450g/1lb orange-fleshed sweet
    potato, peeled
  salt and ground black pepper
For the dressing
  1 garlic clove, chopped
  15g/½oz/½ cup flat leaf parsley
  30ml/2 tbsp chopped fresh
    coriander (cilantro)
  15ml/1 tbsp salted capers, rinsed
  ½–1 fresh green chilli, seeded
    and chopped
  10ml/2 tsp Dijon mustard
  10–15ml/2–3 tsp white wine vinegar
  75ml/5 tbsp extra virgin olive oil
  2 shallots, finely chopped

1 Roll the beef fillet in the crushed peppercorns and thyme, then set aside to marinate for a few hours. Preheat the oven to 200°C/400°F/Gas 6.

2 Heat half the olive oil in a heavy frying pan. Add the beef and brown it all over, turning frequently, to seal it. Place on a baking tray and cook in the oven for 10–15 minutes.

3 Remove the beef from the oven, and cover with foil, then leave to rest for 10–15 minutes.

4 Meanwhile, preheat the grill (broiler). Cut the sweet potatoes into 1cm/½in slices. Brush with the remaining olive oil, season to taste with salt and pepper, and grill (broil) for about 5–6 minutes on each side, until tender and browned. Cut the sweet potato slices into strips and place them in a bowl.

5 Cut the beef into slices or strips and toss with the sweet potato, then set the bowl aside.

6 For the dressing, process the garlic, parsley, coriander, capers, chilli, mustard and 10ml/2 tsp of the vinegar in a food processor or blender until chopped. With the motor still running, gradually pour in the oil to make a smooth dressing. Season the dressing with salt and pepper and add more vinegar, to taste. Stir in the shallots.

7 Toss the dressing into the sweet potatoes and beef and leave to stand for up to 2 hours before serving.

COOK'S TIP
Not only do orange-fleshed sweet potatoes look more appetizing than white ones, but they are also better for you, as they contain antioxidant vitamins that help protect against disease.

Per portion: Energy 400Kcal/1670kJ; Protein 29.2g; Carbohydrate 16g, of which sugars 4.3g; Fat 24.9g, of which saturates 6.2g; Cholesterol 81mg; Calcium 23mg; Fibre 1.8g; Sodium 89mg.

THAI BEEF SALAD

ALL THE INGREDIENTS FOR THIS TRADITIONAL THAI DISH — KNOWN AS YAM NUA YANG — ARE WIDELY AVAILABLE IN LARGER SUPERMARKETS.

SERVES FOUR

INGREDIENTS
  675g/1½lb fillet steak
    (beef tenderloin)
  30ml/2 tbsp olive oil
  2 small mild red chillies, seeded
    and sliced
  225g/8oz/3¼ cups shiitake
    mushrooms, sliced
For the dressing
  3 spring onions (scallions), chopped
  2 garlic cloves, finely chopped
  juice of 1 lime
  15–30ml/1–2 tbsp fish or oyster
    sauce, to taste
  5ml/1 tsp soft light brown sugar
  30ml/2 tbsp chopped fresh
    coriander (cilantro)
To serve
  1 cos or romaine lettuce, torn
    into strips
  175g/6oz cherry tomatoes, halved
  5cm/2in piece cucumber, peeled,
    halved and thinly sliced
  45ml/3 tbsp toasted sesame seeds

1 Preheat the grill (broiler), then cook the steak for 2–4 minutes on each side depending on how well done you like steak. Leave to cool for at least 15 minutes.

2 Use a very sharp knife to slice the meat as thinly as possible and place the slices in a bowl.

VARIATION
If you can find them, yellow chillies make a colourful addition to this dish. Substitute one for one of the red chillies.

3 Heat the olive oil in a small frying pan. Add the seeded and sliced red chillies and the sliced mushrooms and cook for 5 minutes, stirring occasionally. Turn off the heat and add the grilled (broiled) steak slices to the pan, then stir well to coat the slices in the chilli and mushroom mixture.

4 Stir all the ingredients for the dressing together, then pour it over the meat mixture and toss gently.

5 Arrange the salad ingredients on a serving plate. Spoon the warm steak mixture into the centre and sprinkle the sesame seeds over, then serve.

Per portion: Energy 381Kcal/1591kJ; Protein 39.8g; Carbohydrate 4.1g, of which sugars 3.8g; Fat 23g, of which saturates 6.6g; Cholesterol 103mg; Calcium 105mg; Fibre 2.5g; Sodium 352mg.

RICE AND RISOTTO

If you're the sort of person who finds cooking relaxing and loves chatting to friends while preparing a meal, rustle up a tasty risotto. You need to stand at the stove and stir the rice for twenty minutes just before serving, but the action is both soothing and satisfying and the results are inevitably delicious. Chicken and Prawn Jambalaya is another wonderful dish for entertaining. Like Seafood Paella, it is full of flavour and the combination of ingredients means that every mouthful brings a taste of the delightfully unexpected.

STUFFED VEGETABLES

COLOURFUL, EASY TO PREPARE AND UTTERLY DELICIOUS, THIS MAKES A POPULAR SUPPER DISH, AND WITH A CHOICE OF VEGETABLES INCLUDED IN THE RECIPE, THERE'S BOUND TO BE SOMETHING TO APPEAL TO EVERY MEMBER OF THE FAMILY.

SERVES FOUR

INGREDIENTS
  1 aubergine (eggplant)
  1 green (bell) pepper
  2 beefsteak tomatoes
  45ml/3 tbsp olive oil
  1 onion, chopped
  2 garlic cloves, crushed
  115g/4oz/1–1½ cups button (white)
    mushrooms, chopped
  1 carrot, grated
  225g/8oz/2 cups cooked white long
    grain rice
  15ml/1 tbsp chopped fresh dill
  90g/3½oz/scant ½ cup crumbled feta
    cheese
  75g/3oz/¾ cup pine nuts,
    lightly toasted
  30ml/2 tbsp currants
  salt and ground black pepper

1 Preheat the oven to 190°C/375°F/Gas 5. Lightly grease a shallow ovenproof dish. Cut the aubergine in half, through the stalk, and scoop out the flesh from each half, taking care not to pierce the skin, to leave two hollow "boats". Dice the aubergine flesh. Cut the pepper in half lengthways and remove the cores and seeds.

2 Cut off the tops from the tomatoes and hollow out the centres with a spoon. Chop the flesh and add it to the diced aubergine. Place the tomatoes upside down on kitchen paper to drain.

3 Bring a pan of water to the boil, add the aubergine halves and blanch for 3 minutes. Add the pepper halves to the boiling water and blanch for 3 minutes more. Drain the vegetables, then place, hollow side up, in the baking dish.

4 Heat 30ml/2 tbsp oil in a pan and cook the onion and garlic for about 5 minutes. Stir in the diced aubergine and tomato mixture with the mushrooms and carrot. Cover, cook for 5 minutes until softened, then mix in the rice, dill, feta, pine nuts and currants. Season to taste.

5 Divide the mixture among the vegetable shells, sprinkle with the remaining olive oil and bake for 20 minutes, until the topping has browned. Serve hot or cold.

Per portion: Energy 544Kcal/2265kJ; Protein 12.9g; Carbohydrate 63.3g, of which sugars 17.2g; Fat 26.8g, of which saturates 5.3g; Cholesterol 16mg; Calcium 134mg; Fibre 4.1g; Sodium 343mg.

ROASTED SQUASH

GEM SQUASH HAS A SWEET, SUBTLE FLAVOUR THAT CONTRASTS WELL WITH OLIVES AND SUN-DRIED TOMATOES IN THIS RECIPE. THE RICE ADDS SUBSTANCE WITHOUT CHANGING ANY OF THE FLAVOURS.

2 Mix the rice, tomatoes, olives, cheese, half the olive oil and basil in a bowl.

3 Oil a shallow ovenproof dish with the remaining oil, just large enough to hold the squash side by side. Divide the rice mixture among the squash and place them in the dish.

SERVES FOUR

INGREDIENTS
   4 whole gem squashes
   225g/8oz/2 cups cooked white
     long grain rice
   75g/3oz/1½ cups sun-dried
     tomatoes in oil, drained
     and chopped
   50g/2oz/½ cup pitted black
     olives, chopped
   60ml/4 tbsp soft goat's cheese
   30ml/2 tbsp olive oil
   15ml/1 tbsp chopped fresh basil
     leaves, plus fresh basil sprigs,
     to serve
   yogurt and mint dressing
     or green salad,
     to serve (optional)

1 Preheat the oven to 180°C/350°F/ Gas 4. Using a sharp knife, trim away the base of each gem squash and then slice off the tops. Using a spoon, scoop out and discard the seeds.

4 Cover with foil and bake for about 45–50 minutes, until the squash is tender when pierced with the point of a sharp knife or skewer. Garnish with basil sprigs and serve with a yogurt and mint dressing or with a green salad if you like.

Per portion: Energy 280Kcal/1170kJ; Protein 8.7g; Carbohydrate 23.6g, of which sugars 5g; Fat 17.4g, of which saturates 6.3g; Cholesterol 23mg; Calcium 125mg; Fibre 3.1g; Sodium 434mg.

BASMATI AND NUT PILAFF

VEGETARIANS WILL LOVE THIS SIMPLE PILAFF. ADD WILD OR CULTIVATED MUSHROOMS, IF YOU LIKE.

SERVES FOUR

INGREDIENTS
15–30ml/1–2 tbsp sunflower oil
1 onion, chopped
1 garlic clove, crushed
1 large carrot, coarsely grated
225g/8oz/generous 1 cup basmati
  rice, soaked
5ml/1 tsp cumin seeds
10ml/2 tsp ground coriander
10ml/2 tsp black mustard
  seeds (optional)
4 green cardamom pods
450ml/¾ pint/scant 2 cups vegetable
  stock or water
1 bay leaf
75g/3oz/¾ cup unsalted walnuts and
  cashew nuts
salt and ground black pepper
fresh parsley or coriander (cilantro)
  sprigs, to garnish

1 Heat the oil in a large, shallow frying pan. Add the onion, garlic and carrot and cook over a low heat, stirring occasionally, for 3–4 minutes, until softened. Thoroughly drain the rice and then add to the pan with the cumin seeds, ground coriander, black mustard seeds and cardamom pods. Cook for 1–2 minutes more, stirring constantly to coat the grains in oil.

2 Pour in the stock or water, add the bay leaf and season well. Bring to the boil, lower the heat, cover and simmer very gently for 10–12 minutes.

3 Remove the pan from the heat without lifting the lid. Leave to stand for about 5 minutes, then check the rice. If it is cooked, there will be small steam holes on the surface of the rice. Remove and discard the bay leaf and the cardamom pods.

4 Stir in the nuts, taste and adjust the seasoning if necessary. Spoon on to a warm platter, garnish with the parsley or coriander and serve.

COOK'S TIP
Use whichever nuts you prefer in this dish – even unsalted peanuts taste good, although almonds, cashew nuts or pistachios are more exotic.

Per portion: Energy 376Kcal/1562kJ; Protein 7.5g; Carbohydrate 50g, of which sugars 4g; Fat 16g, of which saturates 1.4g; Cholesterol 0mg; Calcium 43mg; Fibre 1.6g; Sodium 7mg.

MUSHROOM PILAFF

THIS DISH IS SIMPLICITY ITSELF, YET IT IS FULL OF DELICIOUS INDIAN FLAVOURS.

SERVES FOUR

INGREDIENTS

    30ml/2 tbsp vegetable oil
    2 shallots, finely chopped
    1 garlic clove, crushed
    3 green cardamom pods
    25g/1oz/2 tbsp ghee or butter
    175g/6oz/2½ cups button (white)
      mushrooms, sliced
    225g/8oz/generous 1 cup basmati
      rice, soaked
    5ml/1 tsp grated fresh root ginger
    good pinch of garam masala
    15ml/1 tbsp chopped fresh
      coriander (cilantro)
    salt

1 Heat the oil in a flameproof casserole and cook the shallots, garlic and cardamom pods over a medium heat for 3–4 minutes, until the shallots have softened and are beginning to brown.

2 Add the ghee or butter. When it has melted, add the mushrooms and cook for 2–3 minutes more.

3 Add the rice, ginger and garam masala. Stir-fry over a low heat for 2–3 minutes, then stir in 450ml/¾ pint/ scant 2 cups water and a little salt. Bring to the boil, then cover tightly and simmer over a low heat for 10 minutes.

4 Remove the casserole from the heat. Leave to stand, still covered, for 5 minutes. Add the chopped coriander and gently fork it through the rice. Spoon into a warm serving bowl and serve immediately.

Per portion: Energy 309Kcal/1286kJ; Protein 5.2g; Carbohydrate 46.3g, of which sugars 1g; Fat 11.2g, of which saturates 4g; Cholesterol 13mg; Calcium 18mg; Fibre 0.7g; Sodium 41mg.

ROASTED PEPPER RISOTTO

THIS MAKES AN EXCELLENT AND COLOURFUL VEGETARIAN LUNCH OR SUPPER DISH.

SERVES THREE TO FOUR

INGREDIENTS
1 red (bell) pepper
1 yellow (bell) pepper
15ml/1 tbsp olive oil
25g/1oz/2 tbsp butter
1 onion, chopped
2 garlic cloves, crushed
275g/10oz/1½ cups risotto rice
1 litre/1¾ pints/4 cups simmering
   vegetable stock
50g/2oz/⅔ cup freshly grated
   Parmesan cheese
salt and ground black pepper
freshly grated Parmesan cheese, to
   serve (optional)

1 Preheat the grill (broiler). Cut the peppers in half, remove the seeds and pith and arrange, cut side down, on a baking sheet. Place under the grill for 5–6 minutes until the skin is charred. Put the peppers in a plastic bag, tie the ends and leave for 4–5 minutes.

2 Peel the peppers when they are cool enough to handle and the steam has loosened the skin. Cut into thin strips.

3 Heat the oil and butter in a pan and cook the onion and garlic for 4–5 minutes over a low heat until the onion begins to soften. Add the peppers and cook the mixture for 3–4 minutes more, stirring occasionally.

4 Stir in the rice. Cook over a medium heat for 3–4 minutes, stirring all the time, until the rice is evenly coated in oil and the outer part of each grain has become translucent.

5 Add a ladleful of stock. Cook, stirring, until all the liquid has been absorbed. Continue to add the stock, a ladleful at a time, making sure each quantity has been absorbed before adding the next.

6 When the rice is tender but retains a little "bite", stir in the Parmesan, and add seasoning to taste. Cover and leave to stand for 3–4 minutes, then serve, with extra Parmesan, if using.

Per portion: Energy 555Kcal/2312kJ; Protein 16.1g; Carbohydrate 80.1g, of which sugars 10g; Fat 18g, of which saturates 8.4g; Cholesterol 34mg; Calcium 238mg; Fibre 2.6g; Sodium 241mg.

RISOTTO WITH FOUR VEGETABLES

THIS IS ONE OF THE PRETTIEST RISOTTOS, ESPECIALLY WHEN MADE WITH ACORN SQUASH.

SERVES THREE TO FOUR

INGREDIENTS
    115g/4oz/1 cup shelled fresh peas
    115g/4oz/1 cup green beans, cut
      into short lengths
    30ml/2 tbsp olive oil
    75g/3oz/6 tbsp butter
    1 acorn squash, skin and seeds
      removed, flesh cut into batons
    1 onion, finely chopped
    275g/10oz/1½ cups risotto rice
    120ml/4fl oz/½ cup Italian dry
      white vermouth
    1 litre/1¾ pints/4 cups boiling
      chicken stock
    75g/3oz/1 cup freshly grated
      Parmesan cheese
    salt and ground black pepper

1 Bring a pan of lightly salted water to the boil, add the peas and beans and cook for 2–3 minutes, until the vegetables are just tender. Drain, refresh under cold running water, drain again and set aside.

2 Heat the oil with 25g/1oz/2 tbsp of the butter in a medium pan until foaming. Add the squash and cook gently for 2–3 minutes, or until just softened. Remove with a slotted spoon and set aside. Add the onion to the pan and cook gently for about 3 minutes, stirring frequently, until softened.

3 Stir in the rice until the grains start to swell and burst, then add the vermouth. Stir until the vermouth stops sizzling and most of it has been absorbed by the rice, then add a few ladlefuls of the stock, with salt and pepper to taste. Stir over a low heat until the stock has been absorbed.

4 Gradually add the remaining stock, a few ladlefuls at a time, allowing the rice to absorb the liquid before adding more, and stirring all the time.

VARIATIONS
Shelled broad (fava) beans can be used instead of the peas, and asparagus tips instead of the green beans. Use courgettes (zucchini) if acorn squash is not available.

5 After about 20 minutes, when all the stock has been absorbed and the rice is cooked and creamy but still has a "bite", gently stir in the vegetables, the remaining butter and about half the grated Parmesan. Heat through, then taste and adjust the seasoning and serve with the remaining grated Parmesan handed around separately.

Per portion: Energy 836Kcal/3472kJ; Protein 22.1g; Carbohydrate 79.4g, of which sugars 6g; Fat 42.6g, of which saturates 22.1g; Cholesterol 89mg; Calcium 379mg; Fibre 3.9g; Sodium 462mg.

RISOTTO WITH FOUR CHEESES

THIS IS A VERY RICH DISH. IT IS THE PERFECT CHOICE FOR A DINNER PARTY WITH AN ITALIAN THEME, SERVED WITH A LIGHT, DRY SPARKLING WHITE WINE.

SERVES FOUR

INGREDIENTS

40g/1½oz/3 tbsp butter
1 small onion, finely chopped
1.2 litres/2 pints/5 cups chicken
  stock, preferably home-made
350g/12oz/1¾ cups risotto rice
200ml/7fl oz/scant 1 cup dry
  white wine
50g/2oz/½ cup grated Gruyère cheese
50g/2oz/½ cup diced taleggio cheese
50g/2oz/½ cup diced
  Gorgonzola cheese
50g/2oz/⅔ cup freshly grated
  Parmesan cheese
salt and ground black pepper
chopped fresh flat leaf parsley,
  to garnish

1 Melt the butter in a large, heavy pan or deep frying pan and cook the onion over a low heat, stirring frequently, for about 4–5 minutes, until softened and lightly browned. Meanwhile, pour the chicken stock into another pan and heat it to simmering point.

2 Add the rice to the onion mixture, stir until the grains start to swell and burst, then add the wine. Stir until it stops sizzling and most of it has been absorbed by the rice, then pour in a little of the hot stock. Add salt and pepper to taste. Stir over a low heat until the stock has been absorbed.

3 Gradually add the remaining stock, a little at a time, allowing the rice to absorb the liquid before adding more, and stirring constantly. After about 20–25 minutes the rice will be *al dente* and the risotto creamy.

4 Turn off the heat under the pan, then add the Gruyère, taleggio, Gorgonzola and 30ml/2 tbsp of the Parmesan cheese. Stir gently until the cheeses have melted, then taste and adjust the seasoning, if necessary. Spoon the risotto into a warm serving bowl and garnish with parsley. Serve immediately, handing the remaining grated Parmesan separately.

Per portion: Energy 640Kcal/2662kJ; Protein 22.1g; Carbohydrate 67.1g, of which sugars 1.2g; Fat 26g, of which saturates 15.9g; Cholesterol 70mg; Calcium 451mg; Fibre 0.2g; Sodium 473mg.

RISOTTO WITH RICOTTA AND BASIL

THIS IS A WELL-FLAVOURED RISOTTO, WHICH BENEFITS FROM THE DISTINCTIVE PUNGENCY OF BASIL, MELLOWED WITH SMOOTH RICOTTA.

SERVES THREE TO FOUR

INGREDIENTS
45ml/3 tbsp olive oil
1 onion, finely chopped
275g/10oz/1½ cups risotto rice
1 litre/1¾ pints/4 cups hot chicken
  or vegetable stock
175g/6oz/¾ cup ricotta cheese
50g/2oz/2 cups fresh basil leaves,
  finely chopped, plus extra
  to garnish
75g/3oz/1 cup freshly grated
  Parmesan cheese
salt and ground black pepper

1 Heat the oil in a large pan or flameproof casserole and cook the onion over a low heat until soft.

2 Tip in the rice. Cook for a few minutes, stirring constantly, until the rice grains are well coated with oil and are slightly translucent.

3 Pour in about a quarter of the stock. Cook, stirring, until all the stock has been absorbed, then add another ladleful. Continue in this manner, adding more stock when the previous ladleful has been absorbed, until the risotto has been cooking for about 20 minutes and the rice is just tender.

4 Spoon the ricotta into a bowl and break it up a little with a fork. Gently stir it into the risotto along with the chopped basil and grated Parmesan. Taste and adjust the seasoning, if necessary, then cover and leave to stand for 2–3 minutes before serving, garnished with basil leaves.

Per portion: Energy 715Kcal/2975kJ; Protein 22.4g; Carbohydrate 72.6g, of which sugars 2.8g; Fat 36.2g, of which saturates 16.4g; Cholesterol 70mg; Calcium 382mg; Fibre 0.7g; Sodium 442mg.

SEARED SCALLOPS WITH CHIVE SAUCE ON LEEK AND CARROT RICE

SCALLOPS ARE ONE OF THE MOST DELICIOUS SHELLFISH. HERE THEY ARE PARTNERED WITH A DELICATE CHIVE SAUCE AND A PILAFF OF WILD AND WHITE RICE WITH SWEET LEEKS AND CARROTS.

SERVES FOUR

INGREDIENTS

    12–16 shelled scallops
    45ml/3 tbsp olive oil
    50g/2oz/⅓ cup wild rice
    65g/2½ oz/5 tbsp butter
    4 carrots, cut into long thin strips
    2 leeks, cut into thick,
      diagonal slices
    1 small onion, finely chopped
    115g/4oz/⅔ cup long grain rice
    1 fresh bay leaf
    200ml/7fl oz/scant 1 cup white wine
    450ml/¾ pint/scant 2 cups fish stock
    60ml/4 tbsp double (heavy) cream
    a little lemon juice
    25ml/5 tsp chopped fresh chives
    30ml/2 tbsp fresh chervil sprigs
    salt and ground black pepper

1 Lightly season the scallops, brush with 15ml/1 tbsp of the olive oil and set aside.

2 Cook the wild rice in plenty of boiling water for about 30 minutes, until tender, then drain well.

3 Melt half the butter in a small frying pan and cook the carrots over a low heat for 4–5 minutes. Add the leeks and cook for a further 2 minutes. Season with salt and pepper and add 30–45ml/ 2–3 tbsp water, then cover and cook for a few minutes more. Uncover and cook until the liquid has reduced. Remove from the heat and set aside.

4 Melt half the rest of the butter with 15ml/1 tbsp of the remaining oil in a heavy pan. Add the onion and cook over a low heat for 3–4 minutes, until softened but not browned.

5 Add the long grain rice and bay leaf and cook, stirring constantly, until the rice looks translucent and the grains are coated with oil.

6 Pour in half the wine and half the stock. Season with 2.5ml/½ tsp salt and bring to the boil. Stir, then cover and cook very gently for 15 minutes, or until the liquid is absorbed and the rice is cooked and tender.

7 Reheat the carrots and leeks gently, then stir them into the long grain rice with the wild rice. Add seasoning to taste, if necessary.

8 Meanwhile, pour the remaining wine and stock into a small pan and boil rapidly until reduced by half.

COOK'S TIP
Choose fresh, rather than frozen, scallops as the frozen ones tend to exude water on cooking. Scallops need only the briefest cooking at high heat, just until they turn opaque and brown on each side, so have the pan very hot. Although some people avoid eating the orange-coloured coral, it is delicious and many people consider it to be the best part.

9 Heat a heavy frying pan over a high heat. Add the remaining butter and oil. Sear the scallops for 1–2 minutes on each side. Set aside and keep warm.

10 Pour the reduced stock into the pan and heat until bubbling, then add the cream and boil until thickened. Season with lemon juice, salt and pepper. Stir in the chives and scallops.

11 Stir the chervil into the rice and pile it on to plates. Arrange the scallops on top and spoon the sauce over the rice.

Per portion: Energy 482Kcal/2014kJ; Protein 28.1g; Carbohydrate 42.7g, of which sugars 6g; Fat 18.6g, of which saturates 6.7g; Cholesterol 68mg; Calcium 80mg; Fibre 3g; Sodium 200mg.

SEAFOOD PAELLA

THERE ARE AS MANY VERSIONS OF PAELLA AS THERE ARE REGIONS OF SPAIN. THOSE FROM NEAR THE COAST CONTAIN A LOT OF SEAFOOD, WHILE INLAND VERSIONS ADD CHICKEN OR PORK. HERE THE ONLY MEAT IS THE CHORIZO, ESSENTIAL FOR AN AUTHENTIC FLAVOUR.

SERVES FOUR

INGREDIENTS

45ml/3 tbsp olive oil
1 Spanish (Bermuda) onion, chopped
2 fat garlic cloves, chopped
150g/5oz chorizo sausage, sliced
300g/11oz small squid, cleaned
1 red (bell) pepper, cut into strips
4 tomatoes, peeled, seeded and
  diced, or 200g/7oz can tomatoes
500ml/17fl oz/generous 2 cups
  chicken stock
105ml/7 tbsp dry white wine
200g/7oz/1 cup short grain Spanish
  rice or risotto rice
a large pinch of saffron threads
150g/5oz/1 cup fresh or frozen peas
12 large cooked prawns (shrimp), in
  the shell, or 8 langoustines
450g/1lb fresh mussels, scrubbed
450g/1lb medium clams, scrubbed
salt and ground black pepper

1 Heat the olive oil in a paella pan or wok, add the onion and garlic and cook until translucent. Add the chorizo and cook until lightly golden.

2 If the squid are very small, leave them whole, otherwise cut the bodies into rings and the tentacles into pieces. Add the squid to the pan and sauté over a high heat for 2 minutes.

3 Stir in the pepper strips and tomatoes and simmer gently for 5 minutes, until the pepper strips are tender. Pour in the stock and white wine, stir well and bring to the boil.

4 Stir in the rice and saffron threads and season well with salt and pepper. Spread the contents of the pan evenly. Bring the liquid back to the boil, then lower the heat and simmer gently for about 10 minutes.

5 Add the peas, prawns or langoustines, mussels and clams, stirring them gently into the rice.

6 Cook the paella over a low heat for a further 15–20 minutes, until the rice is tender and all the mussels and clams have opened. If any remain closed, discard them. If the paella seems dry, add a little more hot chicken stock. Gently stir everything together and serve while piping hot.

Per portion: Energy 618Kcal/2600kJ; Protein 41.4g; Carbohydrate 63.8g, of which sugars 10.3g; Fat 21.9g, of which saturates 5.4g; Cholesterol 290mg; Calcium 179mg; Fibre 4.6g; Sodium 1117mg.

KEDGEREE

THIS CLASSIC DISH ORIGINATED IN INDIA. IT IS BEST MADE WITH BASMATI RICE, WHICH GOES WELL WITH THE MILD CURRY FLAVOUR, BUT LONG GRAIN RICE WILL DO. FOR A COLOURFUL GARNISH, ADD SOME FINELY SLICED RED ONION AND A LITTLE RED ONION MARMALADE.

SERVES FOUR

INGREDIENTS
    450g/1lb undyed smoked
      haddock fillet
    750ml/1¼ pints/3 cups milk
    2 bay leaves
    ½ lemon, sliced
    50g/2oz/¼ cup butter
    1 onion, chopped
    2.5ml/½ tsp ground turmeric
    5ml/1 tsp mild Madras curry powder
    2 green cardamom pods
    350g/12oz/1¾ cups basmati or long
      grain rice, washed and drained
    4 hard-boiled eggs (not *too* hard),
      coarsely chopped
    150ml/¼ pint/⅔ cup single (light)
      cream (optional)
    30ml/2 tbsp chopped fresh parsley
    salt and ground black pepper

1 Put the haddock in a shallow pan and add the milk, bay leaves and lemon slices. Poach gently for 8–10 minutes, until the haddock flakes easily when tested with the tip of a sharp knife. Strain the milk into a jug (pitcher), discarding the bay leaves and lemon slices. Remove the skin from the haddock and flake the flesh into large pieces. Keep hot until required.

2 Melt the butter in the pan, add the onion and cook over a low heat for about 3 minutes, until softened. Stir in the turmeric, the curry powder and cardamom pods and cook for 1 minute.

3 Add the rice, stirring to coat it well with the butter. Pour in the reserved milk, stir and bring to the boil. Lower the heat and simmer the rice for 10–12 minutes, until all the milk has been absorbed and the rice is tender. Season to taste, going easy on the salt.

4 Gently stir in the fish and hard-boiled eggs, with the cream, if using. Sprinkle with the parsley and serve.

VARIATION
Use smoked or poached fresh salmon for a delicious change from haddock.

Per portion: Energy 579Kcal/2421kJ; Protein 34.4g; Carbohydrate 71.1g, of which sugars 0.9g; Fat 17g, of which saturates 8.2g; Cholesterol 257mg; Calcium 76mg; Fibre 0.2g; Sodium 1001mg.

Chicken and Prawn Jambalaya

The mixture of chicken, seafood and rice suggests a close relationship to the Spanish paella, but the Creole name is more likely to have derived from jambon (the French for ham), and à la ya (Creole for rice). Jambalayas are a colourful mixture of highly flavoured ingredients, and are made in large quantities for feasts and celebration meals.

SERVES TEN

INGREDIENTS

    2 chickens, each about 1.5kg/3–3½lb
    450g/1lb piece raw smoked gammon
      (cured ham)
    50g/2oz/4 tbsp lard or bacon fat
    50g/2oz/½ cup plain (all-
      purpose) flour
    3 onions, finely sliced
    2 green (bell) peppers, seeded
      and sliced
    675g/1½lb tomatoes, peeled
      and chopped
    2–3 garlic cloves, crushed
    10ml/2 tsp chopped fresh thyme
    24 large raw prawns (shrimp), peeled
      and deveined
    500g/1¼lb/3 cups white long grain rice
    2–3 dashes Tabasco sauce
    45ml/3 tbsp chopped fresh flat leaf
      parsley, plus sprigs, to garnish
    salt and ground black pepper

4 Add the diced gammon, onions, green peppers, tomatoes, garlic and thyme. Cook, stirring regularly, for 10 minutes, then add the prawns and mix lightly.

5 Stir the rice into the pan and pour in 1.2 litres/2 pints/5 cups water. Season to taste with salt, pepper and Tabasco sauce. Bring to the boil over a medium heat, then lower the heat, cover and cook gently until the rice is tender and all the liquid has been absorbed. Add a little extra boiling water if the rice looks as if it might be drying out before it is cooked.

6 Add the chopped flat leaf parsley and gently stir it into the finished dish, garnish with tiny sprigs of flat leaf parsley and serve immediately while piping hot.

1 Cut each chicken into 10 pieces and season with salt and pepper. Dice the gammon, discarding the rind and fat.

2 Melt the lard or bacon fat in a large, heavy frying pan. Add the chicken pieces, in batches, brown them all over, then lift them out with a slotted spoon and set them aside.

3 Reduce the heat. Sprinkle the flour into the fat in the pan and stir until the roux turns golden brown. Return the chicken pieces to the pan.

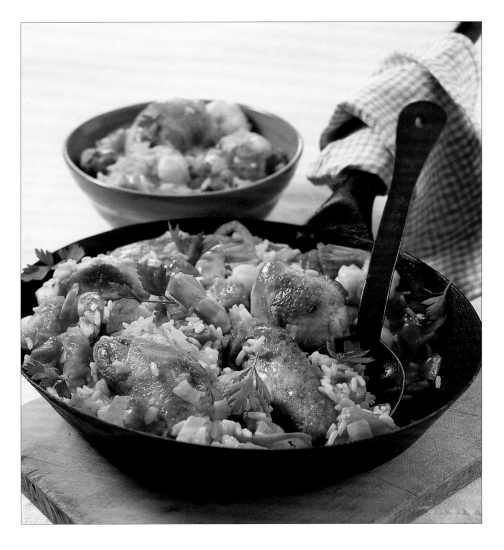

Per portion: Energy 748Kcal/3117kJ; Protein 54.9g; Carbohydrate 50.3g, of which sugars 5.5g; Fat 36.2g, of which saturates 10.8g; Cholesterol 262mg; Calcium 70mg; Fibre 2g; Sodium 588mg.

CARIBBEAN PEANUT CHICKEN

PEANUT BUTTER IS USED A LOT IN MANY CARIBBEAN DISHES. IT ADDS A RICHNESS TO THE DISH, AS WELL AS A DELICIOUS DEPTH OF FLAVOUR ALL OF ITS OWN.

SERVES FOUR

INGREDIENTS

  4 skinless, boneless chicken breast
    portions, cut into thin strips
  225g/8oz/generous 1 cup white long
    grain rice
  30ml/2 tbsp groundnut (peanut) oil
  15g/½oz/1 tbsp butter, plus extra
    for greasing
  1 onion, finely chopped
  2 tomatoes, peeled, seeded
    and chopped
  1 fresh green chilli, seeded
    and sliced
  60ml/4 tbsp smooth peanut butter
  450ml/¾ pint/scant 2 cups
    chicken stock
  lemon juice, to taste
  salt and ground black pepper
  lime wedges and fresh flat leaf
    parsley sprigs, to garnish
For the marinade
  15ml/1 tbsp sunflower oil
  1–2 garlic cloves, crushed
  5ml/1 tsp chopped fresh thyme
  25ml/1½ tbsp medium curry powder
  juice of half a lemon

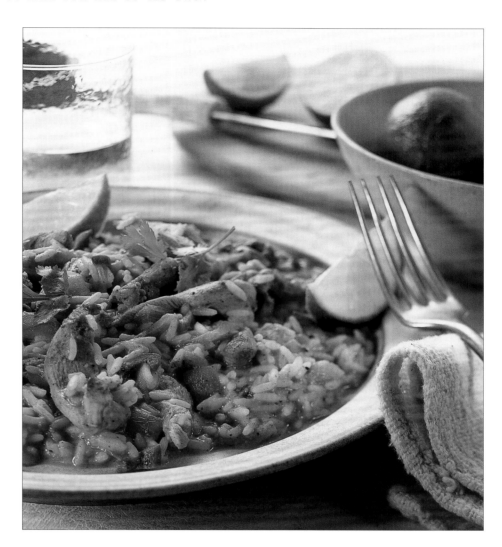

1 Mix all the marinade ingredients in a large bowl and stir in the chicken. Cover loosely with clear film (plastic wrap) and set aside in a cool place for 2–3 hours.

2 Meanwhile, cook the rice in plenty of lightly salted, boiling water until tender. Drain well and turn into a generously buttered casserole.

3 Preheat the oven to 180°C/350°F/Gas 4. Heat 15ml/1 tbsp of the oil and butter in a flameproof casserole and cook the chicken pieces for 4–5 minutes, until evenly brown. Add more oil if necessary.

4 Transfer the chicken to a plate. Add the onion to the casserole and cook for 5–6 minutes until lightly browned. Stir in the tomatoes and chilli. Cook over a low heat for 3–4 minutes, stirring occasionally. Remove from the heat.

5 Mix the peanut butter with the chicken stock. Stir into the tomato and onion mixture, then add the chicken. Stir in the lemon juice, season to taste, then spoon the mixture over the rice in the casserole.

6 Cover the casserole, transfer it to the oven and cook for 15–20 minutes, or until piping hot. Use a large spoon to toss the rice with the chicken mixture. Serve immediately, garnished with the lime wedges and parsley sprigs.

COOK'S TIP
If the casserole is not large enough to let you toss the rice with the chicken mixture before serving, invert a large, deep plate over the casserole, turn both over and toss the mixture on the plate.

Per portion: Energy 606Kcal/2532kJ; Protein 46.4g; Carbohydrate 52.6g, of which sugars 5.3g; Fat 23.2g, of which saturates 6.6g; Cholesterol 113mg; Calcium 41mg; Fibre 2.3g; Sodium 202mg.

BURRITOS WITH CHICKEN AND RICE

IN MEXICO, BURRITOS ARE A POPULAR STREET FOOD, EATEN ON THE HOOF. THE SECRET OF A SUCCESSFUL BURRITO IS TO HAVE ALL THE FILLING NEATLY PACKAGED INSIDE THE TORTILLA FOR EASY EATING, SO THESE SNACKS ARE SELDOM SERVED WITH A POUR-OVER SAUCE.

SERVES FOUR

INGREDIENTS
90g/3½oz/½ cup long grain rice
15ml/1 tbsp vegetable oil
1 onion, chopped
2.5ml/½ tsp ground cloves
5ml/1 tsp dried, or fresh oregano
200g/7oz can chopped tomatoes
2 skinless, boneless chicken
  breast portions
150g/5oz/1¼ cups grated Monterey
  Jack or mild Cheddar cheese
60ml/4 tbsp sour cream (optional)
8 x 20–25cm/8–10in fresh wheat
  flour tortillas
salt
fresh oregano, to garnish (optional)

1 Bring a pan of lightly salted water to the boil. Add the rice, bring back to the boil and cook for 8 minutes. Drain, rinse and then drain again.

2 Heat the oil in a large pan. Add the onion, with the ground cloves and oregano, and cook, stirring occasionally, for 2–3 minutes. Stir in the rice and tomatoes, with their can juice, and cook over a low heat until all the tomato juice has been absorbed. Remove the pan from the heat and set aside.

VARIATION
For an extra touch of spice, you can add 3–4 canned or bottled jalapeño chillies to the filling, with the chicken, and substitute fresh coriander (cilantro) for the oregano. Rinse, seed and finely chopped the chillies first.

3 Put the chicken portions in a large pan, pour in enough water to cover and bring to the boil. Lower the heat and simmer for about 10 minutes, or until the chicken is cooked through. Lift the chicken out of the pan, put on a plate and leave to cool slightly.

4 Preheat the oven to 160°C/325°F/ Gas 3. Shred the chicken by pulling the flesh apart with two forks, then add the chicken to the rice mixture, with the grated cheese. Gently stir in the sour cream, if using.

COOK'S TIP
If you use very fresh tortillas, you may be able to dispense with the cocktail sticks. Secure the tortilla parcels by damping the final fold with a little water. When you lay the burritos in the dish, place them with the folded surfaces down.

5 Wrap the tortillas in foil and place them on a plate. Stand the plate over boiling water for about 5 minutes. Alternatively, wrap in microwave-safe film and heat in a microwave on full power for 1 minute.

6 Spoon one-eighth of the filling into the centre of a tortilla and fold in both sides. Fold the bottom up and the top down to form a parcel. Secure with a cocktail stick (toothpick).

7 Put the filled burrito in a shallow dish or casserole, cover with foil and keep warm in the oven while you make seven more. Remove the cocktail sticks before serving, sprinkled with fresh oregano.

Per portion: Energy 625Kcal/2628kJ; Protein 37.4g; Carbohydrate 82.2g, of which sugars 4.6g; Fat 17.1g, of which saturates 8.7g; Cholesterol 89mg; Calcium 411mg; Fibre 3.3g; Sodium 617mg.

BEEF BIRYANI

THE MOGULS INTRODUCED THIS DRY, SPICY RICE DISH TO CENTRAL INDIA.

SERVES FOUR

INGREDIENTS
2 large onions
2 garlic cloves, chopped
2.5cm/1in piece of fresh root ginger,
  peeled and coarsely chopped
½–1 fresh green chilli, seeded and
  coarsely chopped
bunch of fresh coriander (cilantro)
60ml/4 tbsp flaked (sliced) almonds
30–45ml/2–3 tbsp water
15ml/1 tbsp ghee or butter, plus
  25g/1oz/2 tbsp butter, for the rice
45ml/3 tbsp sunflower oil
30ml/2 tbsp sultanas (golden raisins)
500g/1¼lb braising or stewing
  steak, cubed
5ml/1 tsp ground coriander
15ml/1 tbsp ground cumin
2.5ml/½ tsp ground turmeric
2.5ml/½ tsp ground fenugreek
good pinch of ground cinnamon
175ml/6fl oz/¾ cup natural
  (plain) yogurt
275g/10oz/1½ cups basmati rice
about 1.2 litres/2 pints/5 cups hot
  chicken stock or water
salt and ground black pepper
2 hard-boiled eggs, quartered,
  to garnish

1 Coarsely chop 1 onion and place it in a food processor or blender. Add the garlic, ginger, chilli, fresh coriander and half the flaked almonds. Pour in the water and process to a smooth paste.

2 Thinly slice the remaining onion into rings or half rings. Heat half the ghee or butter with half the oil in a heavy, flameproof casserole and cook the onion rings over a medium heat for 10–15 minutes, until they are a deep golden brown. Transfer to a plate with a slotted spoon. Cook the remaining flaked almonds briefly until golden and set aside with the onion rings, then quickly cook the sultanas until they swell. Transfer to the plate.

3 Heat the remaining ghee or butter in the casserole with a further 15ml/1 tbsp of the oil. Cook the meat, in batches, until evenly browned. Transfer to a plate and set aside.

4 Wipe the casserole clean with kitchen paper, heat the remaining oil and pour in the onion and ginger paste. Cook over a medium heat, stirring constantly, for 2–3 minutes, until the mixture begins to brown lightly. Stir in the ground coriander, cumin, turmeric, fenugreek and cinnamon, season to taste with salt and pepper and cook for 1 minute more.

5 Lower the heat, then gradually stir in the yogurt, a little at a time. When all of it has been incorporated into the spice mixture, return the meat to the casserole. Stir to coat, cover tightly and simmer over a gentle heat for about 40–45 minutes, until the meat is tender.

6 Meanwhile, place the rice in a large bowl, pour in cold water to cover and leave to soak for 15–20 minutes.

7 Preheat the oven to 160°C/325°F/ Gas 3. Drain the rice, place it in a pan and add the hot chicken stock or water, together with a little salt. Bring back to the boil, cover, lower the heat and cook for 5–6 minutes.

8 Drain the rice and pile it in a mound on top of the meat in the casserole. Using the handle of a spoon, make a hole through the rice and meat mixture, to the base of the pan. Sprinkle the onion rings, almonds and sultanas over the top and dot with butter. Cover the casserole tightly with a double layer of foil and secure with a lid.

9 Cook the biryani in the oven for 30–40 minutes. To serve, spoon the mixture on to a warmed serving plate and garnish with the quartered hard-boiled eggs. Serve with parathas, naan bread or chapatis, if you like.

COOK'S TIP
When you are cooking the onion and ginger paste and the ground spices, reduce the heat to very low and stir constantly to avoid scorching them.

Per portion: Energy 778Kcal/3240kJ; Protein 40g; Carbohydrate 70.4g, of which sugars 13.4g; Fat 37.4g, of which saturates 11.8g; Cholesterol 94mg; Calcium 164mg; Fibre 2.3g; Sodium 183mg.

PASTA, GNOCCHI AND NOODLES

For sheer all-round popularity, pasta dishes top the bill. Pasta cooks quickly and looks as good as it tastes. It is easy to digest and gives slow-release energy. This chapter includes dishes suitable for vegetarians and vegans, as well as such classics as Clams with Neapolitan Tomato Sauce, which features vermicelli. Asian noodles are well represented, too. For a special treat, try Thai Crispy Noodles with Beef, or give your tastebuds a treat with Potato Gnocchi with Simple Tomato and Butter Sauce.

PASTA WITH GARLIC AND CHILLI

THIS IS THE SIMPLEST OF PASTA DISHES AND ONE OF THE BEST. MINT AND OREGANO GIVE VERY DIFFERENT RESULTS, BOTH GOOD. THERE IS NO NEED TO SERVE GRATED PARMESAN WITH THIS DISH — INSTEAD, LET THE CLEAR FLAVOUR OF THE GARLIC AND OLIVE OIL SING OUT.

SERVES THREE TO FOUR

INGREDIENTS
  400g/14oz dried spaghetti
  105ml/7 tbsp extra virgin olive oil,
    plus extra to taste
  1.5ml/¼ tsp dried red chilli flakes or
    2 small whole dried red chillies
  6 large garlic cloves, finely chopped
  15ml/1 tbsp chopped fresh mint
    or oregano
  15g/½ oz chopped fresh flat
    leaf parsley
  salt and ground black pepper

1 Cook the spaghetti in lightly salted, boiling water for 9–11 minutes, or according to the packet instructions, until just tender.

2 Meanwhile, heat the oil in a large frying pan or pan over a very gentle heat. Add the chilli flakes or whole chillies and cook very gently for 2–3 minutes.

COOK'S TIP
If you use fresh spaghetti, cook for only 2–3 minutes in salted, boiling water.

3 Add the garlic to the pan. Keep the heat very low, so that the garlic barely bubbles and does not brown, then cook, shaking the pan occasionally, for about 2 minutes. Remove the pan from the heat and cool a little, then add the fresh mint or oregano.

4 Drain the pasta, then immediately add it to the oil and garlic mixture, with the parsley. Toss thoroughly. Season with freshly ground black pepper and transfer to warmed serving bowls. Serve immediately, offering more olive oil for drizzling at the table.

VARIATION
Cook 250g/9oz broccoli florets in salted, boiling water for 4 minutes. Add to the chilli oil and cook for 5–8 minutes.

Per portion: Energy 688Kcal/2897kJ; Protein 16.2g; Carbohydrate 98.9g, of which sugars 4.5g; Fat 28.1g, of which saturates 3.9g; Cholesterol 0mg; Calcium 43mg; Fibre 4.1g; Sodium 6mg.

RIGATONI WITH TOMATOES AND FRESH HERBS

This pretty and colourful pasta dish relies for its success on the best Italian canned tomatoes and tender young herbs, freshly picked. For a real treat, use fresh tomatoes, peeled and puréed. Add a little sugar if the tomatoes are not at the peak of ripeness.

SERVES SIX TO EIGHT

INGREDIENTS
1 onion
1 carrot
1 celery stick
60ml/4 tbsp olive oil
1 garlic clove, thinly sliced
a few leaves each of fresh basil,
  thyme and oregano or marjoram
2 x 400g/14oz cans chopped Italian
  plum tomatoes
15ml/1 tbsp sun-dried tomato paste
5ml/1 tsp granulated sugar
about 90ml/6 tbsp dry red or white
  wine (optional)
350g/12oz/3 cups dried rigatoni
salt and ground black pepper
coarsely shaved Parmesan cheese,
  to serve

COOK'S TIP
Large pasta tubes are best for this recipe, as they capture the wonderful tomato and herb sauce. If you can't get rigatoni, try penne or penne rigate (ridged penne).

1 Chop the onion, carrot and celery stick finely, either in a food processor or by hand, with a sharp knife.

2 Heat the olive oil in a medium pan, add the garlic slices and stir over a very low heat for 1–2 minutes. Do not let the garlic burn or it will taste bitter.

3 Add the chopped vegetables and the fresh herbs, reserving a few to garnish. Cook over a low heat, stirring frequently, for 5–7 minutes, until the vegetables have softened and are lightly coloured.

4 Add the canned tomatoes, tomato paste and sugar, then stir in the wine, if using. Add salt and pepper to taste. Bring to the boil, stirring, then lower the heat to a gentle simmer. Cook, stirring frequently, for about 45 minutes.

5 Cook the pasta in lightly salted, boiling water for 10–12 minutes, drain and tip into a warmed bowl. Pour the sauce over the pasta and toss well. Garnish with the reserved herbs. Serve immediately, with shavings of Parmesan handed separately.

Per portion: Energy 313Kcal/1323kJ; Protein 8.8g; Carbohydrate 51g, of which sugars 8.8g; Fat 8.6g, of which saturates 1.2g; Cholesterol 0mg; Calcium 43mg; Fibre 3.3g; Sodium 62mg.

CLAMS WITH NEAPOLITAN TOMATO SAUCE

THIS RECIPE TAKES ITS NAME FROM THE CITY OF NAPLES, WHERE BOTH FRESH TOMATO SAUCE AND SHELLFISH ARE TRADITIONALLY SERVED WITH VERMICELLI. HERE THE TWO ARE COMBINED TO MAKE A VERY TASTY DISH THAT IS PERFECT FOR A COLD WINTER'S EVENING.

SERVES FOUR

INGREDIENTS

1kg/2¼lb fresh clams
250ml/8fl oz/1 cup dry white wine,
  or vegetable stock
2 garlic cloves, bruised
1 large handful fresh flat leaf parsley
30ml/2 tbsp extra virgin olive oil or
  sunflower oil
1 small onion, finely chopped
8 ripe plum tomatoes, peeled, seeded
  and finely chopped
½–1 fresh red chilli, seeded and
  finely chopped
350g/12oz dried vermicelli
salt and ground black pepper

1 Scrub the clams thoroughly with a brush under cold running water and discard any that are open or do not close their shells when sharply tapped against the work surface.

2 Pour the white wine or vegetable stock into a large, heavy pan and add the bruised garlic cloves. Shred half the parsley finely, add to the wine or stock, then add the clams.

3 Cover the pan tightly with the lid and bring to the boil over a high heat. Cook for about 5 minutes, shaking the pan frequently, until the clams have opened.

4 Tip the clams into a large colander set over a bowl and let the liquid drain through. Leave the clams until cool enough to handle, then remove about two-thirds of them from their shells, tipping the clam liquor into the bowl of cooking liquid. Discard any clams that have failed to open.

5 Set both shelled and unshelled clams aside, keeping the unshelled clams warm in a bowl covered with a lid or thick cloth.

6 Heat the oil in a pan, add the onion and cook gently, stirring frequently, for about 5 minutes, until softened and lightly coloured. Add the tomatoes, then strain in the clam cooking liquid. Add the chilli, and salt and pepper to taste.

7 Bring to the boil, half cover the pan and simmer gently for 15–20 minutes. Meanwhile, cook the pasta according to the packet instructions. Chop the remaining parsley finely.

8 Add the shelled clams to the tomato sauce, stir well and heat through very gently for 2–3 minutes.

9 Drain the cooked pasta well and tip it into a warmed bowl. Taste the sauce for seasoning, then pour the sauce over the pasta and toss everything together well. Garnish with the reserved clams, sprinkle the parsley over the pasta and serve immediately.

Per portion: Energy 500Kcal/2091kJ; Protein 21.6g; Carbohydrate 77.3g, of which sugars 6.9g; Fat 7.1g, of which saturates 1.1g; Cholesterol 50mg; Calcium 134mg; Fibre 2.9g; Sodium 932mg.

PASTA WITH TOMATOES AND SHELLFISH

COLOURFUL AND DELICIOUS, THIS TYPICAL GENOESE DISH IS IDEAL FOR A DINNER PARTY. THE TOMATO SAUCE IS QUITE RUNNY, SO SERVE IT WITH CRUSTY BREAD AND SPOONS AS WELL AS FORKS. FOR A REAL TASTE OF ITALY, CHOOSE A DRY WHITE ITALIAN WINE TO SERVE WITH THE MEAL.

SERVES FOUR

INGREDIENTS

45ml/3 tbsp olive oil
1 small onion, chopped
1 garlic clove, crushed
½ fresh red chilli, seeded
  and chopped
200g/7oz can chopped
  plum tomatoes
30ml/2 tbsp chopped fresh flat
  leaf parsley
400g/14oz fresh clams
400g/14oz fresh mussels
60ml/4 tbsp dry white wine
400g/14oz/3½ cups dried trenette
  or spaghetti
a few fresh basil leaves
90g/3½oz/⅔ cup cooked, peeled
  prawns (shrimp), thawed and
  thoroughly dried if frozen
salt and ground black pepper
lemon wedges and chopped fresh herbs,
  such as parsley or thyme, to garnish

1 Heat 30ml/2tbsp of the oil in a frying pan or medium pan. Add the onion, garlic and chilli and cook over a medium heat for 1–2 minutes, stirring constantly. Stir in the tomatoes, half the parsley and pepper to taste. Bring to the boil, lower the heat, cover and simmer for 15 minutes.

2 Meanwhile, scrub the clams and mussels under cold running water. Discard any that are open and that do not close when sharply tapped against the work surface.

3 In a large pan, heat the remaining oil. Add the clams and mussels, with the rest of the parsley and toss over a high heat for a few seconds. Pour in the wine, then cover tightly. Cook for about 5 minutes, shaking the pan frequently, until the clams and mussels have opened.

4 Transfer the clams and mussels to a bowl, discarding any shellfish that have failed to open. Strain the cooking liquid and set aside. Reserve eight clams and four mussels for the garnish, then remove the rest from their shells.

5 Cook the pasta according to the instructions on the packet. Meanwhile, add 120ml/4fl oz/ ½ cup of the reserved shellfish liquid to the tomato sauce. Add the basil, prawns, shelled clams and mussels to the sauce. Season.

6 Drain the pasta and tip it into a warmed bowl. Add the sauce and toss well to combine. Serve in individual bowls. Sprinkle with herbs and garnish each portion with lemon, two clams and one mussel in their shells.

Per portion: Energy 510Kcal/2160kJ; Protein 27.2g; Carbohydrate 77.1g, of which sugars 5.6g; Fat 11.5g, of which saturates 1.6g; Cholesterol 68mg; Calcium 180mg; Fibre 3.5g; Sodium 193mg.

LOBSTER RAVIOLI

IT IS ESSENTIAL TO USE HOME-MADE PASTA TO OBTAIN THE DELICACY AND THINNESS THAT THIS
SUPERB FILLING DESERVES. BEFORE YOU START THE RECIPE, MAKE A WELL-FLAVOURED FISH STOCK,
USING THE LOBSTER SHELL AND HEAD.

SERVES FOUR

INGREDIENTS
  1 lobster, about 450g/1lb, cooked
    and taken out of the shell
  2 soft white bread slices, about
    50g/2oz, crusts removed
  200ml/7fl oz/scant 1 cup fish stock
  1 egg
  250ml/8fl oz/1 cup double
    (heavy) cream
  15ml/1 tbsp chopped fresh chives,
    plus extra to garnish
  15ml/1 tbsp finely chopped
    fresh chervil
  salt and ground white pepper
  fresh chives, to garnish
For the pasta dough
  225g/8oz/2 cups strong plain (all-
    purpose) flour
  2 eggs, plus 2 egg yolks
For the mushroom sauce
  a large pinch of saffron threads
  25g/1oz/2 tbsp butter
  2 shallots, finely chopped
  200g/7oz/3 cups button (white)
    mushrooms, finely chopped
  juice of ½ lemon
  200ml/7fl oz/scant 1 cup
    double (heavy) cream

2 Meanwhile, make the lobster filling. Cut the lobster meat into large chunks and place in a bowl. Tear the white bread into small pieces and soak them in 45ml/3 tbsp of the fish stock. Place in a food processor with half the egg and 30–45ml/2–3 tbsp of the double cream and process until smooth. Stir the mixture into the lobster meat, then add the chives and chervil and season to taste with salt and white pepper.

3 Roll the ravioli dough to a thickness of 3mm/⅛in, preferably using a pasta machine. The process can be done by hand with a rolling pin but is quite hard work. Divide the dough into four rectangles and dust each rectangle lightly with flour.

4 Spoon six equal heaps of filling on to one sheet of pasta, leaving about 3cm/1¼in between each pile of filling. Lightly beat the remaining egg with a tablespoon of water and brush it over the pasta between the piles of filling. Cover with a second sheet of pasta. Repeat with the other two sheets of pasta and remaining filling.

5 Using your fingertips, press the top layer of dough down well between the piles of filling, making sure each is well sealed. Cut between the heaps with a 7.5cm/3in fluted pastry cutter or a pasta wheel to make twelve ravioli.

6 Place the ravioli in a single layer on a baking sheet, cover with clear film or a damp cloth, and put in the refrigerator while you make the sauces.

7 Make the mushroom sauce. Soak the saffron in 15ml/1 tbsp warm water. Melt the butter in a pan and cook the shallots over a low heat until they are soft but not coloured.

8 Add the chopped mushrooms and lemon juice and continue to cook over a low heat until almost all the liquid has evaporated. Stir in the saffron, with its soaking water, and the cream, then cook gently, stirring occasionally, until the sauce has thickened. Keep warm while you cook the ravioli.

1 Make the pasta dough. Sift the flour with a pinch of salt. Put into a food processor with the eggs and yolks and process until the mixture resembles breadcrumbs. Turn out on to a floured surface; knead to a smooth dough. Wrap in clear film (plastic wrap) and leave to rest in the refrigerator for 1 hour.

Per portion: Energy 652Kcal/2722kJ; Protein 23g; Carbohydrate 52.2g, of which sugars 3.1g; Fat 40.5g, of which saturates 22.2g; Cholesterol 361mg; Calcium 186mg; Fibre 2.9g; Sodium 298mg.

9 In another pan, bring the remaining fish stock to the boil, stir in the rest of the cream and bubble to make a slightly thickened sauce. Season to taste with salt and pepper and keep warm. Bring a large pan of lightly salted water to a rolling boil. Gently drop in the ravioli (left) and cook for 3–4 minutes, until the pasta is just tender.

10 Place three ravioli on to the centre of each of four individual warmed plates, spoon over a little of the mushroom sauce and pour a ribbon of fish sauce around the edge. Serve immediately, garnished with chopped and whole fresh chives.

SEAFOOD LASAGNE

THIS DISH CAN BE AS SIMPLE OR AS ELEGANT AS YOU LIKE. FOR A DINNER PARTY, DRESS IT UP WITH SCALLOPS, MUSSELS OR PRAWNS AND A REALLY GENEROUS PINCH OF SAFFRON IN THE SAUCE; FOR A FAMILY SUPPER, USE SIMPLE FISH, SUCH AS COD AND SMOKED HADDOCK. THE LASAGNE CAN BE PREPARED IN ADVANCE AND BAKED AT THE LAST MOMENT.

SERVES EIGHT

INGREDIENTS
  350g/12oz monkfish
  350g/12oz salmon fillet
  350g/12oz undyed smoked haddock
  1 litre/1¾ pints/4 cups milk
  500ml/17fl oz/generous 2 cups
    fish stock
  2 bay leaves or a good pinch of
    saffron threads
  1 small onion, peeled and halved
  75g/3oz/6 tbsp butter, plus extra
    for greasing
  45ml/3 tbsp plain (all-purpose) flour
  150g/5oz/2 cups mushrooms, sliced
  225–300g/8–11oz no-precook or
    fresh lasagne
  60ml/4 tbsp freshly grated
    Parmesan cheese
  salt, ground black pepper, grated
    nutmeg and paprika
  rocket (arugula) leaves, to garnish
For the tomato sauce
  30ml/2 tbsp olive oil
  1 red onion, finely chopped
  1 garlic clove, finely chopped
  400g/14oz can chopped tomatoes
  15ml/1 tbsp tomato purée (paste)
  15ml/1 tbsp torn fresh basil leaves

1 Make the tomato sauce. Heat the oil in a pan and cook the onion and garlic over a low heat for 5 minutes, until softened and golden. Stir in the tomatoes and tomato purée and simmer for 20–30 minutes, stirring occasionally. Season to taste with salt and pepper and stir in the basil.

COOK'S TIP
It is preferable to use fresh lasagne, if available, as it has a better flavour and texture. Cook the sheets, in batches if necessary, in a large pan of lightly salted, boiling water for 3 minutes. Do not overcrowd the pan or the sheets will stick together.

2 Put all the fish in a shallow flameproof dish or pan with the milk, stock, bay leaves or saffron and onion. Bring to the boil over a medium heat. Poach for 5 minutes, until almost cooked. Leave to cool.

3 When the fish is almost cold, strain it, reserving the liquid. Remove the skin and any bones and flake the flesh.

4 Preheat the oven to 180°C/350°F/Gas 4. Melt the butter in a pan, stir in the flour; cook for 2 minutes, stirring. Gradually add the poaching liquid and bring to the boil, stirring. Add the mushrooms, cook for 2–3 minutes; season with salt, pepper and nutmeg.

5 Lightly grease a shallow ovenproof dish. Spoon a thin layer of the mushroom sauce over the base of the dish and spread it with a spatula. Stir the fish into the remaining mushroom sauce in the pan.

6 Make a layer of lasagne, then a layer of fish and sauce. Add another layer of lasagne, then spread over all the tomato sauce. Continue to layer the lasagne and fish, finish with a layer of lasagne.

7 Sprinkle over the grated Parmesan cheese. Bake for 30–45 minutes, until bubbling and golden. Before serving, sprinkle with paprika and garnish with rocket leaves.

Per portion: Energy 411Kcal/1724kJ; Protein 32.2g; Carbohydrate 29.8g, of which sugars 3.6g; Fat 18.9g, of which saturates 7.8g; Cholesterol 71mg; Calcium 143mg; Fibre 1.9g; Sodium 525mg.

SPAGHETTI WITH EGGS, BACON AND CREAM

THIS ITALIAN CLASSIC, FLAVOURED WITH PANCETTA AND A GARLIC AND EGG SAUCE THAT COOKS AROUND THE HOT SPAGHETTI, IS POPULAR WORLDWIDE. IT MAKES A GREAT LAST-MINUTE SUPPER.

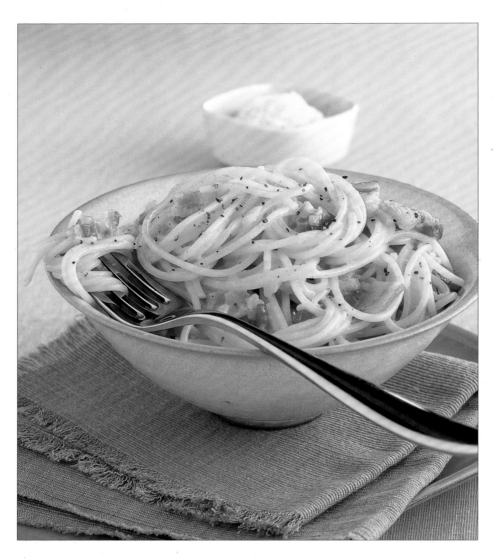

3 Meanwhile, cook the spaghetti in a large pan of salted, boiling water according to the instructions on the packet until *al dente*.

4 Put the eggs, crème fraîche and grated Parmesan in a bowl. Stir in plenty of black pepper, then beat together well.

5 Drain the pasta thoroughly, tip it into the pan with the pancetta or bacon and toss well to mix.

6 Turn off the heat under the pan, then immediately add the egg mixture and toss thoroughly so that it cooks lightly and coats the pasta.

7 Season to taste, then divide the spaghetti among four warmed bowls and sprinkle with freshly ground black pepper. Serve immediately, with extra grated Parmesan handed separately.

COOK'S TIP

You can replace the crème fraîche with either double (heavy) cream or sour cream, if you like.

SERVES FOUR

INGREDIENTS

    30ml/2 tbsp olive oil
    1 small onion, finely chopped
    1 large garlic clove, crushed
    8 pancetta or rindless smoked
      streaky (fatty) bacon rashers
      (strips), cut into 1cm/½in strips
    350g/12oz fresh or dried spaghetti
    4 eggs
    90–120ml/6–8 tbsp/½ cup
      crème fraîche
    60ml/4 tbsp freshly grated
      Parmesan cheese, plus extra
      to serve
    salt and ground black pepper

1 Heat the oil in a large pan, add the onion and garlic and cook gently for about 5 minutes, until softened.

2 Add the pancetta or bacon to the pan and cook for 10 minutes, stirring.

Per portion: Energy 686Kcal/2873kJ; Protein 31.1g; Carbohydrate 66.6g, of which sugars 4.2g; Fat 34.5g, of which saturates 14.8g; Cholesterol 213mg; Calcium 243mg; Fibre 2.8g; Sodium 1098mg.

TURKEY LASAGNE

THIS EASY MEAL-IN-ONE BAKED PASTA DISH IS DELICIOUS MADE WITH COOKED TURKEY PIECES AND BROCCOLI IN A RICH, CREAMY PARMESAN SAUCE.

SERVES FOUR

INGREDIENTS
30ml/2 tbsp light olive oil
1 onion, chopped
2 garlic cloves, chopped
450g/1lb cooked turkey meat,
   finely diced
225g/8oz/1 cup mascarpone cheese
30ml/2 tbsp chopped fresh tarragon
300g/11oz broccoli, broken
   into florets
salt and ground black pepper
For the sauce
50g/2oz/¼ cup butter
30ml/2 tbsp plain (all-purpose) flour
600ml/1 pint/2½ cups milk
75g/3oz/1 cup freshly grated
   Parmesan cheese
115g/4oz no pre-cook lasagne verdi

3 To make the sauce, melt the butter in a pan, stir in the flour and cook for 1 minute, still stirring. Remove from the heat and gradually stir in the milk. Return to the heat and bring the sauce to the boil, stirring constantly. Simmer for 1 minute, then add 50g/2oz/⅔ cup of the Parmesan and plenty of salt and pepper.

4 Spoon a layer of the turkey mixture into a large, shallow ovenproof dish. Add a layer of broccoli and cover with sheets of lasagne. Coat with cheese sauce. Repeat these layers, finishing with a layer of cheese sauce on top. Sprinkle with the remaining Parmesan and bake for 35–40 minutes.

1 Preheat the oven to 180°C/350°F/Gas 4. Heat the oil in a heavy pan and cook the onion and garlic until softened but not coloured. Remove the pan from the heat and stir in the diced turkey, mascarpone and tarragon and season with salt and pepper to taste.

2 Blanch the broccoli in a large pan of salted, boiling water for 1 minute, then drain and rinse thoroughly under cold water to prevent the broccoli from overcooking. Drain well and set aside.

COOK'S TIP

This is a delicious way of using up any cooked turkey that is left over after Christmas or Thanksgiving celebrations. It is also especially good made with half ham and half turkey.

Per portion: Energy 732Kcal/3072kJ; Protein 61.6g; Carbohydrate 43g, of which sugars 13.1g; Fat 36.2g, of which saturates 19.4g; Cholesterol 138mg; Calcium 539mg; Fibre 3.6g; Sodium 475mg.

POTATO GNOCCHI

GNOCCHI CAN BE MADE EITHER WITH MASHED POTATO AND FLOUR, OR WITH SEMOLINA. TO MAKE SURE THAT THEY ARE LIGHT AND FLUFFY, TAKE CARE NOT TO OVERMIX THE DOUGH.

4 Divide the dough into four pieces. On a lightly floured surface, form each into a roll about 2cm/¾in in diameter. Cut the rolls crossways into pieces about 2cm/¾in long.

SERVES FOUR TO SIX

INGREDIENTS
1kg/2¼lb waxy potatoes
250–300g/9–11oz/2¼–2¾ cups
  plain flour (all-purpose), plus more
  if necessary
1 egg
pinch of freshly grated nutmeg
25g/1oz/2 tbsp butter
salt
fresh basil leaves, to garnish
Parmesan cheese cut in shavings,
  to garnish

COOK'S TIP
Gnocchi are also excellent served with a heated sauce, such as Bolognese or a simple cheese sauce.

1 Cook the potatoes in their skins in a large pan of lightly salted, boiling water until tender but not falling apart. Drain and peel while the potatoes are still hot.

2 Spread a layer of flour on a work surface. Pass the hot potatoes through a food mill, dropping them directly on to the flour. Sprinkle with about half of the remaining flour and mix in very lightly. Break the egg into the mixture.

3 Finally, add the nutmeg to the dough and knead lightly, adding more flour if the mixture is too loose. When the dough is light to the touch and no longer moist, it is ready to be rolled.

5 Hold an ordinary table fork with tines sideways, leaning on the board. Then one by one, press and roll the gnocchi lightly along the tines of the fork towards the points, making ridges on one side, and a depression from your thumb on the other.

6 Bring a large pan of salted water to a fast boil, then drop in about half the prepared gnocchi.

7 When the gnocchi rise to the surface, after 3–4 minutes, they are done. Lift them out with a slotted spoon, drain well, and place in a warmed serving bowl. Dot with butter. Cover to keep warm while cooking the remainder. As soon as they are cooked, toss the gnocchi with the butter, garnish with Parmesan shavings and fresh basil leaves, and serve immediately.

Per portion: Energy 454Kcal/1921kJ; Protein 11.7g; Carbohydrate 88.9g, of which sugars 4.2g; Fat 8.1g, of which saturates 4g; Cholesterol 61mg; Calcium 111mg; Fibre 4.5g; Sodium 85mg.

POTATO GNOCCHI WITH SIMPLE TOMATO AND BUTTER SAUCE

GNOCCHI MAKE A SUBSTANTIAL AND TASTY ALTERNATIVE TO PASTA. IN THIS DISH THEY ARE SERVED WITH A VERY SIMPLE, BUT DELICIOUS, FRESH TOMATO SAUCE.

SERVES FOUR

INGREDIENTS
  675g/1½lb floury potatoes
  2 egg yolks
  75g/3oz/¾ cup plain (all-purpose) flour
  60ml/4 tbsp finely chopped fresh
    parsley, to garnish
For the sauce
  25g/1oz/2 tbsp butter, melted
  450g/1lb plum tomatoes, peeled,
    seeded and chopped
  salt

1 Preheat the oven to 200°C/400°F/ Gas 6. Scrub the potatoes, then bake them in their skins in the oven for 1 hour, or until the flesh feels soft when pricked with a fork.

2 While the potatoes are still warm, cut them in half and gently squeeze the flesh into a bowl, or use a spoon to scrape the flesh out of the shells. Mash the potato well, then season with a little salt. Add the egg yolks and mix lightly with a fork or spoon.

3 Add the flour and mix to a coarse dough. Place on a floured work surface and knead for 5 minutes, until the dough is smooth and elastic.

4 Shape the dough into thumb-sized shapes by making long rolls and cutting them into segments. Press each of these with the back of a fork. Place the gnocchi on a floured work surface.

5 Preheat the oven to 140°C/275°F/ Gas 1. Cook the gnocchi, in small batches, in barely simmering, slightly salted water for about 10 minutes. Remove with a slotted spoon, drain well and tip into a dish. Cover and keep hot in the oven.

6 To make the sauce, heat the butter in a small pan for 1 minute, then add the tomatoes and cook over a low heat until the juice starts to run. Sprinkle the gnocchi with chopped parsley and serve with the sauce.

Per portion: Energy 278Kcal/1174kJ; Protein 6.9g; Carbohydrate 45.3g, of which sugars 6g; Fat 9g, of which saturates 4.4g; Cholesterol 114mg; Calcium 57mg; Fibre 3.4g; Sodium 72mg.

INDIAN MEE GORENG

THIS IS A TRULY INTERNATIONAL DISH COMBINING INDIAN, CHINESE AND WESTERN INGREDIENTS. IT IS A DELICIOUS TREAT FOR LUNCH OR SUPPER AND IN SINGAPORE AND MALAYSIA CAN BE BOUGHT IN MANY STREETS FROM ONE OF THE NUMEROUS HAWKERS' STALLS.

2 If using fried tofu, cut each cube in half, refresh it in a pan of boiling water, then drain well. Heat 30ml/2 tbsp of the oil in a large frying pan. If using plain tofu, cut it into cubes and cook until brown, then lift it out with a slotted spoon and set aside.

3 Beat the eggs with the water and seasoning. Add to the oil in the frying pan and cook without stirring until set. Flip over, cook the other side, then slide it out of the pan, roll up and slice thinly.

SERVES FOUR TO SIX

INGREDIENTS
    450g/1lb fresh yellow egg noodles
    60–90ml/4–6 tbsp vegetable oil
    115g/4oz fried tofu or 150g/5oz
      firm tofu
    2 eggs
    30ml/2 tbsp water
    1 onion, sliced
    1 garlic clove, crushed
    15ml/1 tbsp light soy sauce
    30–45ml/2–3 tbsp tomato ketchup
    15ml/1 tbsp chilli sauce (or to taste)
    1 large cooked potato, diced
    4 spring onions (scallions), shredded
    1–2 fresh green chillies, seeded
      and thinly sliced (optional)

1 Bring a large pan of water to the boil, add the fresh egg noodles and cook for just 2 minutes. Drain the noodles and immediately rinse them under cold water to halt cooking. Drain again and set aside.

4 Heat the remaining oil in a wok and cook the onion and garlic for 2–3 minutes. Add the drained noodles, soy sauce, ketchup and chilli sauce. Toss well over medium heat for 2 minutes, then add the diced potato. Reserve a few spring onions for garnish and stir the rest into the noodles with the chilli, if using, and the tofu.

5 When hot, stir in the omelette. Serve on a hot platter, garnished with the remaining spring onion.

Per portion: Energy 662Kcal/2788kJ; Protein 20.7g; Carbohydrate 95.8g, of which sugars 8.8g; Fat 24.5g, of which saturates 4.9g; Cholesterol 129mg; Calcium 210mg; Fibre 4.5g; Sodium 715mg.

SICHUAN NOODLES WITH SESAME SAUCE

THIS TASTY CHINESE VEGETARIAN DISH RESEMBLES THAMIN LETHOK, A BURMESE DISH, WHICH ALSO CONSISTS OF FLAVOURED NOODLES SERVED WITH SEPARATE VEGETABLES THAT ARE TOSSED AT THE TABLE. THIS ILLUSTRATES NEATLY HOW RECIPES MIGRATE FROM ONE COUNTRY TO ANOTHER.

SERVES THREE TO FOUR

INGREDIENTS

450g/1lb fresh or 225g/8oz dried egg noodles
½ cucumber, sliced lengthways, seeded and diced
4–6 spring onions (scallions)
a bunch of radishes, about 115g/4oz
225g/8oz mooli (daikon), peeled
115g/4oz/2 cups beansprouts, rinsed then left in iced water and drained
60ml/4 tbsp groundnut (peanut) oil or sunflower oil
2 garlic cloves, crushed
45ml/3 tbsp toasted sesame paste
15ml/1 tbsp sesame oil
15ml/1 tbsp light soy sauce
5–10ml/1–2 tsp chilli sauce, to taste
15ml/1 tbsp rice vinegar
120ml/4fl oz/½ cup chicken stock or water
5ml/1 tsp sugar, or to taste
salt and ground black pepper
roasted peanuts or cashew nuts, to garnish

1 If using fresh noodles, cook them in boiling water for 1 minute, then drain well. Rinse the noodles in fresh water and drain again. Cook dried noodles according to the instructions on the packet, draining and rinsing them as for fresh noodles.

2 Sprinkle the cucumber with salt, leave for 15 minutes, rinse well, then drain and pat dry on kitchen paper. Place in a large salad bowl.

3 Cut the spring onions into fine shreds. Cut the radishes in half and slice finely. Coarsely grate the mooli using a mandolin or a food processor. Add all the vegetables to the cucumber and toss gently.

4 Heat half the oil in a wok or frying pan and stir-fry the noodles for about 1 minute. Using a slotted spoon, transfer the noodles to a large serving bowl and keep warm.

5 Add the remaining oil to the wok. When it is hot, cook the garlic to flavour the oil. Remove from the heat and stir in the sesame paste, with the sesame oil, soy and chilli sauces, vinegar and stock or water. Add a little sugar and season to taste. Warm through over a gentle heat. Do not overheat or the sauce will thicken too much. Pour the sauce over the noodles and toss well. Garnish with peanuts or cashew nuts and serve with the vegetables.

Per portion: Energy 383Kcal/1592kJ; Protein 8.7g; Carbohydrate 24.9g, of which sugars 4.8g; Fat 28.3g, of which saturates 3.9g; Cholesterol 9mg; Calcium 153mg; Fibre 4.2g; Sodium 398mg.

FIVE-FLAVOUR NOODLES

THE JAPANESE NAME FOR THIS DISH IS GOMOKU YAKISOBA, *MEANING FIVE DIFFERENT INGREDIENTS; HOWEVER, YOU CAN ADD AS MANY DIFFERENT INGREDIENTS AS YOU WISH TO MAKE AN EXCITING AND TASTY NOODLE STIR-FRY.*

SERVES FOUR

INGREDIENTS
  300g/11oz dried Chinese thin egg
    noodles or 500g/1¼lb fresh yaki-
    soba noodles
  200g/7oz lean boneless pork,
    thinly sliced
  22.5ml/4½ tsp sunflower oil
  10g/¼oz grated fresh root ginger
  1 garlic clove, crushed
  200g/7oz green cabbage,
    coarsely chopped
  115g/4oz/2 cups beansprouts
  1 green (bell) pepper, seeded and cut
    into fine strips
  1 red (bell) pepper, seeded and cut
    into fine strips
  salt and ground black pepper
  20ml/4 tsp ao-nori seaweed, to
    garnish (optional)

For the seasoning mix
  60ml/4 tbsp Worcestershire sauce
  15ml/1 tbsp Japanese soy sauce
  15ml/1 tbsp oyster sauce
  15ml/1 tbsp sugar
  2.5ml/½ tsp salt
  ground white pepper

1 Cook the noodles according to the instructions on the packet. Drain well and set aside.

2 Cut the pork into 3–4cm/1¼–1½in strips and season with salt and pepper.

3 Heat 7.5ml/1½ tsp of the oil in a large wok or frying pan. Add the pork and stir-fry until it is just cooked, then remove it from the pan.

4 Wipe the wok with kitchen paper, and heat the remaining oil in it. Add the ginger, garlic and cabbage and stir-fry for 1 minute.

5 Add the beansprouts, stir until softened, then add the green and red peppers and stir-fry for 1 minute more.

6 Return the pork to the pan and add the noodles. Stir in all the ingredients for the seasoning mix and stir-fry for 2–3 minutes. Serve immediately, sprinkled with ao-nori seaweed, if using.

Per portion: Energy 437Kcal/1848kJ; Protein 22.7g; Carbohydrate 65.6g, of which sugars 12.4g; Fat 11.2g, of which saturates 2.8g; Cholesterol 54mg; Calcium 64mg; Fibre 5.1g; Sodium 686mg.

RICE NOODLES WITH PORK

ALTHOUGH RICE NOODLES HAVE LITTLE FLAVOUR THEMSELVES, THEY HAVE A WONDERFUL ABILITY TO TAKE ON THE FLAVOUR OF OTHER INGREDIENTS.

SERVES FOUR TO SIX

INGREDIENTS
  450g/1lb pork fillet (tenderloin)
  225g/8oz dried rice noodles
  115g/4oz/1 cup broccoli florets
  1 red (bell) pepper, quartered
    and seeded
  45ml/3 tbsp groundnut (peanut) oil
  2 garlic cloves, crushed
  10 spring onions (scallions), cut into
    5cm/2in diagonal slices
  1 lemon grass stalk, finely chopped
  1–2 fresh red chillies, seeded and
    finely chopped
  300ml/½ pint/1¼ cups coconut milk
  15ml/1 tbsp tomato purée (paste)
  3 kaffir lime leaves (optional)
For the marinade
  45ml/3 tbsp light soy sauce
  15ml/1 tbsp rice wine
  30ml/2 tbsp groundnut (peanut) oil
  2.5cm/1in piece of fresh root ginger

1 Cut the pork into strips 2.5cm/1in long and 1cm/½in wide. Mix all the marinade ingredients in a bowl, add the pork, stir and marinate for 1 hour.

2 Spread out the rice noodles in a large, shallow dish, pour over enough hot water to cover and leave to soak for 20 minutes, until soft. Drain well and set aside.

3 Meanwhile, blanch the broccoli florets in a small pan of boiling water for 2 minutes, then drain, refresh under cold water and drain well again. Set aside until required.

4 Place the pepper pieces under a hot grill (broiler) for a few minutes until the skin blackens and blisters. Put in a plastic bag for about 10 minutes and then, when cool enough to handle, peel off the skin and slice the flesh thinly.

5 Drain the pork, reserving the marinade. Heat 30ml/2 tbsp of the oil in a large frying pan. Stir-fry the pork, in batches if necessary, for about 3–4 minutes, until the meat is tender. Transfer to a plate and keep warm.

6 Add a little more oil to the pan if necessary and stir-fry the garlic, spring onions, lemon grass and chillies over a low to medium heat for 2–3 minutes. Add the broccoli and pepper slices and stir-fry for a few minutes more.

7 Stir in the reserved marinade, coconut milk and tomato purée, with the kaffir lime leaves, if using. Simmer gently until the broccoli is nearly tender, then add the pork and noodles. Toss over the heat for 3–4 minutes until completely heated through. Transfer to a warm dish and serve immediately.

Per portion: Energy 454Kcal/1901kJ; Protein 30.1g; Carbohydrate 53.2g, of which sugars 7.1g; Fat 12.8g, of which saturates 3.2g; Cholesterol 70mg; Calcium 57mg; Fibre 1.5g; Sodium 428mg.

CANTONESE FRIED NOODLES

CHOW MEIN IS HUGELY POPULAR WITH THE THRIFTY CHINESE WHO BELIEVE IN TURNING LEFTOVERS INTO TASTY DISHES. FOR THIS DELICIOUS DISH, BOILED NOODLES ARE FRIED TO FORM A CRISPY CRUST, WHICH IS TOPPED WITH A SAVOURY SAUCE CONTAINING WHATEVER TASTES GOOD AND NEEDS EATING UP.

SERVES TWO TO THREE

INGREDIENTS

225g/8oz lean beef steak or pork
fillet (tenderloin)
225g/8oz can bamboo shoots, drained
1 leek, trimmed
25g/1oz Chinese dried mushrooms,
soaked for 30 minutes in 120ml/
4fl oz/½ cup warm water
150g/5oz Chinese leaves
(Chinese cabbage)
450g/1lb cooked egg noodles
(255g/8oz dried), drained well
90ml/6 tbsp vegetable oil
30ml/2 tbsp dark soy sauce
15ml/1 tbsp cornflour (cornstarch)
15ml/1 tbsp rice wine or dry sherry
5ml/1 tsp sesame oil
5ml/1 tsp caster (superfine) sugar
salt and ground black pepper

1 Slice the beef or pork, bamboo shoots and leek into thin batons. Drain the mushrooms, reserving 90ml/6 tbsp of the soaking water. Cut off and discard the stems, then slice the caps finely. Cut the Chinese leaves into 2.5cm/1in diamond-shaped pieces and sprinkle with salt. Pat the noodles dry with kitchen paper.

2 Heat a third of the oil in a large wok or frying pan and sauté the noodles. After turning them over once, press the noodles evenly against the base of the pan with a wooden spatula until they form a flat, even cake. Cook over a medium heat for about 4 minutes, or until the noodles on the underside have become crisp.

3 Turn the noodle cake over with a spatula or fish slice or invert on to a large plate and slide back into the wok. Cook for 3 minutes more, then slide on to a heated plate. Keep warm.

4 Heat 30ml/2 tbsp of the remaining oil in the wok. Add the strips of leek, then the meat strips and stir-fry for 10–15 seconds. Sprinkle over half the soy sauce and then add the bamboo shoots and mushrooms, with salt and pepper to taste. Toss over the heat for 1 minute, then transfer this mixture to a plate and set aside.

5 Heat the remaining oil in the wok and sauté the Chinese leaves for 1 minute. Return the meat and vegetable mixture to the wok and sauté with the leaves for 30 seconds, stirring constantly.

6 Mix the cornflour with the reserved mushroom water. Stir into the wok along with the rice wine or sherry, sesame oil, sugar and remaining soy sauce. Cook for 15 seconds to thicken. Divide the noodles among serving dishes and pile the meat and vegetables on top.

Per portion: Energy 695Kcal/2895kJ; Protein 35.3g; Carbohydrate 38.8g, of which sugars 7.7g; Fat 45.3g, of which saturates 8.5g; Cholesterol 79mg; Calcium 79mg; Fibre 4.6g; Sodium 1185mg.

THAI CRISPY NOODLES WITH BEEF

RICE VERMICELLI ARE VERY FINE, DRY, WHITE NOODLES BUNDLED IN LARGE FRAGILE LOOPS AND SOLD IN PACKETS. THEY ARE DEEP-FRIED BEFORE BEING ADDED TO THIS DISH, AND IN THE PROCESS THEY EXPAND TO AT LEAST FOUR TIMES THEIR ORIGINAL SIZE.

SERVES FOUR

INGREDIENTS
about 450g/1lb rump (round) or
   sirloin steak
teriyaki sauce, for sprinkling
175g/6oz rice vermicelli
groundnut (peanut) oil for deep-frying
   and stir-frying
8 spring onions (scallions),
   diagonally sliced
2 garlic cloves, crushed
4–5 carrots, cut into julienne strips
1–2 fresh red chillies, seeded and
   finely sliced
2 small courgettes (zucchini),
   diagonally sliced
5ml/1 tsp grated fresh root ginger
60ml/4 tbsp white or yellow
   rice vinegar
90ml/6 tbsp light soy sauce
about 475ml/16fl oz/2 cups
   spicy stock

1 Using a meat mallet or the side of a rolling pin, beat out the steak, if necessary, to about 2.5cm/1in thick. Place in a shallow dish, brush generously with the teriyaki sauce and set aside for 2–4 hours to marinate.

2 Separate the rice vermicelli into manageable loops and spread several layers of kitchen paper on a very large plate. Pour the oil into a large wok to a depth of about 5cm/2in, and heat until a strand of vermicelli cooks as soon as it is lowered into the oil.

3 Carefully add a loop of rice vermicelli to the oil. It should immediately expand and become opaque. Turn the noodles over so that the strands cook on both sides and then transfer the cooked noodles to the prepared plate to drain. Repeat the process until all the noodles have been cooked. Transfer the cooked rice vermicelli to a separate wok or a deep serving bowl and keep them warm while you are cooking the steak and vegetables.

4 Strain the oil from the wok into a heatproof bowl and set it aside. Heat 15ml/1 tbsp groundnut oil in the clean wok. When it sizzles, cook the steak for about 30 seconds on each side until browned. Transfer to a board and cut into thick slices. The meat should be well browned on the outside but still pink inside. Set aside.

5 Add a little extra oil to the wok and stir-fry the spring onions, garlic and carrots over a medium heat for about 5–6 minutes until the carrots are slightly soft and glazed. Add the chillies, courgettes and ginger and stir-fry for 1–2 minutes more.

6 Stir in the rice vinegar, soy sauce and stock. Cook for about 4 minutes, until the sauce has slightly thickened. Add the steak and cook for a further 1–2 minutes (or longer, if you prefer your meat well done).

7 Pour the steak, vegetables and all the mixture over the noodles and toss lightly and carefully to mix, then serve.

COOK'S TIP
As soon as you add the meat mixture to the noodles, they will soften. If you wish to keep a few crispy noodles, stir some to the surface so they do not come into contact with the hot liquid.

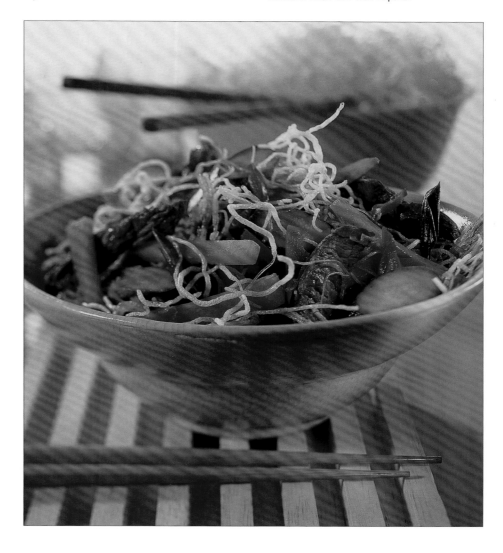

Per portion: Energy 510Kcal/2122kJ; Protein 30.7g; Carbohydrate 41.6g, of which sugars 6.8g; Fat 24.5g, of which saturates 5.7g; Cholesterol 66mg; Calcium 51mg; Fibre 2.1g; Sodium 1262mg.

PAN-FRIED DISHES

Some of the simplest dishes are those that sizzle on top of the stove, leaving the oven free for a baked potato accompaniment, or a hot dessert. With wok or frying pan at the ready, sample such delights as Kofta Kebabs or Salmon with Tequila Cream Sauce. Pan-fried dishes include fritters and fish cakes of various kinds, including completely irresistible Salt Cod Fritters with Aioli. On nights when poultry is on the menu, plump for Stir-fried Chicken with Basil and Chilli for a deliciously spicy stir-fry supper.

  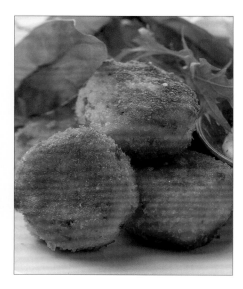

CHEESE AND LEEK SAUSAGES WITH TOMATO, GARLIC AND CHILLI SAUCE

THESE ARE BASED ON THE WELSH SPECIALITY OF GLAMORGAN SAUSAGES, WHICH ARE TRADITIONALLY MADE USING WHITE OR WHOLEMEAL BREADCRUMBS ALONE. HOWEVER, ADDING A LITTLE MASHED POTATO LIGHTENS THE SAUSAGES AND MAKES THEM MUCH EASIER TO HANDLE.

SERVES FOUR

INGREDIENTS
    25g/1oz/2 tbsp butter
    175g/6oz leeks, finely chopped
    90ml/6 tbsp cold mashed potato
    115g/4oz/2 cups fresh white or
        wholemeal (whole-wheat)
        breadcrumbs
    150g/5oz/1¼ cups grated Caerphilly,
        Lancashire or Cantal cheese
    30ml/2 tbsp chopped fresh parsley
    5ml/1 tsp chopped fresh sage
        or marjoram
    2 large (US extra large) eggs, beaten
    cayenne pepper
    65g/2½oz/1 cup dry
        white breadcrumbs
    oil for shallow frying
For the sauce
    30ml/2 tbsp olive oil
    2 garlic cloves, thinly sliced
    1 fresh red chilli, seeded and finely
        chopped, or a good pinch of dried
        red chilli flakes
    1 small onion, finely chopped
    500g/1¼lb tomatoes, peeled, seeded
        and chopped
    few fresh thyme sprigs
    10ml/2 tsp balsamic vinegar or red
        wine vinegar
    pinch of light muscovado
        (brown) sugar
    15–30ml/1–2 tbsp chopped fresh
        marjoram or oregano
    salt and ground black pepper

1 Melt the butter and cook the leeks for 4–5 minutes, until softened but not browned. Mix with the mashed potato, fresh breadcrumbs, cheese, parsley and sage or marjoram. Add sufficient beaten egg (about two-thirds of the quantity) to bind the mixture. Season well and add a good pinch of cayenne.

COOK'S TIP
These sausages are also delicious served with garlic mayonnaise.

2 Shape the mixture into 12 sausage shapes. Dip in the remaining egg, then coat with the dry breadcrumbs. Chill the coated sausages.

3 To make the sauce, heat the oil over a low heat in a pan, add the garlic, chilli and onion and cook for 3–4 minutes. Add the tomatoes, thyme and vinegar. Season with salt, pepper and sugar.

4 Cook the sauce for 40–50 minutes, until much reduced. Remove the thyme and purée the sauce in a blender. Reheat with the marjoram or oregano, then adjust the seasoning, adding more sugar, if necessary.

5 Cook the sausages in shallow oil until golden brown on all sides. Drain on kitchen paper and serve with the sauce.

Per portion: Energy 580Kcal/2416kJ; Protein 19.2g; Carbohydrate 35.5g, of which sugars 7g; Fat 40.3g, of which saturates 15.2g; Cholesterol 164mg; Calcium 361mg; Fibre 3.5g; Sodium 604mg.

POTATO AND ONION CAKES WITH BEETROOT RELISH

THESE IRRESISTIBLE PANCAKES ARE BASED ON TRADITIONAL EASTERN EUROPEAN LATKE, GRATED POTATO CAKES. THEY ARE DELICIOUS WITH A SWEET-SHARP BEETROOT RELISH AND SOUR CREAM.

SERVES FOUR

INGREDIENTS

500g/1¼lb potatoes
1 small cooking apple, peeled, cored and coarsely grated
1 small onion, finely chopped
50g/2oz/½ cup plain (all-purpose) flour
2 large (US extra large) eggs, beaten
30ml/2 tbsp chopped chives
vegetable oil, for shallow frying
salt and ground black pepper
250ml/8fl oz/1 cup sour cream or crème fraîche
fresh dill sprigs and fresh chives or chive flowers, to garnish

For the beetroot (beet) relish

250g/9oz beetroot (beet), cooked and peeled
1 large eating apple, cored and finely diced
15ml/1 tbsp finely chopped red onion
15–30ml/1–2 tbsp tarragon vinegar
15ml/1 tbsp chopped fresh dill
15–30ml/1–2 tbsp light olive oil
pinch of caster (superfine) sugar

1 To make the relish, finely dice the beetroot, then mix it with the apple and onion. Add 15ml/1 tbsp of the vinegar, the dill and 15ml/1 tbsp of the oil. Season, adding more vinegar and oil, and a pinch of caster sugar to taste.

2 Coarsely grate the potatoes, then rinse in cold water, drain and dry them on a clean dishtowel.

3 Mix the potatoes, apple and onion in a bowl. Stir in the flour, eggs and chives. Season and mix again.

4 Heat about 5mm/¼in depth of oil in a frying pan and cook spoonfuls of the mixture. Flatten them to make pancakes 7.5–10cm/3–4in across and cook for 3–4 minutes on each side, until browned. Drain on kitchen paper and keep warm until the mixture is used up.

5 Serve a stack of pancakes – there should be about 16–20 in total – with spoonfuls of sour cream or crème fraîche, and beetroot relish. Garnish with dill sprigs and chives or chive flowers and grind black pepper on top just before serving.

VARIATION
To make a leek and potato cake, melt 25g/1oz/2 tbsp butter in a pan, add 400g/14oz thinly sliced leeks and cook until tender. Season well. Coarsely grate 500g/1¼lb peeled potatoes, then season. Melt another 25g/1oz/2 tbsp butter in a medium frying pan and add a layer of half the potatoes. Cover with the leeks, then add the remaining potatoes, pressing down with a spatula to form a cake. Cook for 20–25 minutes over a low heat until the potatoes are browned, then turn over and cook for 15–20 minutes to brown the other side.

Per portion: Energy 471Kcal/1964kJ; Protein 10.3g; Carbohydrate 42.1g, of which sugars 13.4g; Fat 30.2g, of which saturates 10.6g; Cholesterol 152mg; Calcium 118mg; Fibre 3.7g; Sodium 125mg.

CRAB CAKES

UNLIKE FISH CAKES, CRAB CAKES ARE BOUND WITH EGG AND MAYONNAISE OR TARTARE SAUCE INSTEAD OF POTATOES, WHICH MAKES THEM LIGHT IN TEXTURE. IF YOU PREFER, THEY CAN BE GRILLED INSTEAD OF FRIED; BRUSH WITH A LITTLE OIL FIRST.

SERVES FOUR

INGREDIENTS

450g/1lb mixed brown and white
    crab meat
30ml/2 tbsp mayonnaise or
    tartare sauce
2.5–5ml/½–1 tsp mustard powder
1 egg, lightly beaten
Tabasco sauce
45ml/3 tbsp chopped
    fresh parsley
4 spring onions (scallions), finely
    chopped (optional)
50–75g/2–3oz/½–¾ cup dried
    breadcrumbs, preferably home-made
sunflower oil, for frying
salt, ground black pepper and
    cayenne pepper
chopped spring onions (scallions),
    to garnish
red onion marmalade, to serve

1 Put the crab meat in a bowl and stir in the mayonnaise or tartare sauce, with the mustard and egg. Season with Tabasco, salt, pepper and cayenne.

2 Stir in the parsley, spring onions, if using, and 50g/2oz/½ cup of the breadcrumbs. The mixture should be just firm enough to hold together; depending on how much brown crab meat there is, you may need to add some more breadcrumbs.

3 Divide the mixture into eight portions, roll each into a ball and flatten slightly to make a thick flat disc. Spread out the crab cakes on a platter and put in the refrigerator for 30 minutes before frying.

4 Pour the oil into a shallow pan to a depth of about 5mm/¼in. Cook the crab cakes, in two batches, until golden brown all over. Drain on kitchen paper and keep hot. Serve with a spring onion garnish and red onion marmalade.

Per portion: Energy 285Kcal/1187kJ; Protein 23.9g; Carbohydrate 10.3g, of which sugars 0.9g; Fat 16.7g, of which saturates 2.4g; Cholesterol 134mg; Calcium 178mg; Fibre 0.8g; Sodium 768mg.

VEGETABLE-STUFFED SQUID

SHIRLEY CONRAN FAMOUSLY SAID THAT LIFE IS TOO SHORT TO STUFF A MUSHROOM. THE SAME MIGHT BE SAID OF SQUID, EXCEPT THAT THE RESULT IS SO DELICIOUS THAT IT MAKES THE EFFORT SEEM WORTHWHILE. SMALL CUTTLEFISH CAN BE PREPARED IN THE SAME WAY. SERVE WITH SAFFRON RICE.

SERVES FOUR

INGREDIENTS

4 medium squid, or 12 small squid,
   skinned and cleaned
75g/3oz/6 tbsp butter
50g/2oz/1 cup fresh
   white breadcrumbs
2 shallots, chopped
4 garlic cloves, chopped
1 leek, thinly diced
2 carrots, finely diced
150ml/¼ pint/⅔ cup fish stock
30ml/2 tbsp olive oil
30ml/2 tbsp chopped fresh parsley
salt and ground black pepper
fresh rosemary sprigs, to garnish
saffron rice, to serve

3 Heat half the olive oil in the frying pan, add the chopped squid and cook over a high heat for 1 minute. Remove the squid with a slotted spoon and stir into the vegetables. Stir in the parsley.

4 Put the stuffing mixture into a piping (pastry) bag or use a teaspoon to stuff the squid tubes with the mixture. Do not overfill them, as the stuffing will swell lightly during cooking. Secure the openings with cocktail sticks (toothpicks) or sew up with fine thread.

5 Heat the remaining olive oil in the frying pan, place the stuffed squid in the pan and cook until they are sealed on all sides and golden brown. Transfer the frying pan to the oven and roast the squid for 20 minutes.

6 Unless the squid are very small, carefully cut them into three or four slices and arrange on a bed of saffron rice. Spoon the cooking juices over the squid and serve immediately, garnished with sprigs of rosemary.

1 Preheat the oven to 220°C/425°F/ Gas 7. Cut off the tentacles and side flaps from the squid and chop these finely. Set the squid aside. Melt half the butter in a large frying pan that can safely be used in the oven. Add the fresh white breadcrumbs and cook until they are golden brown, stirring to prevent them from burning. Transfer the breadcrumbs to a bowl and set aside until required.

2 Heat the remaining butter in the frying pan and add the chopped and diced vegetables. Cook until softened but not browned, then stir in the fish stock and cook until it has reduced and the vegetables are very soft. Season to taste with salt and ground black pepper and transfer to the bowl with the breadcrumbs. Mix lightly together.

Per portion: Energy 356Kcal/1486kJ; Protein 21.8g; Carbohydrate 15.2g, of which sugars 3.6g; Fat 23.6g, of which saturates 11.1g; Cholesterol 321mg; Calcium 55mg; Fibre 1.9g; Sodium 352mg.

SALT COD FRITTERS WITH AIOLI

AIOLI IS A FIERCELY GARLICKY, OLIVE OIL MAYONNAISE FROM PROVENCE IN THE SOUTH OF FRANCE AND IS A TRADITIONAL ACCOMPANIMENT TO SALT COD.

SERVES SIX

INGREDIENTS
450g/1lb salt cod
500g/1¼lb floury potatoes
300ml/½ pint/1¼ cups milk
6 spring onions (scallions),
   finely chopped
30ml/2 tbsp extra virgin olive oil
30ml/2 tbsp chopped fresh parsley
juice of ½ lemon, to taste
2 eggs, beaten
60ml/4 tbsp plain (all-purpose) flour
90g/3½oz/1⅓ cups dry
   white breadcrumbs
vegetable oil, for shallow frying
salt and ground black pepper
lemon wedges and salad, to serve
For the aioli
   2 large garlic cloves
   2 egg yolks
   300ml/½ pint/1¼ cups olive oil
   lemon juice, to taste

1 Soak the salt cod in cold water for 24–36 hours, changing the water 5–6 times. It swells as it rehydrates and a tiny piece should not taste too salty when tried. Drain well.

2 Cook the potatoes, unpeeled, in a pan of boiling salted water for about 20 minutes, until tender. Drain, then peel and mash the potatoes.

3 Poach the cod very gently in the milk with half the spring onions for 10–15 minutes, or until it flakes easily. Remove the cod and flake it with a fork into a bowl, discarding bones and skin.

4 Add 60ml/4 tbsp mashed potato to the flaked cod and beat with a wooden spoon. Work in the olive oil, then gradually add the remaining potato. Beat in the remaining spring onions and the parsley. Season with lemon juice and pepper to taste – the mixture may need a little salt. Beat in one egg, then chill the mixture until firm.

5 Shape the mixture into 12–18 small round cakes. Coat them in flour, then dip them in the remaining egg and coat with the breadcrumbs. Chill.

COOK'S TIPS
• Try to find a thick, creamy white piece of salt cod, preferably cut from the middle of the fish rather than the tail and fin ends. Avoid thin, yellowish salt cod, as it will be too dry and salty.
• Mash potatoes by hand, never in a food processor, as it makes them gluey.
• Aioli traditionally has a sharp bite from the raw garlic. However, if you prefer a milder flavour, blanch the garlic once or twice in boiling water for about 3 minutes each time before using it.

6 Meanwhile, make the aioli. Place the garlic and a good pinch of salt in a mortar and pound to a paste with a pestle. Transfer to a bowl and using a small whisk or a wooden spoon, gradually work in the egg yolks.

7 Add the olive oil, a drop at a time, until half is incorporated. When the sauce is as thick as soft butter, beat in 5–10ml/ 1–2 tsp lemon juice, then continue adding oil until the aioli is very thick. Adjust the seasoning, adding lemon juice to taste.

8 Heat about 2cm/¾in depth of oil in a large, heavy frying pan. Add the salt cod fritters and cook over a medium-high heat for about 4 minutes. Turn them over and cook for a further 4 minutes on the other side, until crisp and golden. Drain on crumpled kitchen paper, then serve with the aioli, lemon wedges and salad leaves.

Per portion: Energy 718Kcal/2980kJ; Protein 21.1g; Carbohydrate 33.1g, of which sugars 1.9g; Fat 56.5g, of which saturates 8.3g; Cholesterol 165mg; Calcium 67mg; Fibre 1.6g; Sodium 196mg.

FRIED FISH WITH TOMATO SAUCE

THIS SIMPLE DISH IS PERENNIALLY POPULAR WITH CHILDREN. IT WORKS EQUALLY WELL WITH LEMON SOLE OR DABS (THESE DO NOT NEED SKINNING), OR FILLETS OF HADDOCK AND WHITING.

SERVES FOUR

INGREDIENTS
    60ml/4 tbsp plain (all-purpose) flour
    2 eggs, beaten
    75g/3oz/¾ cup dried breadcrumbs
    4 small plaice or flounder, dark
      skin removed
    15g/½oz/1 tbsp butter
    15ml/1 tbsp sunflower oil
    salt and ground black pepper
    1 lemon, quartered, to serve
    fresh basil leaves, to garnish
For the tomato sauce
    30ml/2 tbsp olive oil
    1 red onion, finely chopped
    1 garlic clove, finely chopped
    400g/14oz can chopped tomatoes
    15ml/1 tbsp tomato purée (paste)
    15ml/1 tbsp torn fresh basil leaves

1 First make the tomato sauce. Heat the olive oil in a large pan, add the finely chopped onion and garlic and cook gently for about 5 minutes, until softened and pale golden. Stir in the chopped tomatoes and tomato purée and simmer for 20–30 minutes, stirring occasionally. Season with salt and pepper and stir in the basil.

2 Spread out the flour in a shallow dish, pour the beaten eggs into another and spread out the breadcrumbs in a third. Season the fish with salt and pepper.

3 Hold a fish in your left hand and dip it first in flour, then in egg and finally in the breadcrumbs, patting the crumbs on with your dry right hand.

4 Heat the butter and oil in a frying pan until foaming. Cook the fish, one at a time, in the hot fat for about 5 minutes on each side, until golden brown and cooked through, but still juicy in the middle. Drain on kitchen paper and keep hot while you cook the rest. Serve with lemon wedges and the tomato sauce, garnished with basil leaves.

Per portion: Energy 345Kcal/1445kJ; Protein 23g; Carbohydrate 28.3g, of which sugars 5.6g; Fat 16.3g, of which saturates 4.2g; Cholesterol 144mg; Calcium 105mg; Fibre 2g; Sodium 338mg.

TROUT WITH TAMARIND AND CHILLI SAUCE

ALTHOUGH VERY ECONOMICAL, TROUT CAN TASTE RATHER BLAND. THIS SPICY THAI-INSPIRED SAUCE REALLY GIVES IT ZING. IF YOU LIKE YOUR FOOD VERY SPICY, ADD AN EXTRA CHILLI.

SERVES FOUR

INGREDIENTS
- 4 trout, 350g/12oz each, cleaned
- 6 spring onions (scallions), sliced
- 60ml/4 tbsp soy sauce
- 15ml/1 tbsp stir-fry oil
- 30ml/2 tbsp chopped fresh coriander (cilantro)

For the sauce
- 50g/2oz tamarind pulp
- 105ml/7 tbsp boiling water
- 2 shallots, coarsely chopped
- 1 fresh red chilli, seeded and chopped
- 1cm/½in piece fresh root ginger, peeled and chopped
- 5ml/1 tsp soft brown sugar
- 45ml/3 tbsp Thai fish sauce

1 Slash the trout diagonally four or five times on each side with a sharp knife and place in a shallow dish.

2 Fill the cavities with spring onions and douse each fish with soy sauce. Carefully turn the fish over to coat both sides with the sauce. Sprinkle on any remaining spring onions and set aside until required.

3 Make the sauce. Put the tamarind pulp in a small bowl and pour on the boiling water. Mash well with a fork until soft. Tip the mixture into a food processor or blender, add the shallots, fresh chilli, chopped ginger, brown sugar and Thai fish sauce and process to a coarse pulp.

4 Heat the stir-fry oil in a large frying pan or wok and cook the trout, one at a time if necessary, for about 5 minutes on each side, until the skin is crisp and browned and the flesh cooked. Put on warmed plates and spoon over some sauce. Sprinkle with the coriander and serve with the remaining sauce.

Per portion: Energy 352Kcal/1481kJ; Protein 55g; Carbohydrate 3.3g, of which sugars 2.8g; Fat 13.4g, of which saturates 2.8g; Cholesterol 224mg; Calcium 95mg; Fibre 0.4g; Sodium 721mg.

SALMON FISH CAKES

THE SECRET OF A GOOD FISH CAKE IS TO MAKE IT WITH FRESHLY PREPARED FISH AND POTATOES, HOME-MADE BREADCRUMBS AND PLENTY OF INTERESTING SEASONING.

SERVES FOUR

INGREDIENTS
    450g/1lb cooked salmon fillet
    450g/1lb cooked potatoes, mashed
    25g/1oz/2 tbsp butter, melted
    10ml/2 tsp wholegrain mustard
    15ml/1 tbsp each chopped fresh dill
        and chopped fresh parsley
    grated rind and juice of ½ lemon
    15g/½oz/1 tbsp plain (all-
        purpose) flour
    1 egg, lightly beaten
    150g/5oz/1¼ cups dried breadcrumbs
    60ml/4 tbsp sunflower oil
    salt and ground black pepper
    rocket (arugula) leaves, chives and
        lemon wedges to garnish

1 Flake the cooked salmon, discarding any skin and bones. Put it in a bowl with the mashed potato, melted butter and wholegrain mustard and mix well. Stir in the dill and parsley and lemon rind and juice. Season to taste with salt and pepper.

2 Divide the mixture into eight portions and shape each into a ball, then flatten into a thick disc. Dip the fish cakes first in flour, then in egg and, finally, in breadcrumbs to coat evenly.

3 Heat the oil in a frying pan until it is very hot. Cook the fish cakes, in batches, until golden brown and crisp all over. As each batch is ready, drain on kitchen paper and keep hot. Garnish with rocket leaves and chives and serve with lemon wedges.

COOK'S TIP
Almost any fresh white or hot-smoked fish is suitable; smoked cod and haddock are particularly good.

Per portion: Energy 586Kcal/2453kJ; Protein 29.8g; Carbohydrate 49.9g, of which sugars 3.2g; Fat 31g, of which saturates 7.2g; Cholesterol 117mg; Calcium 79mg; Fibre 1.3g; Sodium 266mg.

SALMON WITH TEQUILA CREAM SAUCE

USE REPOSADA TEQUILA, WHICH IS LIGHTLY AGED, FOR THIS SAUCE. IT HAS A SMOOTHER, MORE ROUNDED FLAVOUR, WHICH GOES WELL WITH THE CREAM.

SERVES FOUR

INGREDIENTS

3 fresh jalapeño chillies
45ml/3 tbsp olive oil
1 small onion, finely chopped
150ml/¼ pint/⅔ cup fish stock
grated rind and juice of 1 lime
120ml/4fl oz/½ cup single
  (light) cream
30ml/2 tbsp reposada tequila
1 firm avocado
4 salmon fillets
salt and ground white pepper
strips of green (bell) pepper

1 Roast the chillies in a frying pan until the skins are blistered, being careful not to let the flesh burn. Put them in a strong plastic bag and tie the top to keep the steam in. Set aside for 20 minutes.

2 Heat 15ml/1 tbsp of the oil in a pan. Cook the onion for 3–4 minutes, then add the stock, lime rind and juice. Cook for 10 minutes, until the stock starts to reduce. Remove the chillies from the bag and peel off the skins, slit them and scrape out the seeds.

3 Stir the cream into the onion and stock mixture. Slice the chilli flesh into strips and add to the pan. Cook over a gentle heat, stirring constantly, for 2–3 minutes. Season to taste with salt and white pepper.

4 Stir the tequila into the onion and chilli mixture. Leave the pan over a very low heat. Peel the avocado, remove the stone (pit) and slice the flesh. Brush the salmon fillets on one side with a little of the remaining oil.

5 Heat a frying pan or ridged griddle pan until very hot and add the salmon, oiled side down. Cook for 2–3 minutes, until the underside is golden, then brush the top with oil, turn each fillet over and cook the other side until the fish is cooked and flakes easily when tested with the tip of a sharp knife.

6 Serve the fish on a pool of sauce, with the avocado slices. Garnish with strips of green pepper and fresh flat leaf parsley, if you like.

Per portion: Energy 445Kcal/1846kJ; Protein 27.1g; Carbohydrate 2.5g, of which sugars 1.7g; Fat 34.8g, of which saturates 8.7g; Cholesterol 79mg; Calcium 61mg; Fibre 1.5g; Sodium 68mg.

CHICKEN WITH PEAS

THIS ITALIAN DISH STRONGLY REFLECTS THE TRADITIONS OF BOTH MEDITERRANEAN AND JEWISH COOKING. JEWS FAVOUR THE ENRICHMENT OF MEAT SAUCES WITH EGG BECAUSE OF THE LAWS OF THE KASHRUT, WHICH FORBIDS THE ADDITION OF CREAM TO MEAT DISHES.

SERVES FOUR

INGREDIENTS
    4 skinless, boneless chicken
      breast portions
    plain (all-purpose) flour, for dusting
    30–45ml/2–3 tbsp olive oil
    1–2 onions, chopped
    ¼ fennel bulb, chopped (optional)
    15ml/1 tbsp chopped fresh parsley,
      plus extra to garnish
    7.5ml/1½ tsp fennel seeds
    75ml/5 tbsp dry Marsala
    120ml/4fl oz/½ cup chicken stock
    300g/11oz/2¼ cups petits pois
      (baby peas)
    juice of 1½ lemons
    2 egg yolks
    salt and ground black pepper

1 Season the chicken with salt and pepper, then dust generously with flour. Shake off the excess flour; set aside.

2 Heat 15ml/1 tbsp oil in a pan, add the onions, fennel, if using, parsley and fennel seeds. Cook for 5 minutes.

3 Add the remaining oil and the chicken to the pan and cook for 2–3 minutes on each side, until lightly browned. Remove the chicken and onion mixture from the pan and set aside.

4 Deglaze the pan by pouring in the Marsala and cooking over a high heat until reduced to about 30ml/2 tbsp, then pour in the stock. Add the peas and return the chicken and onion mixture to the pan. Cook over a very low heat while you prepare the egg mixture.

5 In a bowl, beat the lemon juice and egg yolks together, then gradually add about 120ml/4fl oz/½ cup of the hot liquid from the chicken and peas, stirring well to combine.

6 Return the mixture to the pan and cook over a low heat, stirring, until the mixture thickens slightly. (Do not allow the mixture to boil or the eggs will curdle and spoil the sauce.) Serve the chicken immediately, sprinkled with a little extra chopped fresh parsley.

Per portion: Energy 319Kcal/1338kJ; Protein 42g; Carbohydrate 9.1g, of which sugars 5.9g; Fat 10.7g, of which saturates 2.2g; Cholesterol 206mg; Calcium 67mg; Fibre 4.2g; Sodium 150mg.

STIR-FRIED CHICKEN WITH BASIL AND CHILLI

THIS QUICK AND EASY CHICKEN DISH IS AN EXCELLENT INTRODUCTION TO THAI CUISINE. THAI BASIL, WHICH IS SOMETIMES KNOWN AS HOLY BASIL, HAS A UNIQUE, PUNGENT FLAVOUR THAT IS BOTH SPICY AND SHARP. DEEP-FRYING THE LEAVES ADDS ANOTHER DIMENSION TO THIS DISH.

SERVES FOUR TO SIX

INGREDIENTS
  45ml/3 tbsp vegetable oil
  4 garlic cloves, thinly sliced
  2–4 fresh red chillies, seeded
    and finely chopped
  450g/1lb skinless boneless chicken
    breast portions, diced
  45ml/3 tbsp Thai fish sauce
  10ml/2 tsp dark soy sauce
  5ml/1 tsp sugar
  10–12 Thai basil leaves
  2 fresh red chillies, seeded and
    finely chopped and about 20 deep-
    fried Thai basil leaves, to garnish

1 Heat the oil in a wok or large frying pan. Add the garlic and chillies and stir-fry over a medium heat for 1–2 minutes, until the garlic is golden.

2 Add the pieces of chicken to the wok or pan and stir-fry until the chicken changes colour.

3 Stir in the Thai fish sauce, soy sauce and sugar. Continue to stir-fry the mixture for 3–4 minutes, or until the chicken is fully cooked with the sauce.

4 Stir in the fresh Thai basil leaves. Spoon the entire mixture on to a warm serving platter or individual serving dishes, and garnish with the sliced chillies and deep-fried Thai basil.

COOK'S TIP
To deep-fry Thai basil leaves, first make sure that the leaves are completely dry or they will splutter when added to the oil. Deep-fry the leaves briefly in hot oil until they are crisp and translucent – this will take only about 30–40 seconds. Lift out the leaves using a slotted spoon or wire basket and leave them to drain on kitchen paper.

Per portion: Energy 196Kcal/819kJ; Protein 27.2g; Carbohydrate 0.4g, of which sugars 0.4g; Fat 9.5g, of which saturates 1.3g; Cholesterol 79mg; Calcium 7mg; Fibre 0g; Sodium 424mg.

TURKEY OR CHICKEN SCHNITZEL

IN AUSTRIA, WHERE THIS DISH ORIGINATED, SCHNITZEL WAS ALWAYS MADE FROM VEAL, POUNDED FLAT, CRISPLY COATED AND THEN FRIED. NOWADAYS, IT MAY BE MADE FROM STEAK, CHICKEN OR TURKEY. THIS IS A POPULAR ISRAELI VERSION. SERVE WITH A SELECTION OF VEGETABLES.

SERVES FOUR

INGREDIENTS

4 boneless turkey or chicken breast
  fillets, each weighing about 175g/6oz
juice of 1 lemon
2 garlic cloves, chopped
plain (all-purpose) flour, for dusting
1–2 eggs
15ml/1 tbsp water
about 50g/2oz/½ cup matzo meal
paprika
a mixture of vegetable and olive oil,
  for shallow frying
salt and ground black pepper
lemon wedges and a selection of
  vegetables, to serve (optional)

1 Lay each piece of meat between two sheets of greaseproof (waxed) paper and pound with a mallet or the end of a rolling pin until it is about half its original thickness and fairly even.

2 In a bowl, combine the lemon juice, garlic, salt and pepper. Coat the meat in it, then leave to marinate.

3 Meanwhile, arrange three wide plates or shallow dishes in a row. Fill one plate or dish with flour, beat the egg and water together in another and mix the matzo meal, salt, pepper and paprika together on the third.

4 Working quickly, dip each fillet into the flour, then the egg, then the matzo meal. Pat everything in well, then arrange the crumbed fillets on a plate and chill for at least 30 minutes and up to 2 hours.

5 In a large, heavy frying pan, heat the oil until it will turn a cube of bread dropped into the oil golden brown in 30–60 seconds. Carefully add the crumbed fillets (in batches if necessary) and cook until golden brown, turning once. Remove and drain on kitchen paper. Serve immediately with lemon wedges and a selection of vegetables.

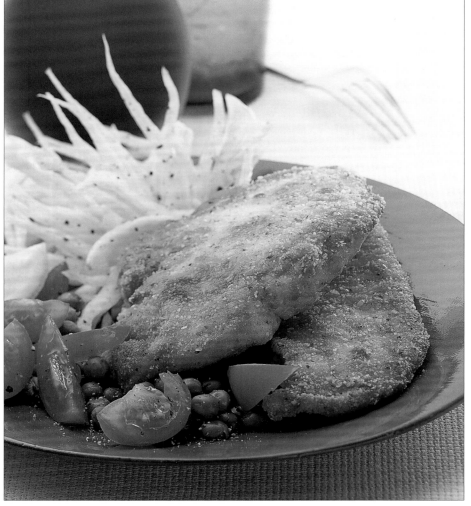

Per portion: Energy 368Kcal/1546kJ; Protein 45.4g; Carbohydrate 14.7g, of which sugars 0.6g; Fat 14.6g, of which saturates 2.3g; Cholesterol 170mg; Calcium 27mg; Fibre 0.5g; Sodium 125mg.

TURKEY CROQUETTES

IN THESE CRISP PATTIES, SMOKED TURKEY IS MIXED WITH MASHED POTATO AND SPRING ONIONS,
ROLLED IN BREADCRUMBS, AND SERVED WITH A TANGY TOMATO SAUCE.

3 Meanwhile, to make the sauce, heat the oil in a frying pan and fry the onion for 5 minutes until softened. Add the tomatoes and purée, stir and simmer for 10 minutes. Stir in the parsley, season with salt and pepper and keep the sauce warm until needed.

SERVES FOUR

INGREDIENTS
   450g/1lb potatoes, diced
   3 eggs
   30ml/2 tbsp milk
   175g/6oz smoked turkey rashers
    (strips), finely chopped
   2 spring onions (scallions),
    thinly sliced
   115g/4oz/2 cups fresh
    white breadcrumbs
   vegetable oil, for deep-frying
For the sauce
   15ml/1 tbsp olive oil
   1 onion, finely chopped
   400g/14oz can tomatoes, drained
   30ml/2 tbsp tomato purée (paste)
   15ml/1 tbsp chopped
    fresh parsley
   salt and ground black pepper

1 Boil the potatoes for 20 minutes, or until tender. Drain and return the pan to a low heat to make sure all the excess water evaporates.

2 Mash the potatoes with two eggs and the milk. Season well with salt and pepper. Stir in the turkey and spring onions. Chill for 1 hour.

4 Remove the potato mixture from the refrigerator and divide into eight pieces. Shape each piece into a sausage shape and dip in the remaining beaten egg and then the breadcrumbs.

5 Heat the vegetable oil in a pan or deep-fryer to 175°C/330°F and deep-fry the croquettes for 5 minutes, or until golden and crisp. Drain and serve immediately with the sauce.

COOK'S TIP
Test the oil is at the correct temperature by dropping a cube of bread on to the surface. If it sinks, rises and sizzles in 10 seconds, the oil is ready to use.

Per portion: Energy 404Kcal/1698kJ; Protein 19.4g; Carbohydrate 47g, of which sugars 7.7g; Fat 16.7g, of which saturates 2.4g; Cholesterol 73mg; Calcium 93mg; Fibre 3.3g; Sodium 315mg.

KOFTA KEBABS

THESE SPICY PATTIES OF MINCED LAMB ARE SPIKED WITH AROMATIC HERBS AND SEASONINGS. THEY ARE VERY POPULAR THROUGHOUT THE MIDDLE EAST RIGHT THROUGH TO THE INDIAN SUBCONTINENT. SERVE WITH FLAT BREAD AND A SELECTION OF REFRESHING AND EXOTIC SALADS, SUCH AS ORANGES SPRINKLED WITH CAYENNE OR PAPRIKA, ONIONS SPRINKLED WITH SUMAC, AND TOMATO WEDGES WITH HERBS AND CHILLIES.

SERVES FOUR

INGREDIENTS
    450g/1lb minced (ground) lamb
    1–2 large slices of French bread,
      very finely crumbled
    ½ bunch fresh coriander (cilantro),
      finely chopped
    5 garlic cloves, chopped
    1 onion, finely chopped
    juice of ½ lemon
    5ml/1 tsp ground cumin
    5ml/1 tsp paprika
    15ml/1 tbsp curry powder
    pinch each of ground cardamom,
      turmeric and cinnamon
    15ml/1 tbsp tomato purée (paste)
    cayenne pepper or chopped fresh
      chillies (optional)
    1 egg, beaten, if needed
    salt and ground black pepper
    flat bread and salads, to serve

1 Put the lamb, crumbled bread, coriander, garlic, onion, lemon juice, spices, tomato purée, cayenne pepper or chillies and seasoning in a large bowl. Mix well. If the mixture does not bind together, add the beaten egg and a little more bread.

2 With wet hands, shape the mixture into four large or eight small patties.

3 Heat a heavy, non-stick frying pan, add the patties and cook, taking care that they do not fall apart, and turning once or twice, until browned. Serve hot with flat bread and salads.

VARIATION
Mix a handful of raisins or sultanas (golden raisins) into the meat mixture before shaping it into patties.

Per portion: Energy 414Kcal/1740kJ; Protein 29.3g; Carbohydrate 36.9g, of which sugars 4.1g; Fat 17.7g, of which saturates 7.6g; Cholesterol 134mg; Calcium 131mg; Fibre 2.5g; Sodium 470mg.

LAMB BURGERS WITH RED ONION AND TOMATO RELISH

A SHARP-SWEET RED ONION RELISH WORKS WELL WITH BURGERS BASED ON MIDDLE-EASTERN STYLE LAMB. SERVE WITH PITTA BREAD AND TABBOULEH OR WITH FRIES AND A CRISP GREEN SALAD.

SERVES FOUR

INGREDIENTS
    25g/1oz/3 tbsp bulgur wheat
    500g/1¼lb lean minced
      (ground) lamb
    1 small red onion, finely chopped
    2 garlic cloves, finely chopped
    1 green chilli, seeded and
      finely chopped
    5ml/1 tsp ground toasted cumin seeds
    2.5ml/½ tsp ground sumac
    15g/½oz chopped fresh flat
      leaf parsley
    30ml/2 tbsp chopped fresh mint
    olive oil, for frying
    salt and ground black pepper
For the relish
    2 red (bell) peppers, halved
      and seeded
    2 red onions, cut into 5mm/¼in
      thick slices
    75–90ml/5–6 tbsp extra virgin olive oil
    350g/12oz cherry tomatoes, chopped
    ½–1 fresh red or green chilli, seeded
      and finely chopped (optional)
    30ml/2 tbsp chopped fresh mint
    30ml/2 tbsp chopped fresh parsley
    15ml/1 tbsp chopped fresh oregano
    2.5–5ml/½–1 tsp each ground toasted
      cumin seeds
    2.5–5ml/½–1 tsp sumac
    juice of ½ lemon
    caster (superfine) sugar, to taste

1 Pour 150ml/¼ pint/⅔ cup hot water over the bulgur wheat in a bowl and leave to stand for 15 minutes, then drain in a sieve and squeeze out the excess moisture.

2 Place the bulgur wheat in a bowl and add the minced lamb, onion, garlic, chilli, cumin, sumac, parsley and mint. Mix the ingredients thoroughly together by hand, then season with 5ml/1 tsp salt and plenty of black pepper and mix again. Form the mixture into eight small burgers and set aside in the refrigerator while you make the relish.

3 Grill (broil) the peppers, skin side up, until the skin chars and blisters. Place in a bowl, cover and leave to stand for 10 minutes. Peel off the skin, dice the peppers finely and place in a bowl.

4 Brush the onions with 15ml/1 tbsp oil and grill for 5 minutes on each side, until browned. Cool, then chop.

5 Add the onions, tomatoes, chilli to taste, the mint, parsley, oregano and 2.5ml/½ tsp each of the cumin and sumac to the peppers. Stir in 60ml/ 4 tbsp of the remaining oil and 15ml/1 tbsp of the lemon juice. Season with salt, pepper and sugar and leave to stand for 20–30 minutes.

6 Heat a heavy frying pan or a ridged, cast-iron griddle pan over a high heat and grease lightly with olive oil. Cook the burgers for about 5–6 minutes on each side, until cooked at the centre.

7 While the burgers are cooking, taste the relish and adjust the seasoning, adding more salt, pepper, sugar, oil, chilli, cumin, sumac and lemon juice to taste. Serve the burgers as soon as they are cooked, with the relish.

Per portion: Energy 537Kcal/2228kJ; Protein 27.2g; Carbohydrate 19g, of which sugars 13.4g; Fat 39.6g, of which saturates 11.1g; Cholesterol 96mg; Calcium 83mg; Fibre 4.2g; Sodium 105mg.

FILLET OF BEEF STROGANOFF

LEGEND HAS IT THAT THIS FAMOUS RUSSIAN RECIPE WAS DEVISED BY COUNT PAUL STROGANOFF'S COOK TO USE BEEF FROZEN BY THE SIBERIAN CLIMATE. THE ONLY WAY IN WHICH IT COULD BE PREPARED WAS CUT INTO VERY THIN STRIPS. THE STRIPS OF LEAN BEEF WERE SERVED IN A SOUR CREAM SAUCE FLAVOURED WITH BRANDY.

3 Add the mushrooms and stir-fry over a high heat. Transfer the vegetables and their juices to a dish and set aside.

4 Wipe the pan, then add and heat the remaining oil. Coat a batch of meat with flour, then stir-fry over a high heat until browned. Remove from the pan, then coat and stir-fry another batch. When the last batch of steak is cooked, replace all the meat and vegetables. Add the brandy and simmer until it has almost evaporated.

5 Stir in the stock or consommé and seasoning and cook for 10–15 minutes, stirring frequently, or until the meat is tender and the sauce is thick and glossy. Add the sour cream and sprinkle with chopped parsley. Serve with rice and a simple salad.

COOK'S TIP

If you do not have a very large pan, it may be easier to cook the meat and vegetables in two separate pans. A large flameproof casserole may be used.

SERVES EIGHT

INGREDIENTS

  1.2kg/2½lb fillet (tenderloin) of beef
  30ml/2 tbsp plain (all-purpose) flour
  large pinch each of cayenne pepper
    and paprika
  75ml/5 tbsp sunflower oil
  1 large onion, chopped
  3 garlic cloves, finely chopped
  450g/1lb/6½ cups chestnut
    mushrooms, sliced
  75ml/5 tbsp brandy
  300ml/½ pint/1¼ cups beef stock
    or consommé
  300ml/½ pint/1¼ cups sour cream
  45ml/3 tbsp chopped fresh flat
    leaf parsley
  salt and ground black pepper

1 Thinly slice the fillet of beef across the grain, then cut it into fine strips. Season the flour with the cayenne pepper and paprika.

2 Heat half the oil in a large frying pan, add the onion and garlic and cook gently until the onion has softened.

Per portion: Energy 407Kcal/1693kJ; Protein 34.9g; Carbohydrate 8.1g, of which sugars 3.4g; Fat 24g, of which saturates 9.8g; Cholesterol 114mg; Calcium 70mg; Fibre 1.5g; Sodium 87mg.

PAN-FRIED CALF'S LIVER
WITH CRISP ONIONS

SAUTÉED OR CREAMY MASHED POTATOES GO WELL WITH FRIED CALF'S LIVER. SERVE A SALAD OF MIXED LEAVES WITH PLENTY OF DELICATE FRESH HERBS, SUCH AS FENNEL, DILL AND PARSLEY, TO COMPLEMENT THE SIMPLE FLAVOURS OF THIS MAIN COURSE.

SERVES FOUR

INGREDIENTS
50g/2oz/¼ cup butter
4 onions, thinly sliced
5ml/1 tsp caster (superfine) sugar
4 slices calf's liver, each weighing
  about 115g/4oz
30ml/2 tbsp plain (all-purpose) flour
30ml/2 tbsp olive oil
salt and ground black pepper
parsley, to garnish

1 Melt the butter in a large, heavy pan with a lid. Add the onions and mix well to coat with butter. Cover the pan with a tight-fitting lid and cook gently for 10 minutes, stirring occasionally.

2 Stir in the sugar and cover the pan. Cook the onions for 10 minutes more, or until they are soft and golden. Increase the heat, remove the lid and stir the onions over a high heat until they are deep gold and crisp. Use a slotted spoon to remove the onions from the pan, draining off the fat.

3 Meanwhile, rinse the calf's liver in cold water and pat it dry on kitchen paper. Season the flour, put it on a plate and turn the slices of liver in it until they are lightly coated in flour.

COOK'S TIP
Take care not to cook the liver for too long as this may cause it to toughen.

4 Heat the oil in a large frying pan, add the liver and cook for about 2 minutes on each side, or until lightly browned and just firm. Arrange the liver on warmed plates, with the crisp onions. Garnish with parsley and serve with sautéed or mashed potatoes.

Per portion: Energy 350Kcal/1458kJ; Protein 23.9g; Carbohydrate 19.7g, of which sugars 8.6g; Fat 20.1g, of which saturates 8.5g; Cholesterol 452mg; Calcium 61mg; Fibre 2.4g; Sodium 162mg.

STEWS, CASSEROLES AND CURRIES

After the fast-food revolution, slow food is enjoying a renaissance as more and more people take time to make — and enjoy — delectable stews and casseroles. It's almost mystical, the way disparate ingredients are transformed by slow cooking into a dish in which all the different flavours blend to create a harmonious whole. Beef Carbonade and Lamb and New Potato Curry are especially fine examples of the genre.

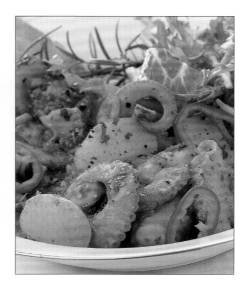

ITALIAN FISH STEW

THIS ROBUST FISH AND TOMATO STEW COMES FROM ITALY WHERE IT IS KNOWN AS BRODETTO.
THERE ARE MANY VERSIONS, BUT ALL REQUIRE FLAVOURSOME SUN-RIPENED TOMATOES AND A GOOD
FISH STOCK. BUY SOME OF THE FISH WHOLE SO THAT YOU CAN SIMPLY SIMMER THEM, REMOVE THE
COOKED FLESH AND STRAIN THE DELICIOUSLY FLAVOURED JUICES TO MAKE THE STOCK.

SERVES FOUR TO FIVE

INGREDIENTS

900g/2lb mixture of fish fillets or
steaks, such as monkfish, cod,
haddock or hake
900g/2lb mixture of conger eel,
red or grey mullet, snapper or
small white fish, prepared
according to type
1 onion, halved
1 celery stick, coarsely chopped
225g/8oz squid
225g/8oz fresh mussels
675g/1½lb ripe tomatoes
60ml/4 tbsp olive oil
1 large onion, thinly sliced
3 garlic cloves, crushed
5ml/1 tsp saffron threads
150ml/¼ pint/⅔ cup dry white wine
90ml/6 tbsp chopped fresh parsley
salt and ground black pepper
croûtons, to serve

1 Remove any skin and bones from the
fish fillets or steaks, cut the fish into large
pieces and reserve. Place the bones in a
pan with all the remaining fish.

2 Add the halved onion and the celery
and just cover with water. Bring almost
to the boil, then reduce the heat and
simmer gently for about 30 minutes. Lift
out the fish and remove the flesh from
the bones. Strain the stock.

3 To prepare the squid, twist the head
and tentacles away from the body. Cut
the head from the tentacles. Discard the
body contents and peel away the
mottled skin. Wash the tentacles and
bodies and dry on kitchen paper.

4 Scrub the mussels, discarding any
that are damaged or open ones that do
not close when sharply tapped.

5 Plunge the tomatoes into boiling
water for 30 seconds, then refresh in
cold water. Peel off the skins and chop
the flesh coarsely.

6 Heat the oil in a large sauté pan. Add
the sliced onion and the garlic, and
cook gently for 3 minutes. Add the
squid and the uncooked white fish,
which you reserved earlier, and cook
quickly on all sides. Remove the fish
from the pan using a slotted spoon.

7 Add 475ml/16fl oz/2 cups strained
reserved fish stock, the saffron and
tomatoes to the pan. Pour in the wine.
Bring to the boil, then reduce the heat
and simmer for about 5 minutes. Add
the mussels, cover, and cook for
3–4 minutes, until the mussels have
opened. Discard any mussels that
remain closed.

8 Season the sauce with salt and
pepper and put all the fish in the pan.
Cook gently for 5 minutes. Sprinkle with
the parsley and serve with the croûtons.

Per portion: Energy 624Kcal/2624kJ; Protein 98.6g; Carbohydrate 12.6g, of which sugars 9.7g; Fat 17.5g, of which saturates 2.9g; Cholesterol 322mg; Calcium 163mg; Fibre 2.8g; Sodium 448mg.

CURRIED PRAWNS IN COCONUT MILK

A WONDERFULLY QUICK AND EASY DISH, THIS FEATURES PRAWNS IN A SPICY YELLOW CURRY GRAVY.

SERVES FOUR TO SIX

INGREDIENTS
- 600ml/1 pint/2¹/₂ cups coconut milk
- 30ml/2 tbsp yellow curry paste (see Cook's Tip)
- 15ml/1 tbsp Thai fish sauce
- 2.5ml/¹/₂ tsp salt
- 5ml/1 tsp sugar
- 450g/1lb raw king prawns (jumbo shrimp) peeled, thawed if frozen
- 225g/8oz cherry tomatoes
- yellow and orange (bell) peppers, seeded and cut into thin strips, chives and juice of ¹/₂ lime, to garnish

VARIATION
Use cooked prawns (shrimp) for an even quicker version. Add after the tomatoes and heat through for 1–2 minutes.

1 Put half the coconut milk in a wok or pan and bring to the boil. Add the yellow curry paste, stir until it disperses, then lower the heat and simmer for about 10 minutes.

2 Add the Thai fish sauce, salt, sugar and remaining coconut milk to the sauce. Simmer for 5 minutes more.

3 Add the prawns and cherry tomatoes. Simmer very gently for about 5 minutes, until the prawns are pink and tender.

4 Spoon into a serving dish, sprinkle with lime juice and garnish with strips of yellow peppers and chives.

COOK'S TIP
To make yellow curry paste, put into a food processor or blender 6–8 fresh yellow chillies, the chopped base of 1 lemon grass stalk, 4 chopped shallots, 4 chopped garlic cloves, 15ml/1 tbsp chopped peeled fresh root ginger, 5ml/1 tsp coriander seeds, 5ml/1 tsp mustard powder, 5ml/1 tsp salt, 2.5ml/¹/₂ tsp ground cinnamon, 15ml/1 tbsp light brown sugar and 30ml/2 tbsp sunflower oil. Process to a paste, scrape into a jar, cover and keep in the refrigerator.

Per portion: Energy 160Kcal/679kJ; Protein 21.5g; Carbohydrate 15.8g, of which sugars 15.5g; Fat 1.7g, of which saturates 0.6g; Cholesterol 219mg; Calcium 144mg; Fibre 2g; Sodium 584mg.

LOUISIANA SEAFOOD GUMBO

GUMBO IS A SOUP, BUT IS SERVED OVER RICE AS A MAIN COURSE. IN LOUISIANA, OYSTERS ARE CHEAP AND PROLIFIC, AND OYSTERS WOULD BE USED THERE INSTEAD OF MUSSELS.

SERVES SIX

INGREDIENTS
  450g/1lb fresh mussels
  450g/1lb raw prawns (shrimp)
  1 cooked crab, about 1kg/2¼lb
  small bunch of fresh parsley, leaves
    chopped and stalks reserved
  150ml/¼ pint/⅔ cup vegetable oil
  115g/4oz/1 cup plain (all-
    purpose) flour
  1 green (bell) pepper, chopped
  1 large onion, chopped
  2 celery sticks, sliced
  3 garlic cloves, finely chopped
  75g/3oz smoked spiced sausage,
    skinned and sliced
  275g/10oz/1½ cups long grain rice
  6 spring onions (scallions), shredded
  cayenne pepper, to taste
  Tabasco sauce, to taste
  salt

1 Wash the mussels in several changes of cold water, pulling away the black beards. Discard any mussels that are broken or do not close when you tap them firmly.

2 Bring 250ml/8fl oz/1 cup water to the boil in a deep pan. Add the mussels, cover the pan tightly and cook over a high heat, shaking frequently, for 3 minutes. As the mussels open, lift them out with tongs into a sieve set over a bowl. Discard any that fail to open. Shell the mussels, discarding the shells. Return the liquid from the bowl to the pan and make the quantity up to 2 litres/3½ pints/8 cups with water.

3 Peel the prawns and set them aside, reserving a few for the garnish. Put the shells and heads into the pan.

4 Remove all the meat from the crab, separating the brown and white meat. Add all the pieces of shell to the pan with 5ml/2 tsp salt.

5 Bring the shellfish stock to the boil, skimming it regularly. When there is no more froth on the surface, add the parsley stalks and simmer for 15 minutes. Cool, then strain it into a measuring jug (cup) and make up to 2 litres/3½ pints/8 cups with water.

6 Heat the oil in a heavy pan and stir in the flour. Stir constantly over a medium heat with a wooden spoon or whisk until the roux reaches a golden-brown colour. Immediately add the pepper, onion, celery and garlic. Continue cooking for about 3 minutes, until the onion is softened. Stir in the sausage. Reheat the stock.

7 Stir the brown crab meat into the roux, then ladle in the hot stock, a little at a time, stirring constantly until it has all been smoothly incorporated. Bring to a low boil, partially cover the pan, then simmer the gumbo for 30 minutes.

8 Meanwhile, cook the rice in plenty of lightly salted, boiling water until the grains are tender.

9 Add the prawns, mussels, white crab meat and spring onions to the gumbo. Return to the boil and season with salt if necessary, cayenne and a dash or two of Tabasco sauce. Simmer for a further minute, then add the chopped parsley leaves. Serve immediately, ladling the soup over the hot rice in soup plates.

COOK'S TIP
It is essential to stir constantly to darken the roux without burning. Should black specks occur at any stage of cooking, discard the roux and start again. Have the onion, green (bell) pepper and celery ready to add to the roux the minute it reaches the correct golden-brown stage, as this arrests its darkening.

Per portion: Energy 559Kcal/2336kJ; Protein 31.1g; Carbohydrate 57.6g, of which sugars 3.7g; Fat 23g, of which saturates 3.4g; Cholesterol 183mg; Calcium 145mg; Fibre 1.9g; Sodium 474mg.

GREEN FISH CURRY

ANY FIRM-FLESHED FISH CAN BE USED FOR THIS DELICIOUS CURRY, WHICH GAINS ITS RICH COLOUR FROM A MIXTURE OF FRESH HERBS; TRY EXOTICS, SUCH AS MAHI-MAHI, HOKI OR SWORDFISH, OR HUMBLER FISH, SUCH AS COLEY. SERVE IT WITH BASMATI OR THAI FRAGRANT RICE AND LIME WEDGES.

SERVES FOUR

INGREDIENTS

4 garlic cloves, coarsely chopped
5cm/2in piece fresh root ginger,
  peeled and coarsely chopped
2 fresh green chillies, seeded and
  coarsely chopped
grated rind and juice of 1 lime
5–10ml/1–2 tsp shrimp paste
5ml/1 tsp coriander seeds
5ml/1 tsp five-spice powder
75ml/5 tbsp sesame oil
2 red onions, finely chopped
900g/2lb hoki fillets, skinned
400ml/14fl oz/1⅔ cups coconut milk
45ml/3 tbsp Thai fish sauce
50g/2oz fresh coriander
  (cilantro) leaves
50g/2oz fresh mint leaves
50g/2oz fresh basil leaves
6 spring onions (scallions), chopped
150ml/¼ pint/⅔ cup sunflower oil
sliced fresh green chilli and finely
  chopped fresh coriander (cilantro),
  to garnish
cooked rice and lime wedges,
  to serve

1 First make the curry paste. Combine the garlic, fresh root ginger, green chillies, the lime juice and shrimp paste in a food processor. Add the coriander seeds and five-spice powder, with half the sesame oil. Process to a fine paste, then set aside until required.

COOK'S TIP
Shrimp paste, also known as blachan or terasi, is available in Asian food stores.

2 Heat a wok or large shallow pan and pour in the remaining sesame oil. When it is hot, stir-fry the red onions over a high heat for 2 minutes. Add the fish and stir-fry for 1–2 minutes to seal the fillets on all sides.

3 Lift out the red onions and fish and put them on a plate. Add the curry paste to the wok or pan and cook for 1 minute, stirring. Return the fish and red onions to the wok or pan, pour in the coconut milk and bring to the boil. Lower the heat, add the Thai fish sauce and simmer for 5–7 minutes, until the fish is cooked through.

4 Meanwhile, process the herbs, spring onions, lime rind and oil in a food processor to a coarse paste. Stir into the fish curry. Garnish with chilli and coriander and serve with rice and lime wedges.

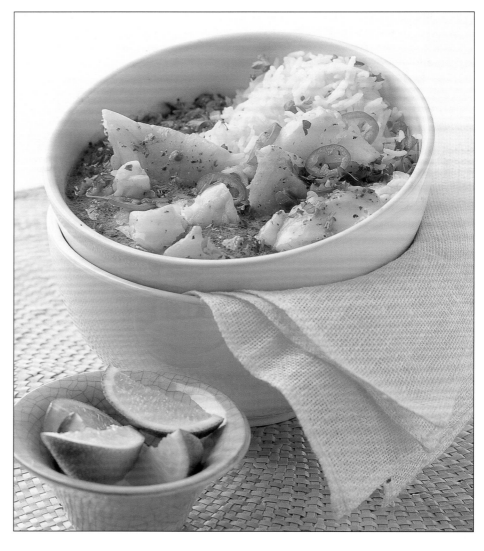

Per portion: Energy 608Kcal/2527kJ; Protein 41g; Carbohydrate 13.3g, of which sugars 9.5g; Fat 43.8g, of which saturates 5.9g; Cholesterol 0mg; Calcium 168mg; Fibre 1.3g; Sodium 313mg.

OCTOPUS STEW

THIS RUSTIC STEW IS A PERFECT DISH FOR ENTERTAINING, AS IT TASTES EVEN BETTER IF MADE A DAY IN ADVANCE. SERVE WITH A COLOURFUL SALAD OF BABY CHARD, ROCKET AND RADICCHIO.

SERVES FOUR TO SIX

INGREDIENTS

    1kg/2¼lb octopus, cleaned
    45ml/3 tbsp olive oil
    1 large red onion, chopped
    3 garlic cloves, finely chopped
    30ml/2 tbsp brandy
    300ml/½ pint/1¼ cups dry
      white wine
    800g/1¾lb ripe plum tomatoes,
      peeled and chopped, or 2 × 400g/
      14oz cans chopped tomatoes
    1 fresh red chilli, seeded and
      chopped (optional)
    450g/1lb small new potatoes
    15ml/1 tbsp chopped fresh rosemary
    15ml/1 tbsp fresh thyme leaves
    1.2 litres/2 pints/5 cups fish stock
    30ml/2 tbsp fresh flat leaf
      parsley leaves
    salt and ground black pepper
    fresh rosemary sprigs, to garnish
For the garlic croûtes
    1 fat garlic clove, peeled
    8 thick slices of baguette or ciabatta
    30ml/2 tbsp olive oil

3 Pour the brandy over the octopus and ignite it. When the flames have died down, add the wine, bring to the boil and bubble gently for about 5 minutes. Stir in the tomatoes, with the chilli, if using, then add the potatoes, rosemary and thyme. Simmer for 5 minutes.

4 Pour in the fish stock and season well. Cover the pan and simmer for 20–30 minutes, stirring occasionally. The octopus and potatoes should be very tender and the sauce should have thickened slightly. At this stage, you can leave the stew to cool, then put it in the refrigerator overnight.

5 Preheat the grill (broiler). To make the garlic croûtes, cut the garlic clove in half and rub both sides of the slices of baguette or ciabatta with the cut side. Crush the garlic, stir it into the oil and brush the mixture over both sides of the bread. Grill (broil) on both sides until the croûtes are golden brown and crisp.

6 To serve the stew, reheat it gently if it has been in the refrigerator overnight, check the seasoning and stir in the parsley leaves. Serve piping hot in individual warmed bowls, garnished with rosemary sprigs and accompanied by the warm garlic croûtes.

1 Cut the octopus into large pieces, put these in a pan and pour in cold water to cover. Season with salt, bring to the boil, then lower the heat and simmer for 30 minutes to tenderize. Drain and cut into bitesize pieces.

2 Heat the oil in a large shallow pan. Cook the onion for 2–3 minutes, until lightly coloured, then add the garlic and cook for 1 minute more. Add the octopus and cook for 2–3 minutes, stirring to colour it lightly on all sides.

Per portion: Energy 588Kcal/2477kJ; Protein 51.6g; Carbohydrate 41.6g, of which sugars 11.5g; Fat 18.1g, of which saturates 2.8g; Cholesterol 120mg; Calcium 163mg; Fibre 3.8g; Sodium 225mg.

RED CHICKEN CURRY WITH BAMBOO SHOOTS

BAMBOO SHOOTS HAVE A LOVELY CRUNCHY TEXTURE. IT IS QUITE ACCEPTABLE TO USE CANNED ONES, AS FRESH BAMBOO IS NOT READILY AVAILABLE IN THE WEST. BUY CANNED WHOLE BAMBOO SHOOTS, WHICH ARE CRISPER AND OF BETTER QUALITY THAN SLICED SHOOTS. RINSE BEFORE USING.

SERVES FOUR TO SIX

INGREDIENTS
   1 litre/1³/₄ pints/4 cups coconut milk
   450g/1lb skinless, boneless chicken
      breast portions, cut into
      bitesize pieces
   30ml/2 tbsp Thai fish sauce
   15ml/1 tbsp sugar
   225g/8oz drained canned bamboo
      shoots, rinsed and sliced
   5 kaffir lime leaves, torn
   salt and ground black pepper
   chopped fresh red chillies and kaffir
      lime leaves, to garnish
For the red curry paste
   5ml/1 tsp coriander seeds
   2.5ml/¹/₂ tsp cumin seeds
   12–15 fresh red chillies, seeded and
      coarsely chopped
   4 shallots, thinly sliced
   2 garlic cloves, chopped
   15ml/1 tbsp chopped galangal
   2 lemon grass stalks, chopped
   3 kaffir lime leaves, chopped
   4 fresh coriander (cilantro) roots
   10 black peppercorns
   good pinch of ground cinnamon
   5ml/1 tsp ground turmeric
   2.5ml/¹/₂ tsp shrimp paste
   5ml/1 tsp salt
   30ml/2 tbsp vegetable oil

1 Make the curry paste. Dry-fry the coriander and cumin seeds for 1–2 minutes, then put in a mortar or food processor with the remaining ingredients, except the oil, and pound or process to a paste.

2 Add the oil, a little at a time, mixing or processing well after each addition. Transfer to a jar and keep in the refrigerator until ready to use.

3 Pour half of the coconut milk into a large, heavy pan. Bring the milk to the boil, stirring constantly until it has separated.

4 Stir in 30ml/2 tbsp of the red curry paste and cook the mixture for 2–3 minutes, stirring constantly. The remaining red curry paste can be kept in the refrigerator for up to 3 months.

5 Add the chicken pieces, Thai fish sauce and sugar to the pan. Stir well, then cook for 5–6 minutes, until the chicken changes colour and is cooked through, stirring constantly to prevent the mixture from sticking to the base of the pan.

6 Pour the remaining coconut milk into the pan, then add the sliced bamboo shoots and torn kaffir lime leaves. Bring the curry back to the boil over a medium heat, stirring constantly to prevent the mixture from sticking, then taste and season with salt and pepper if necessary.

7 To serve, spoon the curry into a warmed serving dish and garnish with chopped chillies and kaffir lime leaves. Boiled Thai jasmine rice would be a good accompaniment.

VARIATION
Instead of, or as well as, bamboo shoots, use straw mushrooms. These are available in cans from Asian stores and supermarkets. Drain well and then stir into the curry at the end of the recipe.

COOK'S TIP
It is essential to use chicken breast portions, rather than any other cut, for this curry, as it is cooked very quickly. Look for diced chicken or strips of chicken (which are often labelled "stir-fry chicken") in the supermarket.

Per portion: Energy 261Kcal/1105kJ; Protein 29.6g; Carbohydrate 19.6g, of which sugars 18.3g; Fat 7.8g, of which saturates 1.5g; Cholesterol 79mg; Calcium 95mg; Fibre 1.1g; Sodium 837mg.

SPANISH PORK AND SAUSAGE CASSEROLE

THIS DISH IS FROM THE CATALAN REGION OF SPAIN, AND COMBINES PORK CHOPS WITH SPICY BUTIFARRA SAUSAGES IN A RICH TOMATO SAUCE. YOU CAN FIND THESE SAUSAGES IN SOME SPANISH DELICATESSENS BUT, IF NOT, SWEET ITALIAN SAUSAGES WILL DO.

SERVES FOUR

INGREDIENTS
    30ml/2 tbsp olive oil
    4 boneless pork chops, about
        175g/6oz each
    4 butifarra or sweet Italian sausages
    1 onion, chopped
    2 garlic cloves, chopped
    120ml/4fl oz/½ cup dry white wine
    6 plum tomatoes, chopped
    1 bay leaf
    30ml/2 tbsp chopped fresh parsley
    salt and ground black pepper
    baked potatoes and green salad,
        to serve

1 Heat the oil in a large, deep frying pan. Cook the pork chops over a high heat until browned on both sides, then transfer to a plate.

2 Add the sausages, onion and garlic to the pan and cook over a medium heat until the sausages are browned and the onion softened, turning the sausages two or three times during cooking. Return the chops to the pan.

3 Stir in the wine, tomatoes, bay leaf and parsley. Season. Cover the pan and cook for 30 minutes.

4 Remove the sausages and cut into thick slices. Return them to the pan and heat through. Serve with baked potatoes and a green salad.

Per portion: Energy 431Kcal/1803kJ; Protein 44.3g; Carbohydrate 12.5g, of which sugars 6.9g; Fat 20.8g, of which saturates 6.5g; Cholesterol 127mg; Calcium 78mg; Fibre 2.4g; Sodium 618mg.

POTATO AND SAUSAGE CASSEROLE

YOU WILL FIND NUMEROUS VARIATIONS OF THIS TRADITIONAL SUPPER DISH THROUGHOUT IRELAND, BUT THE BASIC INGREDIENTS ARE THE SAME WHEREVER YOU GO — POTATOES, SAUSAGES AND BACON.

SERVES FOUR

INGREDIENTS
  15ml/1 tbsp vegetable oil
  4 bacon rashers (strips), cut into
   2.5cm/1in pieces
  2 large onions, chopped
  2 garlic cloves, crushed
  8 large pork sausages
  4 large baking potatoes,
   thinly sliced
  1.5ml/¼ tsp fresh sage
  300ml/½ pint/1¼ cups
   vegetable stock
  salt and ground black pepper
  freshly baked soda bread,
   to serve (optional)

1 Preheat the oven to 180°C/350°F/ Gas 4. Grease a large ovenproof dish and set aside.

2 Heat the oil in a frying pan. Add the bacon and cook for 2 minutes, then add the onions and cook for 5–6 minutes, until golden. Add the garlic and cook for 1 minute, then remove the mixture from the pan and set aside.

3 Add the sausages to the pan and cook for 5–6 minutes, until golden.

4 Arrange the potatoes in the base of the prepared dish. Spoon the bacon and onion mixture on top. Season with the salt and pepper and sprinkle with the fresh sage.

5 Pour on the stock and top with the sausages. Cover and bake for 1 hour. Serve hot with soda bread if you like.

Per portion: Energy 553Kcal/2305kJ; Protein 17.4g; Carbohydrate 48.7g, of which sugars 10g; Fat 33.4g, of which saturates 11.8g; Cholesterol 51mg; Calcium 74mg; Fibre 4g; Sodium 1019mg.

LAMB'S LIVER AND BACON CASSEROLE

BOILED NEW POTATOES TOSSED IN LOTS OF BUTTER GO WELL WITH THIS SIMPLE CASSEROLE. THE TRICK WHEN COOKING LIVER IS TO SEAL IT QUICKLY, THEN SIMMER IT GENTLY AND BRIEFLY. PROLONGED AND/OR FIERCE COOKING MAKES LIVER HARD AND GRAINY.

SERVES FOUR

INGREDIENTS
  30ml/2 tbsp sunflower oil
  225g/8oz rindless unsmoked back
    (lean) bacon rashers (strips), cut
    into pieces
  2 onions, halved and sliced
  175g/6oz/2⅓ cups chestnut
    mushrooms, halved
  450g/1lb lamb's liver, trimmed
    and sliced
  25g/1oz/2 tbsp butter
  15ml/1 tbsp soy sauce
  30ml/2 tbsp plain (all-purpose) flour
  150ml/¼ pint/⅔ cup chicken stock
  salt and ground black pepper

1 Heat the oil in a frying pan and cook the bacon until crisp. Add the onions to the pan and cook for about 10 minutes, stirring frequently, or until softened. Add the mushrooms to the pan and cook for a further 1 minute.

2 Use a slotted spoon to remove the bacon and vegetables from the pan and set aside. Add the liver to the pan and cook over a high heat for 3–4 minutes, turning once to seal the slices on both sides. Remove the liver from the pan and keep warm.

3 Melt the butter in the pan, add the soy sauce and flour and blend together. Stir in the stock and bring to the boil, stirring until thickened. Return the liver and vegetables to the pan and heat through for 1 minute. Season with salt and pepper to taste, and serve with new potatoes and lightly cooked green beans.

Per portion: Energy 434Kcal/1809kJ; Protein 34.7g; Carbohydrate 13g, of which sugars 3.9g; Fat 27.4g, of which saturates 9.4g; Cholesterol 527mg; Calcium 43mg; Fibre 1.6g; Sodium 1258mg.

LAMB AND NEW POTATO CURRY

THIS DISH MAKES THE MOST OF AN ECONOMICAL CUT OF MEAT BY COOKING IT SLOWLY UNTIL THE MEAT IS FALLING FROM THE BONE. CHILLIES AND COCONUT CREAM GIVE IT LOTS OF FLAVOUR.

SERVES FOUR

INGREDIENTS
    25g/1oz/2 tbsp butter
    4 garlic cloves, crushed
    2 onions, sliced into rings
    2.5ml/½ tsp each ground cumin,
      ground coriander, turmeric and
      cayenne pepper
    2–3 fresh red chillies, seeded and
      finely chopped
    300ml/½ pint/1¼ cups hot
      chicken stock
    200ml/7fl oz/scant 1 cup
      coconut cream
    4 lamb shanks, trimmed of fat
    450g/1lb new potatoes, halved
    6 ripe tomatoes, quartered
    salt and ground black pepper
    fresh coriander (cilantro) leaves,
      to garnish
    spicy rice, to serve

2 Stir in the hot stock and coconut cream. Place the lamb shanks in the liquid and cover the casserole with foil. Cook in the oven for 2 hours, turning the shanks twice, first after about an hour or so and again about half an hour later.

3 Par-boil the potatoes for 10 minutes, drain and add to the casserole with the tomatoes, then cook uncovered in the oven for a further 35 minutes. Season to taste, garnish with coriander leaves and serve with the spicy rice.

1 Preheat the oven to 160°C/325°F/Gas 3. Melt the butter in a large flameproof casserole, add the garlic and onions and cook over a low heat for 15 minutes, until golden. Stir in the cumin, ground coriander, turmeric, cayenne and chillies, then cook for a further 2 minutes.

COOK'S TIP
Make this dish a day in advance if possible. Cool and chill overnight, then it will be easy to skim off the excess fat that has risen to the surface and solidified. Reheat the curry thoroughly before you serve it.

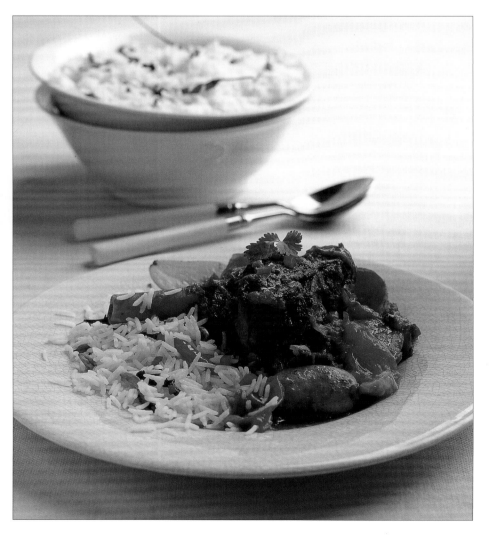

Per portion: Energy 364Kcal/1528kJ; Protein 23.5g; Carbohydrate 30.5g, of which sugars 12.1g; Fat 17.4g, of which saturates 8.8g; Cholesterol 89mg; Calcium 58mg; Fibre 3.5g; Sodium 205mg.

LAMB STEW WITH SHALLOTS AND NEW POTATOES

THIS FRESH LEMON-SEASONED STEW IS FINISHED WITH AN ITALIAN MIXTURE OF CHOPPED GARLIC, PARSLEY AND LEMON RIND KNOWN AS GREMOLATA, THE TRADITIONAL TOPPING FOR OSSO BUCCO.

SERVES SIX

INGREDIENTS
  1kg/2¼lb boneless shoulder of lamb, trimmed of fat and cut into 5cm/ 2in cubes
  1 garlic clove, finely chopped
  finely grated rind of ½ lemon and juice of 1 lemon
  90ml/6 tbsp olive oil
  45ml/3 tbsp plain (all-purpose) flour
  1 large onion, sliced
  5 anchovy fillets in olive oil, drained
  2.5ml/½ tsp caster (superfine) sugar
  300ml/½ pint/1¼ cups white wine
  475ml/16fl oz/2 cups lamb stock or half stock and half water
  1 fresh bay leaf
  fresh thyme sprig
  fresh parsley sprig
  500g/1¼lb small new potatoes
  250g/9oz shallots, peeled but left whole
  45ml/3 tbsp double (heavy) cream (optional)
  salt and ground black pepper
For the gremolata
  1 garlic clove, finely chopped
  finely shredded rind of ½ lemon
  45ml/3 tbsp chopped fresh flat leaf parsley

1 Mix the lamb with the garlic and the rind and juice of ½ lemon. Season with pepper and mix in 15ml/1 tbsp olive oil, then leave to marinate for 12–24 hours.

2 Drain the lamb, reserving the marinade, and pat the lamb dry with kitchen paper. Preheat the oven to 180°C/350°F/Gas 4.

COOK'S TIP
A mezzaluna (double-handled, half-moon shaped, curved chopping blade) makes a very good job of chopping gremolata ingredients. If using a food processor or electric chopper, take care not to overprocess the mixture as it is easy to reduce the ingredients to a paste.

3 Heat 30ml/2 tbsp olive oil in a large, heavy frying pan. Season the flour with salt and pepper and toss the lamb in it to coat, shaking off any excess. Seal the lamb on all sides in the hot oil. Do this in batches, transferring each batch of lamb to an ovenproof pan or flameproof casserole as you brown it. You may need to add an extra 15ml/1 tbsp olive oil to the pan.

4 Reduce the heat, add another 15ml/ 1 tbsp oil to the pan and cook the onion gently over a very low heat, stirring frequently, for 10 minutes, until softened and golden but not browned. Add the anchovies and caster sugar and cook, mashing the anchovies into the soft onion with a wooden spoon.

5 Add the reserved marinade, increase the heat a little and cook for about 1–2 minutes, then pour in the wine and stock or stock and water and bring to the boil. Simmer gently for about 5 minutes, then pour over the lamb.

6 Tie the bay leaf, thyme and parsley together and add to the lamb. Season with salt and pepper, then cover tightly and cook in the oven for 1 hour. Stir the potatoes into the stew and cook for a further 20 minutes.

7 Meanwhile, to make the gremolata, chop all the ingredients together finely. Place in a dish, cover and set aside.

8 Heat the remaining oil in a frying pan and brown the shallots on all sides, then stir them into the lamb. Cover and cook for a further 30–40 minutes, until the lamb is tender. Transfer the lamb and vegetables to a dish and keep warm. Discard the herbs.

9 Boil the cooking juices to reduce and concentrate them, then add the cream, if using, and simmer for 2–3 minutes. Adjust the seasoning, adding a little lemon juice to taste. Pour this sauce over the lamb, sprinkle the gremolata on top and serve immediately.

Per portion: Energy 553Kcal/2311kJ; Protein 37g; Carbohydrate 26.2g, of which sugars 5.3g; Fat 30.6g, of which saturates 10.4g; Cholesterol 128mg; Calcium 79mg; Fibre 2.7g; Sodium 261mg.

SPICED LAMB WITH TOMATOES AND PEPPERS

SELECT LEAN TENDER LAMB FROM THE LEG FOR THIS LIGHTLY SPICED CURRY WITH SUCCULENT PEPPERS AND ONION WEDGES. SERVE WITH WARM NAAN BREAD TO MOP UP THE TOMATO-RICH JUICES.

SERVES SIX

INGREDIENTS

1.5kg/3¼lb boneless lamb, cubed
250ml/8fl oz/1 cup natural
  (plain) yogurt
30ml/2 tbsp sunflower oil
3 onions
2 red (bell) peppers, seeded and cut
  into chunks
3 garlic cloves, finely chopped
1 red chilli, seeded and chopped
2.5cm/1in piece fresh root ginger,
  peeled and chopped
30ml/2 tbsp mild curry paste
2 x 400g/14oz cans tomatoes
large pinch of saffron threads
800g/1¾lb plum tomatoes, halved,
  seeded and cut into chunks
salt and ground black pepper
chopped fresh coriander (cilantro),
  to garnish

1 Mix the lamb with the yogurt in a bowl. Cover and chill for about 1 hour. (Marinating in yogurt helps to tenderize the meat and reduce the cooking time.)

2 Heat the oil in a karahi, wok or large pan. Drain the lamb and reserve the yogurt, then cook the lamb, in batches, until it is golden on all sides – this takes about 15 minutes in total. Remove from the pan and set aside.

3 Cut two of the onions into wedges (six from each onion) and add to the oil remaining in the pan. Cook the onion wedges over a medium heat for about 10 minutes, or until they are beginning to colour. Add the peppers and cook for a further 5 minutes. Use a slotted spoon to remove the vegetables from the pan and set aside.

4 Meanwhile, chop the remaining onion. Add it to the oil remaining in the pan with the garlic, chilli and ginger, and cook, stirring frequently, until softened.

5 Stir in the curry paste and canned tomatoes with the reserved yogurt marinade. Replace the lamb, add seasoning to taste and stir well. Bring to the boil, reduce the heat and simmer for about 30 minutes.

6 Pound the saffron to a powder in a mortar, then stir in a little boiling water to dissolve it. Add this liquid to the curry. Replace the onion and pepper mixture. Stir in the fresh tomatoes and bring back to simmering point, then cook for 15 minutes. Garnish with chopped coriander to serve.

Per portion: Energy 587Kcal/2456kJ; Protein 54.7g; Carbohydrate 19.5g, of which sugars 17.7g; Fat 33g, of which saturates 13.8g; Cholesterol 191mg; Calcium 143mg; Fibre 4g; Sodium 318mg.

OSSO BUCCO WITH RISOTTO MILANESE

LITERALLY MEANING BONE WITH A HOLE, OSSO BUCCO IS A TRADITIONAL MILANESE STEW OF VEAL, ONIONS AND LEEKS IN WHITE WINE. MANY OF TODAY'S VERSIONS ALSO INCLUDE TOMATOES. RISOTTO MILANESE IS THE ARCHETYPAL ITALIAN RISOTTO AND THE CLASSIC ACCOMPANIMENT FOR OSSO BUCCO.

SERVES FOUR

INGREDIENTS
 50g/2oz/¼ cup butter
 15ml/1 tbsp olive oil
 1 large onion, chopped
 1 leek, finely chopped
 45ml/3 tbsp plain (all-purpose) flour
 4 large portions of veal shin (shank)
 600ml/1 pint/2½ cups dry white wine
 salt and ground black pepper
For the risotto
 25g/1oz/2 tbsp butter
 1 onion, finely chopped
 350g/12oz/1⅔ cups risotto rice
 1 litre/1¾ pints/4 cups boiling
  chicken stock
 2.5ml/½ tsp saffron threads
 60ml/4 tbsp white wine
 50g/2oz/⅔ cup Parmesan cheese,
  coarsely grated
For the gremolata
 grated rind of 1 lemon
 30ml/2 tbsp chopped fresh parsley
 1 garlic clove, finely chopped

1 Heat the butter and oil until sizzling in a large frying pan. Add the onion and leek, and cook gently for about 5 minutes without browning the onions. Season the flour and toss the veal in it, then add it to the pan and cook over a high heat until browned.

COOK'S TIP
When buying veal shin, ask for the pieces to be cut thickly so that they will retain the marrow during cooking (or check that they are prepared this way if purchasing prepacked meat).

2 Gradually stir in the wine and heat until simmering. Cover the pan and simmer for 1½ hours, stirring occasionally, or until the meat is very tender. Use a slotted spoon to transfer the veal to a warm serving dish, then boil the sauce rapidly until reduced and thickened to the required consistency.

3 Make the risotto about 30 minutes before the end of the cooking time for the stew. Melt the butter in a large pan and cook the onion until softened.

4 Stir in the rice to coat all the grains in butter. Add a ladleful of boiling chicken stock and mix well. Continue adding the boiling stock a ladleful at a time, letting each portion be absorbed before adding the next. The whole process takes about 20 minutes.

5 Pound the saffron threads in a mortar, then stir in the wine. Add the saffron-scented wine to the risotto and cook for a final 5 minutes. Remove the pan from the heat and stir in the Parmesan.

6 Mix the lemon rind, parsley and garlic for the gremolata. Spoon some risotto on to each plate, then add the veal. Sprinkle with gremolata and serve immediately.

Per portion: Energy 901Kcal/3764kJ; Protein 49.1g; Carbohydrate 92g, of which sugars 8g; Fat 25.9g, of which saturates 13.7g; Cholesterol 130mg; Calcium 248mg; Fibre 2.9g; Sodium 350mg.

BEEF CARBONADE

THIS RICH, DARK STEW OF BEEF, COOKED SLOWLY WITH LOTS OF ONIONS, GARLIC AND BEER, IS A CLASSIC CASSEROLE FROM THE NORTH OF FRANCE AND NEIGHBOURING BELGIUM.

3 Reduce the heat and return the onions to the pan. Add the garlic, cook briefly, then add the beer or ale, water and sugar. Tie the thyme and bay leaf together and add to the pan with the celery. Bring to the boil, stirring, then season with salt and pepper.

4 Pour the sauce over the beef and mix well. Cover tightly, then place in the oven for 2½ hours. Check the beef once or twice to make sure that it is not too dry, adding a little water, if necessary. Test for tenderness, allowing an extra 30–40 minutes' cooking if necessary.

SERVES SIX

INGREDIENTS
    45ml/3 tbsp vegetable oil or
        beef dripping (drippings)
    3 onions, sliced
    45ml/3 tbsp plain (all-purpose) flour
    2.5ml/½ tsp mustard powder
    1kg/2¼lb boneless beef shin (shank)
        or chuck, cut into large cubes
    2–3 garlic cloves, finely chopped
    300ml/½ pint/1¼ cups dark beer or ale
    150ml/¼ pint/⅔ cup water
    5ml/1 tsp dark brown sugar
    1 fresh thyme sprig
    1 fresh bay leaf
    1 piece celery stick
    salt and ground black pepper
For the topping
    50g/2oz/¼ cup butter
    1 garlic clove, crushed
    15ml/1 tbsp Dijon mustard
    45ml/3 tbsp chopped fresh parsley
    6–12 slices baguette or ficelle loaf

1 Preheat the oven to 160°C/325°F/ Gas 3. Heat 30ml/2 tbsp of the oil or dripping in a frying pan and cook the onions over a low heat until softened. Remove from the pan and set aside.

2 Meanwhile, mix together the flour and mustard and season. Toss the beef in the flour. Add the remaining oil or dripping to the pan and heat over a high heat. Brown the beef all over, then transfer it to a casserole.

5 To make the topping, cream the butter with the garlic, mustard and 30ml/2 tbsp of the parsley. Spread the butter thickly over the bread. Increase the oven temperature to 190°C/375°F/ Gas 5. Taste and season the casserole, then arrange the bread slices, buttered side uppermost, on top. Bake for 20–25 minutes, until the bread is browned and crisp. Sprinkle the remaining parsley over the top and serve immediately.

Per portion: Energy 577Kcal/2410kJ; Protein 42.8g; Carbohydrate 32.8g, of which sugars 9.6g; Fat 28.8g, of which saturates 11.5g; Cholesterol 114mg; Calcium 87mg; Fibre 2.1g; Sodium 414mg.

CHILLI CON CARNE

ORIGINALLY MADE WITH FINELY CHOPPED BEEF, CHILLIES AND KIDNEY BEANS BY HUNGRY LABOURERS WORKING ON THE TEXAN RAILROAD, THIS FAMOUS TEX-MEX STEW HAS BECOME AN INTERNATIONAL FAVOURITE. SERVE WITH RICE OR BAKED POTATOES TO COMPLETE THIS HEARTY MEAL.

SERVES EIGHT

INGREDIENTS
- 1.2kg/2½lb lean braising steak
- 30ml/2 tbsp sunflower oil
- 1 large onion, chopped
- 2 garlic cloves, finely chopped
- 15ml/1 tbsp plain (all-purpose) flour
- 300ml/½ pint/1¼ cups red wine
- 300ml/½ pint/1¼ cups beef stock
- 30ml/2 tbsp tomato purée (paste)
- fresh coriander (cilantro) leaves
- salt and ground black pepper

For the beans
- 30ml/2 tbsp olive oil
- 1 onion, chopped
- 1 red chilli, seeded and chopped
- 2 x 400g/14oz cans red kidney beans, drained and rinsed
- 400g/14oz can chopped tomatoes

For the topping
- 6 tomatoes, peeled and chopped
- 1 green chilli, seeded and chopped
- 30ml/2 tbsp chopped fresh chives
- 30ml/2 tbsp fresh coriander (cilantro)
- 150ml/¼ pint/⅔ cup sour cream

2 Use a slotted spoon to remove the onion from the pan, then add the floured beef and cook over a high heat until browned on all sides. Remove from the pan and set aside, then flour and brown another batch of meat.

3 When the last batch of meat is browned, return the first batches with the onion to the pan. Stir in the wine, stock and tomato purée. Bring to the boil, reduce the heat and simmer for 45 minutes, or until the beef is tender.

4 Meanwhile, for the beans, heat the olive oil in a frying pan and cook the onion and chilli until softened. Add the kidney beans and tomatoes and simmer gently for 20–25 minutes, or until thickened and reduced.

5 Mix the tomatoes, chilli, chives and coriander for the topping. Ladle the meat mixture on to warmed plates. Add a layer of bean mixture and tomato topping. Finish with sour cream and garnish with coriander leaves.

1 Cut the meat into thick strips and then cut it crossways into small cubes. Heat the oil in a large, flameproof casserole. Add the chopped onion and garlic, and cook until softened but not coloured. Meanwhile, season the flour and place it on a plate, then toss a batch of meat in it.

VARIATION
This stew is equally good served with tortillas instead of rice. Wrap the tortillas in foil and warm through in the oven.

Per portion: Energy 470Kcal/1969kJ; Protein 42g; Carbohydrate 28.4g, of which sugars 11.2g; Fat 18.9g, of which saturates 6.9g; Cholesterol 106mg; Calcium 124mg; Fibre 8.2g; Sodium 517mg.

STOVE-TOP DISHES

It is remarkable how many main meals can be cooked entirely on top of the stove, from Classic Fish and Chips to steamed specialities like Sea Bass with Orange Chilli Salsa. This is very much hands-on cooking and often achieves better results than when food is cooked in the oven, largely because the cook is more likely to stir and check the dish regularly. The aroma of the cooking food stimulates the appetite, doubling the enjoyment of those lucky enough to tuck into such tasty dishes as Bang Bang Chicken or Pot-roasted Brisket.

MOULES PROVENÇALES

EATING THESE DELECTABLE MUSSELS IS A MESSY AFFAIR, WHICH IS PART OF THEIR CHARM. HAND ROUND PLENTY OF CRUSTY FRENCH BREAD FOR MOPPING UP THE JUICES AND DON'T FORGET FINGERBOWLS OF WARM WATER AND A PLATE FOR DISCARDED SHELLS.

SERVES FOUR

INGREDIENTS

    30ml/2 tbsp olive oil
    200g/7oz rindless unsmoked streaky
      (fatty) bacon, cubed
    1 onion, finely chopped
    3 garlic cloves, finely chopped
    1 bay leaf
    15ml/1 tbsp chopped fresh mixed
      Provençal herbs, such as thyme,
      marjoram, basil, oregano and savory
    15–30ml/1–2 tbsp sun-dried
      tomatoes in oil, chopped
    4 large, very ripe tomatoes, peeled,
      seeded and chopped
    50g/2oz/½ cup pitted black
      olives, chopped
    105ml/7 tbsp dry white wine
    2.25kg/5–5¼lb fresh mussels,
      scrubbed and bearded
    salt and ground black pepper
    60ml/4 tbsp coarsely chopped
      fresh parsley, to garnish

1 Heat the oil in a large pan. Cook the bacon until golden and crisp. Remove with a slotted spoon; set aside. Add the onion and garlic to the pan and cook gently until softened. Add the herbs, with both types of tomatoes. Cook gently for 5 minutes, stirring frequently. Stir in the olives and season.

2 Put the wine and mussels in another pan. Cover and shake over a high heat for 5 minutes, until the mussels open. Discard any that remain closed.

3 Strain the mussel cooking liquid into the pan containing the tomato sauce through a sieve lined with muslin (cheesecloth) and boil until the mixture is reduced by about one-third. Add the mussels and stir to coat them thoroughly with the sauce. Remove and discard the bay leaf.

4 Divide the mussels and sauce among four heated dishes. Sprinkle over the fried bacon and chopped parsley and serve piping hot.

Per portion: Energy 439Kcal/1836kJ; Protein 34.9g; Carbohydrate 12.8g, of which sugars 6.9g; Fat 25.9g, of which saturates 6.2g; Cholesterol 123mg; Calcium 112mg; Fibre 2.4g; Sodium 1467mg.

FRENCH MUSSELS

THIS IS A TRADITIONAL DISH OF MUSSELS COOKED WITH SHALLOTS, GARLIC AND SAFFRON FROM THE WEST ATLANTIC COAST OF FRANCE. IT TASTES AS SUPERB AS IT LOOKS.

SERVES SIX

INGREDIENTS

2kg/4½lb fresh mussels, scrubbed
  and bearded
250g/9oz shallots, finely chopped
300ml/½ pint/1¼ cups medium white
  wine, such as Vouvray
generous pinch of saffron threads
  (about 12 strands)
75g/3oz/6 tbsp butter
2 celery sticks, finely chopped
5ml/1 tsp fennel seeds,
  lightly crushed
2 large garlic cloves, finely chopped
250ml/8fl oz/1 cup fish or stock
1 bay leaf
pinch of cayenne pepper
2 large (US extra large) egg yolks
150ml/¼ pint/⅔ cup double
  (heavy) cream
juice of ½–1 lemon
30–45ml/2–3 tbsp chopped
  fresh parsley
salt and ground black pepper

1 Discard any mussels that do not shut when tapped sharply.

2 Place 30ml/2 tbsp of the shallots with the wine in a wide pan and bring to the boil. Add half the mussels and cover, then boil rapidly for 1 minute, shaking the pan once. Remove all the mussels, discarding any that remain closed. Repeat with the remaining mussels. Remove the top half-shell from each mussel. Strain the cooking liquid through a fine sieve into a bowl and stir in the saffron, then set aside.

3 Melt 50g/2oz/4 tbsp of the butter in a heavy pan. Add the remaining shallots and celery and cook over a low heat, stirring occasionally, for 5–6 minutes, until softened but not browned. Add the fennel seeds and half of the garlic, then cook for another 2–3 minutes.

4 Pour in the reserved mussel liquid, bring to the boil and then simmer for 5 minutes before adding the stock, bay leaf and cayenne. Season with salt and pepper to taste, then simmer, uncovered, for 5–10 minutes.

5 Beat the egg yolks with the cream, then whisk in a ladleful of the hot liquid followed by the juice of ½ lemon. Whisk this mixture back into the sauce. Cook over a very low heat, without allowing it to boil, for 5–10 minutes until slightly thickened. Taste for seasoning and add more lemon juice if necessary.

6 Stir the remaining garlic, butter and most of the parsley into the sauce with the mussels and reheat for 30–60 seconds. Distribute the mussels among six soup plates and ladle the sauce over. Sprinkle with the remaining parsley and serve.

Per portion: Energy 568Kcal/2360kJ; Protein 26g; Carbohydrate 9.9g, of which sugars 5.4g; Fat 42.1g, of which saturates 23.6g; Cholesterol 272mg; Calcium 149mg; Fibre 1.4g; Sodium 632mg.

STEAMED FISH WITH FIVE WILLOW SAUCE

A FISH KETTLE WILL COME IN USEFUL FOR THIS RECIPE. CARP IS TRADITIONALLY USED, BUT ANY CHUNKY FISH THAT CAN BE COOKED WHOLE, SUCH AS SALMON OR SEA BREAM, CAN BE GIVEN THIS TREATMENT. MAKE SURE YOU HAVE A SUITABLE LARGE PLATTER FOR SERVING THIS SPECTACULAR DISH.

SERVES FOUR

INGREDIENTS
- 1–2 carp or similar whole fish, total weight about 1kg/2¼ lb, cleaned and scaled
- 2.5cm/1in piece fresh root ginger, peeled and thinly sliced
- 4 spring onions (scallions), cut into thin strips
- 2.5ml/½ tsp salt

For the five willow sauce
- 375g/13oz jar chow chow (Chinese sweet mixed pickles)
- 300ml/½ pint/1¼ cups water
- 30ml/2 tbsp rice vinegar
- 25ml/1½ tbsp sugar
- 25ml/1½ tbsp cornflour (cornstarch)
- 15ml/1 tbsp light soy sauce
- 15ml/1 tbsp rice wine or medium-dry sherry
- 1 small green (bell) pepper, seeded and diced
- 1 carrot, peeled and cut into batons
- 1 tomato, peeled, seeded and diced

2 Fold up one or two pieces of foil to make a long wide strip. You will need one for each fish. Place the fish on the foil and then lift the fish on to the trivet. Lower the trivet into the fish kettle and tuck the ends of the foil over the fish.

3 Pour boiling water into the fish kettle to a depth of 2.5cm/1in. Bring to a full rolling boil, then lower the heat and cook the fish until the flesh flakes, topping up the kettle with boiling water as necessary. (See Cook's Tip for cooking times.)

5 In a small bowl, mix the cornflour to a paste with the remaining water. Stir in the soy sauce and rice wine or sherry.

6 Add the mixture to the sauce and bring to the boil, stirring until it thickens and becomes glossy. Add all the vegetables, the chopped pickles and the pickle liquid and cook over a gentle heat for 2 minutes.

7 Using the foil strips as a support, carefully transfer the cooked fish to a platter, then ease the foil away. Spoon the warm sauce over the fish and serve.

COOK'S TIP
If using one large fish that is too long to fit in a fish kettle, cut it in half and cook it on a rack placed over a large roasting pan. Pour in a similar quantity of boiling water as for the fish kettle, cover with foil and cook on top of the stove. Allow about 20–25 minutes for a 1kg/2¼ lb fish; 15–20 minutes for a 675g/1½lb fish. Reassemble the halved fish before coating it with the sauce.

1 Rinse the fish inside and out. Dry with kitchen paper. Create a support for each fish by placing a broad strip of oiled foil on the work surface. Place the fish on the foil. Mix the ginger, spring onions and salt, then tuck the mixture into the body cavity.

4 Meanwhile, prepare the sauce. Tip the chow chow into a sieve placed over a bowl and reserve the liquid. Cut each of the pickles in half. Pour 250ml/8fl oz/ 1 cup of the water into a pan and bring to the boil. Add the vinegar and sugar and stir until dissolved.

Per portion: Energy 156Kcal/655kJ; Protein 19.1g; Carbohydrate 7.8g, of which sugars 6.3g; Fat 5.1g, of which saturates 1g; Cholesterol 67mg; Calcium 77mg; Fibre 2.4g; Sodium 739mg.

CHINESE-STYLE STEAMED FISH

THIS IS A CLASSIC CHINESE WAY OF COOKING WHOLE FISH, WITH GARLIC, SPRING ONIONS, GINGER AND BLACK BEANS. THE FISH MAKES A SPLENDID CENTREPIECE FOR A CHINESE MEAL OR IT CAN BE SERVED MORE SIMPLY, WITH BOILED RICE AND SOME STIR-FRIED CHINESE GREENS.

SERVES FOUR TO SIX

INGREDIENTS

    2 sea bass, or trout, each weighing about 675–800g/1½–1¾lb
    25ml/1½ tbsp salted black beans
    2.5ml/½ tsp sugar
    30ml/2 tbsp finely shredded fresh root ginger
    4 garlic cloves, thinly sliced
    30ml/2 tbsp Chinese rice wine or dry sherry
    30ml/2 tbsp light soy sauce
    4–6 spring onions (scallions), finely shredded or sliced diagonally
    45ml/3 tbsp groundnut (peanut) oil
    10ml/2 tsp sesame oil

1 Wash the fish inside and out under cold running water, then pat them dry on kitchen paper. Using a sharp knife, slash three or four deep cross shapes on each side of each fish.

2 Mash half the black beans with the sugar in a small bowl and then stir in the remaining whole beans.

3 Place a little ginger and garlic inside the cavity of each fish and then lay them on a plate or dish that will fit inside a large steamer. Rub the bean mixture into the fish, especially into the slashes, then sprinkle the remaining ginger and garlic over the top. Cover and chill for 30 minutes.

4 Place the steamer over a pan of boiling water. Sprinkle the rice wine or sherry and half the soy sauce over the fish and steam them for 15–20 minutes, or until just cooked.

5 Sprinkle with the remaining soy sauce and sprinkle the spring onions over the fish.

6 In a small pan, heat the groundnut oil until smoking, then trickle it over the spring onions. Sprinkle with the sesame oil and serve immediately.

Per portion: Energy 415Kcal/1741kJ; Protein 54.7g; Carbohydrate 1.6g, of which sugars 1.5g; Fat 20.3g, of which saturates 4.3g; Cholesterol 224mg; Calcium 90mg; Fibre 0.2g; Sodium 739mg.

SEA BASS WITH ORANGE CHILLI SALSA

THE CHILLI CITRUS SALSA HAS A FRESHNESS WHICH PROVIDES THE PERFECT CONTRAST TO THE WONDERFUL FLAVOUR OF FRESH SEA BASS.

SERVES FOUR

INGREDIENTS
    4 sea bass fillets
    salt and ground black pepper
    fresh coriander (cilantro), to garnish
For the salsa
    2 fresh green chillies
    2 oranges or pink grapefruit
    1 small onion

1 Make the salsa. Roast the chillies in a dry griddle pan until the skins are blistered, being careful not to let the flesh burn. Put them in a strong plastic bag and tie the top to keep the steam in. Set aside for 20 minutes.

COOK'S TIP
If the fish has not been scaled, do this by running the back of a small filleting knife against the grain of the scales. They should come away cleanly. Rinse and pat dry with kitchen paper.

2 Slice the top and bottom off each orange or grapefruit and cut off all the peel and pith. Cut between the membranes and put each segment in a bowl.

3 Remove the chillies from the bag and peel off the skins. Cut off the stalks, then slit the chillies and scrape out the seeds. Chop the flesh finely. Cut the onion in half and slice it thinly. Add the onion and chillies to the orange pieces and mix lightly. Season and chill.

4 Season the sea bass fillets. Line a steamer with greaseproof (waxed) paper, allowing extra to hang over the sides to help lift out the fish after cooking. Place the empty steamer over a pan of water and bring to the boil.

5 Place the fish in a single layer in the steamer. Cover with a lid and steam for about 8 minutes, or until just cooked. Garnish with fresh coriander and serve with the salsa and a vegetable side dish of your choice.

Per portion: Energy 181Kcal/763kJ; Protein 30.2g; Carbohydrate 6.6g, of which sugars 6.3g; Fat 3.9g, of which saturates 0.6g; Cholesterol 120mg; Calcium 232mg; Fibre 1.3g; Sodium 108mg.

FILLETS OF TURBOT WITH OYSTERS

THIS LUXURIOUS DISH IS PERFECT FOR SPECIAL OCCASIONS. IT IS WORTH BUYING A WHOLE TURBOT AND ASKING THE FISHMONGER TO FILLET AND SKIN IT FOR YOU. KEEP THE HEAD, BONES AND TRIMMINGS FOR STOCK. SOLE, BRILL AND HALIBUT CAN ALL BE SUBSTITUTED FOR THE TURBOT.

SERVES FOUR

INGREDIENTS
    12 Pacific (rock) oysters
    115g/4oz/½ cup butter
    2 carrots, cut into julienne strips
    200g/7oz celeriac, cut into
        julienne strips
    the white parts of 2 leeks, cut into
        julienne strips
    375ml/13fl oz/generous 1½ cups
        Champagne or dry white sparkling
        wine (about ½ bottle)
    105ml/7 tbsp whipping cream
    1 turbot, about 1.75kg/4–4½lb,
        filleted and skinned
    salt and ground white pepper

1 Using an oyster knife, open the oysters over a bowl to catch the juices, then carefully remove them from their shells, discarding the shells, and place them in a separate bowl. Set aside until required.

2 Melt 25g/1oz/2 tbsp of the butter in a shallow pan, add the vegetable julienne and cook over a low heat until tender but not coloured. Pour in half the Champagne or sparkling wine and cook very gently until all the liquid has evaporated. Keep the heat low so that the vegetables do not colour.

3 Strain the oyster juices into a small pan and add the cream and the remaining Champagne or sparkling wine. Place over a medium heat until the mixture has reduced to the consistency of thin cream. Dice half the remaining butter and whisk it into the sauce, one piece at a time, until smooth. Season to taste, then pour the sauce into a blender and process until velvety smooth.

4 Return the sauce to the pan, bring it to just below boiling point, then drop in the oysters. Poach for about 1 minute, to warm but barely cook. Keep warm, but do not let the sauce boil.

5 Season the turbot fillets with salt and pepper. Heat the remaining butter in a large frying pan until foaming, then cook the fillets over a medium heat for about 2–3 minutes on each side, until cooked through and golden.

6 Cut each turbot fillet into three pieces and arrange on individual warmed plates. Pile the vegetable julienne on top, place three oysters around the turbot fillets on each plate and pour the sauce around the edge.

Per portion: Energy 752Kcal/3125kJ; Protein 66.7g; Carbohydrate 9.2g, of which sugars 8g; Fat 44.1g, of which saturates 23.9g; Cholesterol 106mg; Calcium 252mg; Fibre 1.4g; Sodium 370mg.

COD CARAMBA

THIS COLOURFUL MEXICAN DISH, WITH ITS CONTRASTING CRUNCHY TOPPING AND TENDER FISH FILLING, CAN BE MADE WITH ANY ECONOMICAL WHITE FISH, SUCH AS COLEY OR HADDOCK.

SERVES FOUR TO SIX

INGREDIENTS
  450g/1lb cod fillets
  225g/8oz smoked cod fillets
  300ml/½ pint/1¼ cups fish stock
  50g/2oz/¼ cup butter
  1 onion, sliced
  2 garlic cloves, crushed
  1 green and 1 red (bell) pepper,
    seeded and diced
  2 courgettes (zucchini), diced
  115g/4oz/⅔ cup drained canned or
    thawed frozen corn kernels
  2 tomatoes, peeled and chopped
  juice of 1 lime
  Tabasco sauce
  salt, ground black pepper and
    cayenne pepper
For the topping
  75g/3oz tortilla chips
  50g/2oz/½ cup grated
    Cheddar cheese
  coriander (cilantro) sprigs, to garnish
  lime wedges, to serve

1 Lay the fish in a shallow pan and pour over the fish stock. Bring to the boil, lower the heat, cover and poach for about 8 minutes, until the flesh flakes easily when tested with the tip of a sharp knife. Leave to cool slightly, then remove the skin and separate the flesh into large flakes. Keep hot.

2 Melt the butter in a pan, add the onion and garlic and cook over a low heat until soft. Add the peppers, stir and cook for 2 minutes. Stir in the courgettes and cook for 3 minutes more, until all the vegetables are tender.

3 Mix the corn and tomatoes, then add lime juice and Tabasco to taste. Add to the pan, season with salt, black pepper and cayenne. Cook for 2 minutes to heat the corn and tomatoes, then stir in the fish and transfer to a dish that can safely be used under the grill (broiler).

4 Preheat the grill. Make the topping by crushing the tortilla chips, then mixing in the grated cheese. Add cayenne pepper to taste and sprinkle over the fish. Place the dish under the grill until the topping is crisp and brown. Garnish with coriander sprigs and lime wedges.

Per portion: Energy 439Kcal/1834kJ; Protein 39.8g; Carbohydrate 23.7g, of which sugars 11.3g; Fat 20.8g, of which saturates 10.4g; Cholesterol 116mg; Calcium 185mg; Fibre 4.8g; Sodium 1391mg.

CLASSIC FISH AND CHIPS

NOTHING BEATS A PIECE OF COD COOKED TO A CRISP WITH FRESHLY MADE CHIPS ON THE SIDE. THE BATTER SHOULD BE LIGHT AND CRISP, BUT NOT TOO GREASY AND THE FISH SHOULD MELT IN THE MOUTH. SERVE WITH LEMON WEDGES, OR LIME WEDGES IF YOU REALLY WANT TO SHOW OFF. THE SECRET OF COOKING FISH AND CHIPS SUCCESSFULLY IS TO MAKE SURE THE OIL IS FRESH AND CLEAN. HEAT THE OIL TO THE CORRECT TEMPERATURE BEFORE COOKING THE CHIPS AND AGAIN BEFORE YOU ADD THE FISH. SERVE THE DISH IMMEDIATELY, WHILE STILL CRISP AND PIPING HOT.

SERVES FOUR

INGREDIENTS
   450g/1lb potatoes
   groundnut (peanut) oil for deep-frying
   4 x 175g/6oz cod fillets, skinned
For the batter
   75g/3oz/⅔ cup plain (all-
      purpose) flour
   1 egg yolk
   10ml/2 tsp oil
   175ml/6fl oz/¾ cup water
   salt

1 Cut the potatoes into 5mm/¼in thick slices. Cut each slice again to make 5mm/¼in chips (French fries).

2 Heat the oil in a deep-fryer to 180ºC/350ºF. Add the chips to the fryer and cook for 3 minutes, then remove from the pan and shake off all fat and set to one side.

3 To make the batter, sift the flour into a bowl and add the remaining ingredients with a pinch of salt. Beat well until smooth. Set aside until ready to use.

4 Cook the chips again in the fat for a further 5 minutes or so, until they are really nice and crisp. Drain on kitchen paper and season with salt. Keep hot in a low oven while you cook the pieces of fish.

VARIATION
Although cod is the traditional choice for fish and chips, you can also use haddock. Rock salmon, sometimes sold as huss or dogfish, also has a good flavour. It has a central length of cartilage which cannot be removed before cooking – otherwise the pieces of fish will fall apart – but can be easily prised out once the fish is served.

5 Dip the fish into the batter, making sure they are evenly coated, and shake off any excess.

6 Carefully lower the fish into the fat and cook for 5 minutes. Drain on kitchen paper. Serve with lemon wedges and the chips.

COOK'S TIPS
• Use fresh rather than frozen fish for the very best texture and flavour. If you have to use frozen fish, thaw it thoroughly and make sure it is dry before coating with batter.
• Ideally, you should use fresh oil for deep-frying each time, but it can usually be safely re-used once more. Do not use the same oil repeatedly, as it gradually breaks down and will smoke or even ignite quite easily. Long storage may cause it to turn rancid. After the first use, cool, then strain the oil to remove any debris. Remember, too, that the oil will be flavoured, to some extent, by the food first cooked in it.
• People keeping an eye on their fat intake may not realize that deep-fried foods absorb less fat during cooking than shallow-fried foods. This is because the initial submersion in the oil, providing it has been heated to the correct temperature, quickly seals the outside, preventing any more fat from being absorbed by the food.

Per portion: Energy 740Kcal/3093kJ; Protein 32.8g; Carbohydrate 61g, of which sugars 0.8g; Fat 42.2g, of which saturates 4.2g; Cholesterol 0mg; Calcium 134mg; Fibre 3.6g; Sodium 313mg.

TANDOORI CHICKEN

THE WORD TANDOORI REFERS TO A METHOD OF COOKING IN A CHARCOAL-FIRED CLAY OVEN CALLED A TANDOOR. IN NORTHERN INDIA AND PAKISTAN, A WIDE VARIETY OF FOODS IS COOKED IN THIS TYPE OF OVEN, BUT IN WESTERN COUNTRIES THE METHOD IS MOST POPULAR FOR CHICKEN. WARM NAAN BREAD AND MANGO CHUTNEY MAY BE OFFERED WITH THE CHICKEN AND RICE.

SERVES FOUR

INGREDIENTS

30ml/2 tbsp vegetable oil
2 small onions, cut into wedges
2 garlic cloves, sliced
4 skinless, boneless chicken breast
  portions, cut into cubes
100ml/3½fl oz/⅓ cup water
300g/11oz jar tandoori sauce
salt and ground black pepper
coriander (cilantro) sprigs, to garnish

To serve
5ml/1 tsp ground turmeric
350g/12oz/1⅔ cups basmati rice

1 Heat the oil in a flameproof casserole. Add the onions and garlic, and cook for about 3 minutes, or until the onion is beginning to soften, stirring frequently.

2 Add the cubes of chicken to the casserole and cook for 6 minutes. Stir the water into the tandoori sauce and pour it over the chicken. Bring to the boil, then reduce the heat and simmer for 10 minutes, or until the chicken pieces are cooked through and the sauce is slightly reduced and thickened.

3 Meanwhile, bring a large pan of lightly salted water to the boil, add the turmeric and rice and bring back to the boil. Stir once, reduce the heat to prevent the water from boiling over and simmer the rice for 12 minutes, or according to the time suggested on the packet, until tender.

4 Drain the rice well and serve with the tandoori chicken on warmed individual serving plates, garnished with sprigs of fresh coriander.

COOK'S TIP
You will find jars of ready-made tandoori sauce in large supermarkets.

Per portion: Energy 592Kcal/2479kJ; Protein 44g; Carbohydrate 77.5g, of which sugars 4.5g; Fat 11.4g, of which saturates 1.1g; Cholesterol 105mg; Calcium 54mg; Fibre 0.4g; Sodium 826mg.

CHICKEN AND VEGETABLE TAGINE

MOROCCAN TAGINES ARE USUALLY SERVED WITH COUSCOUS, BUT RICE MAKES AN EQUALLY DELICIOUS ACCOMPANIMENT. HERE, COUSCOUS IS STIRRED INTO THE RICE TO CREATE AN UNUSUAL AND TASTY DISH, ALTHOUGH YOU COULD USE RICE BY ITSELF.

SERVES FOUR

INGREDIENTS
 30ml/2 tbsp groundnut (peanut) oil
 4 skinless, boneless chicken breast
   portions, cut into large pieces
 1 large onion, chopped
 2 garlic cloves, crushed
 1 parsnip, cut into 2.5cm/1in pieces
 1 turnip, cut into 2cm/¾in pieces
 3 carrots, cut into 4cm/1½in pieces
 4 tomatoes, chopped
 1 cinnamon stick
 4 cloves
 5ml/1 tsp ground ginger
 1 bay leaf
 1.5–2.5ml/¼–½ tsp cayenne pepper
 350ml/12fl oz/1½ cups chicken stock
 400g/14oz can chickpeas, drained
   and skinned
 1 red (bell) pepper, seeded
   and sliced
 150g/5oz green beans, halved
 1 piece of preserved lemon peel,
   thinly sliced
 20–30 pitted brown or green olives
 salt
For the rice and couscous
 750ml/1¼ pints/3 cups chicken stock
 225g/8oz/generous 1 cup
   long grain rice
 115g/4oz/⅔ cup couscous
 45ml/3 tbsp chopped fresh
   coriander (cilantro)

1 Heat half of the oil in a large, flameproof casserole and cook the chicken pieces for a few minutes until evenly browned. Transfer to a plate.

2 Heat the remaining oil and cook the onion, garlic, parsnip, turnip and carrots together over a medium heat for 4–5 minutes until the vegetables are lightly flecked with brown, stirring frequently. Lower the heat, cover and sweat the vegetables for 5 minutes more, stirring occasionally.

3 Add the tomatoes, cook for a few minutes, then add the cinnamon stick, cloves, ginger, bay leaf and cayenne. Cook for 1–2 minutes.

4 Pour in the chicken stock, add the chickpeas and browned chicken pieces, and season with salt. Cover and simmer for 25 minutes.

5 Meanwhile, cook the rice and couscous mixture. Bring the chicken stock to the boil. Add the rice and simmer for about 5 minutes until almost tender. Remove the pan from the heat, stir in the couscous, cover tightly and leave for about 5 minutes.

6 When the vegetables in the tagine are almost tender, stir in the pepper slices and green beans and simmer for 10 minutes. Add the preserved lemon and olives, stir well and cook for 5 minutes more, or until the vegetables are perfectly tender.

7 Stir the chopped coriander into the rice and couscous mixture and pile it on to a plate. Serve the chicken tagine in the traditional dish, if you have one, or in a casserole.

Per portion: Energy 707Kcal/2985kJ; Protein 52.6g; Carbohydrate 99.5g, of which sugars 16.9g; Fat 13.7g, of which saturates 2.6g; Cholesterol 105mg; Calcium 164mg; Fibre 10.8g; Sodium 344mg.

BANG BANG CHICKEN

WHAT A DESCRIPTIVE NAME THIS SPECIAL DISH FROM SICHUAN HAS! USE TOASTED SESAME PASTE TO GIVE THE SAUCE AN AUTHENTIC FLAVOUR, ALTHOUGH CRUNCHY PEANUT BUTTER CAN BE USED INSTEAD. BANG BANG CHICKEN IS PERFECT FOR PARTIES AND IDEAL FOR A BUFFET.

SERVES FOUR

INGREDIENTS
   3 skinless, boneless chicken
      breast portions, total weight
      about 450g/1lb
   1 garlic clove, crushed
   2.5ml/½ tsp black peppercorns
   1 small onion, halved
   1 large cucumber, peeled, seeded
      and cut into thin strips
   salt and ground black pepper
For the sauce
   45ml/3 tbsp toasted sesame paste
   15ml/1 tbsp light soy sauce
   15ml/1 tbsp wine vinegar
   2 spring onions (scallions),
      finely chopped
   2 garlic cloves, crushed
   5 x 1cm/2 x ½in piece fresh
      root ginger, peeled and cut
      into thin batons
   15ml/1 tbsp Sichuan peppercorns,
      dry-fried and crushed
   5ml/1 tsp light brown sugar
For the chilli oil
   60ml/4 tbsp groundnut (peanut) oil
   5ml/1 tsp chilli powder

1 Place the chicken in a large, heavy pan. Pour in sufficient water just to cover, add the garlic, peppercorns and onion and bring to the boil over a medium heat. Skim off any foam that rises to the surface, stir in salt and pepper to taste, then cover the pan. Lower the heat and cook for about 25 minutes, or until the chicken is just tender. Drain, reserving the stock.

2 Make the sauce by mixing the toasted sesame paste with 45ml/3 tbsp of the chicken stock, saving the rest for soup. Add the soy sauce, vinegar, spring onions, garlic, ginger and crushed peppercorns to the sesame mixture. Stir in sugar to taste.

3 Make the chilli oil by gently heating the oil and chilli powder together until foaming. Simmer for 2 minutes, cool, then strain off the red-coloured oil and discard the sediment.

4 Spread out the cucumber batons on a platter. Cut the chicken breast portions into pieces of about the same size as the cucumber strips and arrange them on top. Pour over the sauce, drizzle on the chilli oil and serve.

VARIATION
Crunchy peanut butter can be used instead of sesame paste, if you like. Mix it with 30ml/2 tbsp sesame oil and proceed as in Step 2.

Per portion: Energy 297Kcal/1239kJ; Protein 29.7g; Carbohydrate 2.3g, of which sugars 1.8g; Fat 18.9g, of which saturates 2.6g; Cholesterol 79mg; Calcium 94mg; Fibre 1.4g; Sodium 339mg.

POT-COOKED DUCK AND GREEN VEGETABLES

PREPARE THE INGREDIENTS FOR THIS JAPANESE DISH BEFOREHAND, SO THAT THE COOKING CAN BE DONE AT THE TABLE. USE A HEAVY PAN OR FLAMEPROOF CASSEROLE WITH A PORTABLE STOVE.

SERVES FOUR

INGREDIENTS
    4 duck breast fillets, about 800g/
        1¾lb total weight
    8 large shiitake mushrooms, stalks
        removed, a cross cut into each cap
    2 leeks, trimmed and cut diagonally
        into 6cm/2½in lengths
    ½ hakusai, stalk part removed and
        cut into 5cm/2in squares
    500g/1¼lb shungiku or mizuna, root
        part removed, cut in half crossways
For the stock
    raw bones from 1 chicken, washed
    1 egg shell
    200g/7oz/scant 1 cup short grain
        rice, washed and drained
    120ml/4fl oz/½ cup sake
    about 10ml/2 tsp coarse sea salt
For the sauce
    75ml/5 tbsp shoyu
    30ml/2 tbsp sake
    juice of 1 lime
    8 white peppercorns, crushed
For the soup
    130g/4½oz Chinese egg noodles,
        cooked and loosened
    1 egg, beaten
    1 bunch of chives
    ground white pepper

1 To make the stock, put the chicken bones into a pan three-quarters full of water. Bring to the boil and drain when it reaches boiling point. Wash the pan and the bones again, then return to the pan with the same amount of water. Add the egg shell and then bring to the boil. Simmer, uncovered, for 1 hour, skimming frequently. Remove the bones and egg shell. Add the rice, sake and salt, then simmer for 30 minutes. Remove from the heat and set aside.

2 Heat a heavy frying pan until just smoking. Remove from the heat for 1 minute, then add the duck breasts, skin side down. Return to a medium heat and sear for 3–4 minutes, or until crisp. Turn over and sear the other side for 1 minute. Remove from the heat.

3 When cool, wipe the duck fat with kitchen paper and cut the breast and skin into 5mm/¼in thick slices. Arrange on a large serving plate with all the prepared vegetables.

4 Heat through all the ingredients for the sauce in a small pan and transfer to a small jug (pitcher) or bowl.

5 Prepare four dipping bowls, four serving bowls and chopsticks. At the table, bring the pan of soup stock to the boil, then reduce to medium-low. Add half of the shiitake and leeks. Wait for 5 minutes and put in half of the stalk part of the hakusai. Add half of the duck and cook for 1–2 minutes for rare or 5–8 minutes for well-done meat.

6 Each person prepares some duck and vegetables in a serving bowl and drizzles over a little sauce. Add the soft hakusai leaves, shungiku and mizuna to the stock as you eat, adjusting the heat as you go. When the stock is less than a quarter of the pot's volume, top up with 3 parts water to 1 part sake.

7 When the duck has been eaten, bring the reduced stock to the boil. Skim the oil from the surface, and reduce the heat to medium. Add the noodles, cook for 1–2 minutes and check the seasoning. Add more salt if required. Pour in the beaten egg and swirl in the stock. Cover, turn off the heat, then leave to stand for 1 minute. Decorate with the chopped chives and serve with ground pepper.

Per portion: Energy 676Kcal/2846kJ; Protein 53.4g; Carbohydrate 81.6g, of which sugars 9.8g; Fat 19.4g, of which saturates 4.1g; Cholesterol 277mg; Calcium 126mg; Fibre 9.3g; Sodium 1296mg.

LAMB POT-ROASTED <u>WITH</u> TOMATOES, BEANS <u>AND</u> ONIONS

THIS SLOW-BRAISED DISH OF LAMB AND TOMATOES, SPICED WITH CINNAMON AND STEWED WITH GREEN BEANS, SHOWS A GREEK INFLUENCE. IT IS ALSO GOOD MADE WITH COURGETTES INSTEAD OF BEANS.

<u>SERVES EIGHT</u>

INGREDIENTS

  1kg/2¼lb lamb on the bone
  8 garlic cloves, chopped
  2.5–5ml/½–1 tsp ground cumin
  45ml/3 tbsp olive oil
  juice of 1 lemon
  2 onions, thinly sliced
  about 500ml/17fl oz/2¼ cups
    lamb, beef or vegetable stock
  75–90ml/5–6 tbsp tomato
    purée (paste)
  1 cinnamon stick
  2–3 large pinches of ground
    allspice or ground cloves
  15–30ml/1–2 tbsp sugar
  400g/14oz/scant 3 cups
    green beans
  salt and ground black pepper
  15–30ml/1–2 tbsp chopped
    fresh parsley, to garnish

1 Preheat the oven to 160°C/325°F/Gas 3. Coat the lamb with the garlic, cumin, olive oil, lemon juice, salt and pepper.

2 Heat a flameproof casserole. Sear the lamb on all sides. Add the onions and pour the stock over the meat to cover. Stir in the tomato purée, spices and sugar. Cover and cook in the oven for 2–3 hours.

3 Remove the casserole from the oven and pour the stock into a pan. Move the onions to the side of the dish and return to the oven, uncovered, for 20 minutes.

4 Meanwhile, add the beans to the hot stock and cook until the beans are tender and the sauce has thickened. Slice the meat and serve with the pan juices and beans. Garnish with parsley.

Per portion: Energy 333Kcal/1394kJ; Protein 39.1g; Carbohydrate 8.2g, of which sugars 6.9g; Fat 16.2g, of which saturates 5.4g; Cholesterol 125mg; Calcium 41mg; Fibre 2g; Sodium 109mg.

POT-ROASTED BRISKET

THIS JEWISH, POT-ROASTED MEAT DISH INCLUDES THE TRADITIONAL KISHKE, A HEAVY, SAUSAGE-SHAPED DUMPLING, WHICH IS ADDED TO THE POT AND COOKED WITH THE MEAT. SERVE WITH KASHA — MEAT GRAVY WITH KASHA IS ONE OF LIFE'S PERFECT COMBINATIONS.

SERVES SIX TO EIGHT

INGREDIENTS
    5 onions, sliced
    3 bay leaves
    1–1.6kg/2¼–3½lb beef brisket
    1 garlic bulb, broken into cloves
    4 carrots, thickly sliced
    5–10ml/1–2 tsp paprika
    about 500ml/17fl oz/2¼ cups
      beef stock
    3–4 baking potatoes, peeled
      and quartered
    salt and ground black pepper
For the kishke
    about 90cm/36in sausage casing
      (see Cook's Tip)
    250g/9oz/2¼ cups plain
      (all-purpose) flour
    120ml/4fl oz/½ cup semolina
      or couscous
    10–15ml/2–3 tsp paprika
    1 carrot, grated and 2 carrots,
      diced (optional)
    250ml/8fl oz/1 cup rendered
      chicken fat
    30ml/2 tbsp crisp, fried onions
    ½ onion, grated and 3 onions,
      thinly sliced
    3 garlic cloves, chopped
    salt and ground black pepper

1 Preheat the oven to 180°C/350°F/Gas 4. Put one-third of the onions and a bay leaf in an ovenproof dish, then top with the brisket. Sprinkle over the garlic, carrots and the remaining bay leaves, sprinkle with salt, pepper and paprika, then top with the remaining onions.

2 Pour in enough stock to fill the dish to about 5–7.5cm/2–3in and cover with foil. Cook in the oven for 2 hours.

3 Meanwhile, make the kishke. In a bowl, combine all the ingredients and stuff the mixture into the casing, leaving enough space for the mixture to expand. Tie into sausage-shaped lengths.

4 When the meat has cooked for about 2 hours, add the kishke and potatoes to the pan, re-cover and cook for a further 1 hour, or until the meat and potatoes are tender.

5 Remove the foil from the dish and increase the oven temperature to 190–200°C/375–400°F/Gas 5–6. Move the onions away from the top of the meat to the side of the dish and return to the oven for a further 30 minutes, or until the meat, onions and potatoes are beginning to brown and become crisp. Serve hot or cold.

COOK'S TIP
Traditionally, sausage casings are used for kishke but, if unavailable, use cooking-strength clear film (plastic wrap) or a piece of muslin (cheesecloth).

Per portion: Energy 781Kcal/3271kJ; Protein 44.2g; Carbohydrate 74g, of which sugars 12.7g; Fat 36.4g, of which saturates 14.4g; Cholesterol 113mg; Calcium 124mg; Fibre 5g; Sodium 124mg.

TACOS WITH SHREDDED BEEF

IN MEXICO, TACOS ARE MOST OFTEN MADE WITH SOFT CORN TORTILLAS, WHICH ARE FILLED AND FOLDED IN HALF. IT IS UNUSUAL TO SEE THE CRISP SHELLS OF CORN WHICH ARE SO WIDELY USED IN TEX-MEX COOKING. TACOS ARE ALWAYS EATEN IN THE HAND.

SERVES SIX

INGREDIENTS

    450g/1lb rump (round) steak, diced
    150g/5oz/1 cup masa harina
    2.5ml/½ tsp salt
    120ml/4fl oz/½ cup warm water
    10ml/2 tsp dried oregano
    5ml/1 tsp ground cumin
    30ml/2 tbsp oil
    1 onion, thinly sliced
    2 garlic cloves, crushed
    fresh coriander (cilantro), to garnish
    shredded lettuce, lime wedges and
      tomato salsa, to serve

1 Put the steak in a deep frying pan and pour over water to cover. Bring to the boil, then lower the heat and simmer for 1–1½ hours.

2 Meanwhile, make the tortilla dough. Mix the masa harina and salt in a large mixing bowl. Add the warm water, a little at a time, to make a dough that can be worked into a ball. Knead the dough on a lightly floured surface for 3–4 minutes until smooth, then wrap the dough in clear film (plastic wrap) and leave to rest for 1 hour.

3 Put the meat on a board, let it cool slightly, then shred it, using two forks. Put the meat in a bowl. Divide the tortilla dough into six equal balls.

4 Open a tortilla press and line both sides with plastic (this can be cut from a new plastic sandwich bag). Put each ball on the press and flatten it into a 15–20cm/6–8in round.

5 Heat a griddle or frying pan until hot. Cook each tortilla for 15–20 seconds on each side, and then for a further 15 seconds on the first side. Keep the tortillas warm and soft by folding them inside a slightly damp dishtowel.

6 Add the oregano and cumin to the shredded meat and mix well. Heat the oil in a frying pan and cook the onion and garlic for 3–4 minutes, until softened. Add the meat mixture and toss over the heat until heated through.

7 Place some shredded lettuce on a tortilla, top with shredded beef and salsa, fold in half and serve with lime wedges. Garnish with fresh coriander.

Per portion: Energy 232Kcal/975kJ; Protein 18.6g; Carbohydrate 21.4g, of which sugars 1.8g; Fat 8.6g, of which saturates 2.6g; Cholesterol 46mg; Calcium 44mg; Fibre 1.1g; Sodium 198mg.

BEEF ENCHILADAS <u>WITH</u> RED SAUCE

ENCHILADAS ARE USUALLY MADE WITH CORN TORTILLAS, ALTHOUGH IN PARTS OF NORTHERN MEXICO WHEAT FLOUR TORTILLAS ARE SOMETIMES USED.

SERVES THREE TO FOUR

INGREDIENTS
    500g/1¼lb rump (round) steak, cut
      into 5cm/2in cubes
    2 ancho chillies, seeded
    2 pasilla chillies, seeded
    2 garlic cloves, crushed
    10ml/2 tsp dried oregano
    2.5ml/½ tsp ground cumin
    30ml/2 tbsp vegetable oil
    7 fresh corn tortillas
    shredded onion and flat leaf parsley
      to garnish
    mango salsa, to serve

1 Put the steak in a deep frying pan and cover with water. Bring to the boil, then lower the heat and simmer for 1–1½ hours, or until very tender.

2 Meanwhile, put the dried chillies in a bowl and pour over the hot water. Leave to soak for 30 minutes, then tip the contents of the bowl into a blender and process to a smooth paste.

3 Drain the steak and let it cool, reserving 250ml/8fl oz/1 cup of the cooking liquid. Meanwhile, cook the garlic, oregano and cumin in the oil for 2 minutes.

4 Stir in the chilli paste and the reserved cooking liquid from the steak. Tear one of the tortillas into small pieces and add it to the mixture. Bring to the boil, then lower the heat. Simmer for 10 minutes, stirring occasionally, until thickened. Shred the steak, using two forks, stir it into the sauce and heat through for a few minutes.

5 Spoon some of the meat mixture on to each tortilla and roll it up to make an enchilada. Keep the enchiladas in a warmed dish until you have rolled them all. Garnish with shreds of onion and fresh flat leaf parsley and then serve immediately with the mango salsa.

VARIATION
For a richer version place the rolled enchiladas side by side in a gratin dish. Pour over 300ml/½ pint/1¼ cups sour cream and 75g/3oz/¾ cup grated Cheddar cheese. Place under a preheated grill (broiler) for 5 minutes, or until the cheese melts and the sauce begins to bubble. Serve with the salsa.

Per portion: Energy 477Kcal/2004kJ; Protein 40.6g; Carbohydrate 39.9g, of which sugars 0.9g; Fat 18.3g, of which saturates 5.5g; Cholesterol 102mg; Calcium 85mg; Fibre 1.6g; Sodium 261mg.

GRILLS AND GRIDDLED DISHES

Whether you grill (broil) inside the oven, on a ridged griddle pan or over an open fire, this is an excellent cooking method. Grilled food looks good, with an all-over tan or the attractive stripes that mark the means of its cooking. There's often a contrast in textures, the outside gaining a crisp crust beneath which the food is beautifully tender. Finally — and perhaps most importantly — grilled food is healthy, as only a minimum amount of oil is used in the process. This chapter includes kebabs, patties and superb grilled vegetable dishes.

  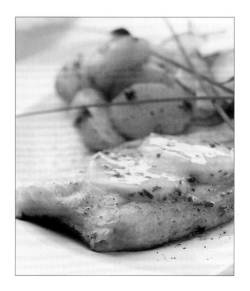

GRILLED AUBERGINE PARCELS

THESE ARE DELICIOUS LITTLE ITALIAN BUNDLES OF PLUM TOMATOES, MOZZARELLA CHEESE AND FRESH BASIL LEAVES, WRAPPED IN SLICES OF AUBERGINE.

SERVES FOUR

INGREDIENTS
   2 large, long aubergines (eggplant)
   225g/8oz mozzarella cheese
   2 plum tomatoes
   16 large fresh basil leaves
   30ml/2 tbsp olive oil
   salt and ground black pepper
For the dressing
   60ml/4 tbsp olive oil
   5ml/1 tsp balsamic vinegar
   15ml/1 tbsp sun-dried tomato paste
   15ml/1 tbsp lemon juice
For the garnish
   30ml/2 tbsp roasted pine nuts
   torn basil leaves

1 Remove and discard the stalks from the aubergines and cut them lengthways into thin slices – the aim is to get 16 slices in total (disregarding the first and last slices), each about 5mm/¼in thick.

2 Bring a large pan of salted water to the boil and cook the aubergine slices for about 2 minutes, until just softened. Drain, then dry on kitchen paper.

3 Cut the mozzarella cheese into eight slices. Cut each tomato into eight slices, not counting the first and last slices.

4 Place two aubergine slices on a baking sheet in a cross. Place a tomato slice in the centre, season, then add a basil leaf, followed by a slice of mozzarella, a basil leaf, a tomato slice and more seasoning.

5 Fold the ends of the aubergine slices around the filling to make a neat parcel. Repeat with the rest of the ingredients to make eight parcels. Chill for about 20 minutes. Preheat the grill (broiler).

6 To make the tomato dressing, whisk all the ingredients together and season to taste.

7 Brush the parcels with the oil and cook for about 5 minutes on each side, until golden. Serve, with the dressing, sprinkled with pine nuts and basil.

Per portion: Energy 370Kcal/1532kJ; Protein 12.9g; Carbohydrate 4.4g, of which sugars 4.2g; Fat 33.6g, of which saturates 10.6g; Cholesterol 33mg; Calcium 219mg; Fibre 2.7g; Sodium 237mg.

GRILLED POLENTA WITH CARAMELIZED ONIONS, RADICCHIO AND TALEGGIO CHEESE

SLICES OF GRILLED POLENTA, ONE OF THE STAPLES OF NORTH ITALIAN COOKING, ARE TASTY TOPPED WITH SLOWLY CARAMELIZED ONIONS AND BUBBLING TALEGGIO, ALSO FROM NORTH ITALY.

SERVES FOUR

INGREDIENTS
  900ml/1½ pints/3¾ cups water
  5ml/1 tsp salt
  150g/5oz/generous 1 cup polenta
    or cornmeal
  50g/2oz/⅓ cup freshly grated
    Parmesan cheese
  5ml/1 tsp chopped fresh thyme
  90ml/6 tbsp olive oil
  675g/1½lb onions, halved and sliced
  2 garlic cloves, chopped
  a few fresh thyme sprigs
  5ml/1 tsp brown sugar
  15–30ml/1–2 tbsp balsamic vinegar
  2 heads radicchio, cut into thick
    slices or wedges
  225g/8oz Taleggio cheese, sliced
  salt and ground black pepper

1 In a large pan, bring the water to the boil and add the salt. Adjust the heat so that it simmers. Stirring constantly, add the polenta in a steady stream, then bring to the boil. Cook over a very low heat, stirring frequently, for about 30–40 minutes, until thick and smooth.

2 Beat in the Parmesan and chopped thyme, then turn on to a work surface or tray. Spread evenly, then leave to cool.

3 Heat 30ml/2 tbsp of the oil in a frying pan over a moderate heat. Add the onions and stir to coat in the oil, then cover and cook over a very low heat for 15 minutes, stirring occasionally.

4 Add the garlic and most of the thyme sprigs and cook, uncovered, for another 10 minutes, or until light brown.

5 Add the sugar, 15ml/1 tbsp of the vinegar and salt and pepper. Cook for another 5–10 minutes, until soft and well-browned. Taste and add more vinegar and seasoning as necessary.

6 Preheat the grill (broiler). Cut the polenta into thick slices and brush with a little of the remaining oil, then grill (broil) until crusty and lightly browned.

7 Turn over the polenta and add the radicchio to the grill rack or pan. Season the radicchio and brush with a little oil. Grill for about 5 minutes, until the polenta and radicchio are browned. Drizzle a little vinegar over the radicchio.

8 Heap the onions on to the polenta. Sprinkle the cheese and a few sprigs of thyme over both polenta and radicchio. Grill until the cheese is bubbling. Season with pepper and serve immediately.

Per portion: Energy 608Kcal/2522kJ; Protein 22.3g; Carbohydrate 42.7g, of which sugars 11.4g; Fat 37.5g, of which saturates 15.2g; Cholesterol 65mg; Calcium 352mg; Fibre 3.7g; Sodium 456mg.

YUCATAN-STYLE SHARK STEAK

A FIRM-FLESHED FISH, SHARK IS WIDELY AVAILABLE, EITHER FRESH OR FROZEN. IT NEEDS CAREFUL WATCHING, AS OVERCOOKING WILL MAKE IT DRY AND TOUGH, BUT THE FLAVOUR IS EXCELLENT.

SERVES FOUR

INGREDIENTS

grated rind and juice of 1 orange
juice of 1 small lime
45ml/3 tbsp white wine
30ml/2 tbsp olive oil
2 garlic cloves, crushed
10ml/2 tsp ground achiote seed
  (annatto powder)
2.5ml/½ tsp cayenne pepper
2.5ml/½ tsp dried marjoram
5ml/1 tsp salt
4 shark steaks
fresh oregano leaves, to garnish
4 wheat-flour tortillas and any
  suitable salsa, to serve

COOK'S TIP
Shark freezes successfully, with little or no loss of flavour on thawing, so use frozen steaks if you can't find fresh.

1 Put the orange rind and juice in a shallow non-metallic dish which is large enough to hold all the shark steaks in a single layer. Add the lime juice, white wine, olive oil, garlic, ground achiote (annatto powder), cayenne, marjoram and salt. Mix well.

2 Add the shark steaks to the dish and spoon the marinade over them. Cover and set aside for 1 hour, turning once.

3 Heat a griddle pan until very hot and cook the marinated shark steaks for 2–3 minutes on each side. Alternatively, they are very good cooked on the barbecue, as long as they are cooked after the coals have lost their fierce initial heat. Do not overcook.

4 Garnish the shark steaks with oregano and serve with the tortillas and salsa. A green vegetable would also go well.

Per portion: Energy 239Kcal/1006kJ; Protein 40.6g; Carbohydrate 0.7g, of which sugars 0.1g; Fat 7.5g, of which saturates 1.2g; Cholesterol 77mg; Calcium 33mg; Fibre 0.2g; Sodium 246mg.

SEARED TUNA STEAKS WITH RED ONION SALSA

RED ONIONS ARE IDEAL FOR THIS SALSA, NOT ONLY FOR THEIR MILD AND SWEET FLAVOUR, BUT ALSO BECAUSE THEY LOOK SO APPETIZING. SALAD, RICE OR BREAD AND A BOWL OF THICK YOGURT FLAVOURED WITH CHOPPED FRESH HERBS ARE GOOD ACCOMPANIMENTS.

SERVES FOUR

INGREDIENTS

4 tuna steaks, each weighing about
175–200g/6–7oz
5ml/1 tsp cumin seeds, toasted
and crushed
pinch of dried red chilli flakes
grated rind and juice of 1 lime
30–60ml/2–4 tbsp extra virgin
olive oil
salt and ground black pepper
lime wedges and fresh coriander
(cilantro) sprigs, to garnish

For the salsa

1 small red onion, finely chopped
200g/7oz red or yellow cherry
tomatoes, coarsely chopped
1 avocado, peeled, stoned
(pitted) and chopped
2 kiwi fruit, peeled and chopped
1 fresh red chilli, seeded and
finely chopped
15g/½oz fresh coriander
(cilantro), chopped
6 fresh mint sprigs, leaves
only, chopped
5–10ml/1–2 tsp Thai fish sauce
about 5ml/1 tsp muscovado
(molasses) sugar

1 Wash the tuna steaks and pat dry. Sprinkle with half the cumin, the dried chilli, salt, pepper and half the lime rind. Rub in 30ml/2 tbsp of the oil and set aside in a glass or china dish for about 30 minutes.

2 Meanwhile, make the salsa. Mix the onion, tomatoes, avocado, kiwi fruit, fresh chilli, chopped coriander and mint. Add the remaining cumin, the rest of the lime rind and half the lime juice. Season with Thai fish sauce and sugar to taste. Set aside for 15–20 minutes, then add more Thai fish sauce, lime juice and olive oil if required.

3 Heat a ridged, cast–iron griddle pan. Cook the tuna, allowing about 2 minutes on each side for rare tuna or a little longer for a medium result.

4 Serve the tuna steaks garnished with lime wedges and coriander sprigs. Serve the salsa separately or spoon on to the plates with the tuna.

Per portion: Energy 389Kcal/1628kJ; Protein 43.2g; Carbohydrate 7.9g, of which sugars 6.8g; Fat 20.7g, of which saturates 4.4g; Cholesterol 49mg; Calcium 55mg; Fibre 2.5g; Sodium 180mg.

GRILLED SKEWERED CHICKEN

THESE JAPANESE-STYLE KEBABS, SERVED WITH DELICIOUS YAKITORI SAUCE FOR DIPPING, ARE PERFECT FOR EASY ENTERTAINING AND ABSOLUTELY IDEAL FOR A BARBECUE PARTY. FOR AUTHENTICITY, SERVE WITH JAPANESE CONDIMENTS AND SMALL DRINKING BOWLS OF WARM RICE WINE.

SERVES FOUR

INGREDIENTS
    8 chicken thighs with skin, boned
    8 large, thick spring onions
      (scallions), trimmed
For the yakitori sauce
    60ml/4 tbsp sake
    75ml/5 tbsp shoyu
    15ml/1 tbsp mirin
    15ml/1 tbsp caster (superfine) sugar
To serve
    shichimi togarashi, sansho or
      lemon wedges

1 First, make the yakitori sauce. Mix all the ingredients together in a small pan. Bring to the boil, then reduce the heat and simmer for 10 minutes, or until the sauce has thickened.

2 Cut the chicken into 2.5cm/1in cubes with a sharp knife. Cut the spring onions into 2.5cm/1in long sticks.

3 To grill (broil), preheat the grill (broiler) to high. Oil the wire rack and spread out the chicken cubes on it. Grill both sides of the chicken until the juices run, then dip the pieces in the sauce and put back on the rack. Grill for 30 seconds on each side, repeating the dipping process twice more.

4 Set aside and keep warm. Gently grill the spring onions until soft and slightly brown outside. Do not dip. Thread about four pieces of chicken and three spring onion pieces on to each of eight bamboo skewers.

5 Alternatively, to cook on a barbecue, soak eight bamboo skewers overnight in water. This prevents the skewers from burning. Prepare the barbecue. Thread the chicken and spring onion pieces on to skewers, as above. Place the sauce in a small bowl.

6 Cook the skewered chicken on the barbecue. Keep the skewer handles away from the fire, turning them frequently until the juices start to run. Brush the chicken with sauce. Return to the coals and repeat this process twice more until the chicken is well cooked.

7 Arrange the skewers on a platter or individual plates and serve sprinkled with shichimi togarashi or sansho, or accompanied by lemon wedges.

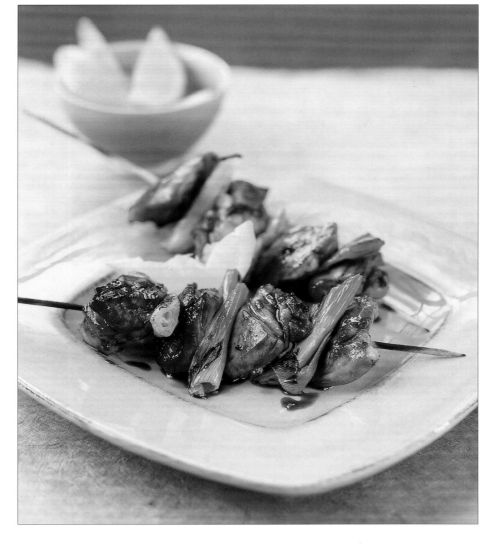

Per portion: Energy 132Kcal/558kJ; Protein 21.6g; Carbohydrate 5.2g, of which sugars 5.1g; Fat 2.9g, of which saturates 0.8g; Cholesterol 105mg; Calcium 18mg; Fibre 0.3g; Sodium 715mg.

GRILLED CHICKEN BALLS COOKED ON BAMBOO SKEWERS

These tasty chicken balls, known as Tsukune, are a yakitori bar regular in Japan, as well as a favourite family dish, as they are easy for children to eat directly from the skewer. You can make the balls in advance up to the end of step 2, and they freeze very well.

SERVES FOUR

INGREDIENTS
  300g/11oz skinless chicken,
    minced (ground)
  2 eggs
  2.5ml/½ tsp salt
  10ml/2 tsp plain (all-purpose) flour
  10ml/2 tsp cornflour (cornstarch)
  90ml/6 tbsp dried breadcrumbs
  2.5cm/1in piece fresh root
    ginger, grated
For the "tare" yakitori sauce
  60ml/4 tbsp sake
  75ml/5 tbsp shoyu
  15ml/1 tbsp mirin
  15ml/1 tbsp caster (superfine) sugar
  2.5ml/½ tsp cornflour (cornstarch)
    blended with 5ml/1 tsp water
To serve
  shichimi togarashi or
    sansho (optional)

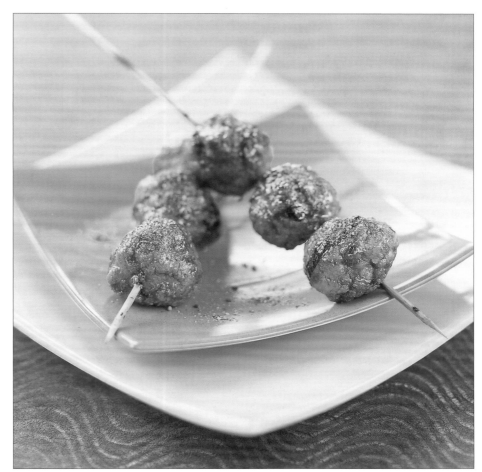

1 Soak eight bamboo skewers overnight in water. Put all the ingredients for the chicken balls, except the ginger, in a food processor and blend well.

2 Wet your hands and scoop about a tablespoonful of the mixture into your palm. Shape it into a small ball about half the size of a golf ball. Make a further 30–32 balls in the same way.

3 Squeeze the juice from the grated ginger into a small mixing bowl. Discard the pulp.

4 Add the ginger juice to a small pan of boiling water. Add the chicken balls, and boil for about 7 minutes, or until the colour of the meat changes and the balls float to the surface. Scoop out using a slotted spoon and drain on a plate covered with kitchen paper.

5 In a small pan, mix all the ingredients for the yakitori sauce, except for the cornflour liquid. Bring to the boil, then reduce the heat and simmer for about 10 minutes, or until the sauce has slightly reduced. Add the cornflour liquid and stir until the sauce is thick. Transfer to a small bowl.

6 Thread three or four balls on to each skewer. Cook under a medium grill (broiler) or on a barbecue, keeping the skewer handles away from the fire. Turn them frequently for a few minutes, or until the balls start to brown. Brush with sauce and return to the heat. Repeat the process twice. Serve, sprinkled with shichimi togarashi or sansho, if you like.

Per portion: Energy 223Kcal/942kJ; Protein 24.2g; Carbohydrate 23.9g, of which sugars 5.1g; Fat 4.1g, of which saturates 1g; Cholesterol 148mg; Calcium 54mg; Fibre 0.6g; Sodium 1031mg.

TURKEY PATTIES

Minced turkey makes deliciously light patties, which are ideal for summer meals. The recipe is a flavourful variation on a classic burger. The patties can also be made using minced lamb, pork or beef. Serve them in split and toasted buns or pieces of crusty bread, with chutney, salad leaves and chunky fries.

SERVES SIX

INGREDIENTS
    675g/1½lb minced (ground) turkey
    1 small red onion, finely chopped
    grated rind and juice of 1 lime
    small handful of fresh thyme leaves
    15–30ml/1–2 tbsp olive oil
    salt and ground black pepper

VARIATIONS
• You could try chopped fresh oregano, parsley or basil in place of the thyme, and lemon rind instead of lime.
• Substitute minced (ground) chicken for the turkey.

1 Mix together the turkey, onion, lime rind and juice, thyme and seasoning. Cover and chill for up to 4 hours to allow the flavours to infuse, then divide the mixture into six equal portions and shape into round patties.

2 Preheat a griddle pan. Brush the patties with oil, then place them on the pan and cook for 10–12 minutes. Turn the patties over, brush with more oil and cook for 10–12 minutes on the second side, or until cooked through.

Per portion: Energy 141Kcal/596kJ; Protein 24.8g; Carbohydrate 0.8g, of which sugars 0.6g; Fat 4.4g, of which saturates 1.1g; Cholesterol 69mg; Calcium 15mg; Fibre 0.2g; Sodium 62mg.

TURKEY BREASTS WITH TOMATO-CORN SALSA

ALTHOUGH AN ECONOMICAL AND USEFUL MEAT, TURKEY CAN BE DISAPPOINTINGLY BLAND, SO MARINATING IT BEFORE COOKING AND SERVING WITH A SPICY SALSA IS THE IDEAL APPROACH.

SERVES FOUR

INGREDIENTS
    4 skinless boneless turkey breast
      halves, about 175g/6oz each
    30ml/2 tbsp fresh lemon juice
    30ml/2 tbsp olive oil
    2.5ml/½ tsp ground cumin
    2.5ml/½ tsp dried oregano
    5ml/1 tsp coarse black pepper
    salt
For the salsa
    1 fresh hot green chilli
    450g/1lb tomatoes, seeded
      and chopped
    250g/9oz/1½ cups corn kernels,
      freshly cooked or thawed frozen
    3 spring onions (scallions), chopped
    15ml/1 tbsp chopped fresh parsley
    30ml/2 tbsp chopped fresh
      coriander (cilantro)
    30ml/2 tbsp fresh lemon juice
    45ml/3 tbsp olive oil
    5ml/1 tsp salt

1 With a meat mallet, pound the turkey breasts between two sheets of greaseproof (waxed) paper until thin.

2 In a shallow dish, combine the lemon juice, oil, cumin, oregano and pepper. Add the turkey and turn to coat. Cover and marinate for at least 2 hours, or overnight in the refrigerator.

COOK'S TIP
Use the flat side of a meat mallet to pound the turkey. If you don't have a meat mallet, use the side of a wooden rolling pin.

3 For the salsa, roast the chilli over a gas flame, holding it with tongs, until charred on all sides. Alternatively, char the skin under the hot grill (broiler). Leave to cool for 5 minutes. Wearing rubber gloves, carefully rub off the charred skin. For a less hot flavour, discard the seeds. Chop the chilli finely and place in a bowl.

4 Add the remaining salsa ingredients and toss well to blend. Set aside.

5 Remove the turkey from the marinade. Season lightly on both sides with salt to taste.

6 Heat a ridged griddle pan. When hot, add the turkey breasts and cook for about 3 minutes, until browned on the undersides. Turn and cook the meat on the other side for a further 3–4 minutes, until it is cooked through. Serve the turkey immediately, accompanied by tomato-corn salsa.

VARIATION
Use the cooked turkey, thinly sliced and combined with the salsa, as a filling for warmed flour tortillas.

Per portion: Energy 407Kcal/1711kJ; Protein 45.7g; Carbohydrate 20.6g, of which sugars 9.9g; Fat 16.4g, of which saturates 2.7g; Cholesterol 100mg; Calcium 36mg; Fibre 2.5g; Sodium 761mg.

PORK CHOPS WITH SOUR GREEN CHILLI SALSA

Thin chops or loin steaks are deliciously tender and cook very quickly, so this tasty dish is ideal for a midweek family supper.

SERVES FOUR

INGREDIENTS
  30ml/2 tbsp vegetable oil
  15ml/1 tbsp fresh lemon juice
  10ml/2 tsp ground cumin
  5ml/1 tsp dried oregano
  8 pork loin chops, about
    5mm/¼ in thick
  salt and ground black pepper
For the salsa
  2 fresh hot green chillies
  2 green (bell) peppers, seeded
    and chopped
  1 tomato, peeled and seeded
  ½ onion, coarsely chopped
  4 spring onions (scallions)
  1 pickled jalapeño chilli
  30ml/2 tbsp olive oil
  30ml/2 tbsp fresh lime juice
  45ml/3 tbsp cider vinegar
  5ml/1 tsp salt

1 In a small bowl, combine the vegetable oil, lemon juice, cumin and oregano. Add pepper to taste and stir to mix well.

2 Arrange the pork chops in one layer in a shallow dish. Brush each of them with the oil mixture on both sides. Cover them with clear film (plastic wrap) and set aside to marinate for 2–3 hours or in the refrigerator overnight.

3 For the salsa, roast the chillies over a gas flame, holding them with tongs, until charred on all sides. Alternatively, char the skins under the grill (broiler). Leave to cool for 5 minutes. Wearing rubber gloves, remove the skin. For a less hot flavour, discard the seeds.

4 Place the chillies in a food processor or blender. Add the remaining salsa ingredients. Process until finely chopped but do not purée.

5 Transfer the salsa to a small, heavy pan and simmer 15 minutes, stirring occasionally. Set aside.

6 Season the pork chops to taste with salt and pepper. Heat a ridged griddle pan. Alternatively, preheat the grill (broiler). When hot, add the pork chops and cook for about 5 minutes, until browned on the undersides. Turn and continue cooking for a further 5–7 minutes, until done. Work in batches, if necessary.

7 Serve immediately, with the sour green chilli salsa.

Per portion: Energy 341Kcal/1427kJ; Protein 38.9g; Carbohydrate 5.2g, of which sugars 4.7g; Fat 18.5g, of which saturates 4g; Cholesterol 110mg; Calcium 30mg; Fibre 2.2g; Sodium 623mg.

PORK <u>AND</u> LEEK SAUSAGES <u>WITH</u> MUSTARD MASHED POTATO <u>AND</u> ONION GRAVY

LONG, SLOW COOKING IS THE TRICK TO REMEMBER FOR GOOD ONION GRAVY AS THIS REDUCES AND CARAMELIZES THE ONIONS TO CREATE A WONDERFULLY SWEET FLAVOUR. DO NOT BE ALARMED AT THE NUMBER OF ONIONS — THEY REDUCE DRAMATICALLY IN VOLUME DURING COOKING.

SERVES FOUR

INGREDIENTS
    12 pork and leek sausages
    salt and ground black pepper
For the onion gravy
    30ml/2 tbsp olive oil
    25g/1oz/2 tbsp butter
    8 onions, sliced
    5ml/1 tsp caster sugar
    15ml/1 tbsp plain (all-purpose) flour
    300ml/½ pint/1¼ cups beef stock
For the mash
    1.5kg/3¼lb potatoes
    50g/2oz/¼ cup butter
    150ml/¼ pint/⅔ cup whipping cream
    15ml/1 tbsp wholegrain mustard

1 Heat the oil and butter in a large pan until foaming. Add the onions and mix well to coat them in the fat. Cover and cook gently for about 30 minutes, stirring frequently. Add the sugar and cook for a further 5 minutes, or until the onions are softened, reduced and caramelized.

2 Remove the pan from the heat and stir in the flour, then gradually stir in the stock. Return the pan to the heat. Bring to the boil, stirring, then simmer for 3 minutes, or until thickened. Season.

VARIATION
Pesto and garlic mash is also good with sausages. Instead of the mustard, add 15ml/1 tbsp pesto, 2 crushed garlic cloves and a little olive oil.

3 Meanwhile, cook the potatoes and the pork and leek sausages. First, cook the potatoes in a pan of salted boiling water for 20 minutes, or until tender.

4 Drain the potatoes well and mash them with the butter, whipping cream and wholegrain mustard. Season with salt and pepper to taste.

5 Meanwhile, preheat the grill (broiler) to medium. Arrange the sausages on the grill rack and cook for 15–20 minutes, or until cooked, turning frequently so that they turn an even golden brown all over.

6 Serve the sausages with the creamy mash and plenty of onion gravy.

Per portion: Energy 939Kcal/3913kJ; Protein 19.9g; Carbohydrate 85g, of which sugars 16.7g; Fat 60g, of which saturates 28.6g; Cholesterol 133mg; Calcium 179mg; Fibre 6.6g; Sodium 942mg.

PORK CHOPS WITH CHILLI-NECTARINE RELISH

A FRUITY SALSA MAKES AN INTERESTING AND TASTY CHANGE FROM THE MORE USUAL APPLE SAUCE.

SERVES FOUR

INGREDIENTS
    250ml/8fl oz/1 cup fresh
      orange juice
    45ml/3 tbsp olive oil
    2 garlic cloves, ground
    5ml/1 tsp ground cumin
    15ml/1 tbsp coarsely ground
      black pepper
    8 pork loin chops, about 2cm/¾in
      thick, well trimmed
    salt
For the relish
    1 small fresh green chilli
    2 nectarines
    30ml/2 tbsp clear honey
    juice of ½ lemon
    250ml/8fl oz/1 cup chicken stock
    1 garlic clove, finely chopped
    ½ onion, finely chopped
    5ml/1 tsp grated fresh root ginger
    1.5ml/¼ tsp salt
    15ml/1 tbsp chopped fresh
      coriander (cilantro)

1 For the relish, roast the chilli over a gas flame, holding it with tongs, until charred on all sides. Alternatively, char the skin under the grill (broiler). Leave to cool for 5 minutes.

2 Wearing rubber gloves, carefully remove the charred skin of the chilli. Discard the seeds if you like a less hot flavour. Finely chop the chilli and place in a heavy pan. Halve the nectarines and remove and discard the stones (pits). Chop the flesh and add to the pan with the chilli.

3 Add the honey, lemon juice, chicken stock, garlic, onion, ginger and salt. Bring to the boil, then simmer, stirring occasionally, for about 30 minutes. Stir in the coriander and set aside.

4 In a small bowl, combine the orange juice, oil, garlic, cumin and pepper. Stir to mix well.

5 Arrange the pork chops, in a single layer, in a shallow, non-metallic dish. Pour over the orange juice mixture and turn to coat. Cover with clear film (plastic wrap) and leave in a cool place to marinate for at least 1 hour or in the refrigerator overnight.

6 Remove the pork chops from the marinade and pat dry with kitchen paper. Season lightly with salt.

7 Heat a ridged griddle pan. When hot, add the pork chops and cook for about 5 minutes, until the undersides are browned. Turn and cook on the other side for a further 10 minutes, until browned. Work in batches if necessary. Serve the chops immediately, with the chilli-nectarine relish.

Per portion: Energy 315Kcal/1321kJ; Protein 43.4g; Carbohydrate 11.4g, of which sugars 11g; Fat 10.9g, of which saturates 3.2g; Cholesterol 126mg; Calcium 28mg; Fibre 0.6g; Sodium 144mg.

ROMANIAN KEBABS

KEBABS ARE POPULAR WORLDWIDE, LARGELY BECAUSE THEY ARE SO EASILY ADAPTED TO SUIT EVERYONE'S TASTE. IN THIS RECIPE, LEAN LAMB IS MARINATED, THEN COOKED WITH CHUNKS OF VEGETABLES TO PRODUCE A DELICIOUS, COLOURFUL AND HEALTHY MEAL.

SERVES SIX

INGREDIENTS
   675g/1½lb lean lamb, cut into
      4cm/1½in cubes
   12 button (pearl) onions
   2 green (bell) peppers, seeded and
      cut into 12 pieces
   12 cherry tomatoes
   12 button (white) mushrooms
   lemon slices and fresh rosemary
      sprigs, to garnish
   freshly cooked rice and crusty bread,
      to serve
For the marinade
   juice of 1 lemon
   120ml/4fl oz/½ cup red wine
   1 onion, finely chopped
   60ml/4 tbsp olive oil
   2.5ml/½ tsp dried sage
   2.5ml/½ tsp chopped fresh rosemary
   salt and ground black pepper

VARIATIONS
• Use rump (round) steak instead of lamb. Cut it into strips, marinate it as suggested, then interleave the strips on the skewers, with the onions, cherry tomatoes and mushrooms. Omit the green (bell) peppers.
• These kebabs are just as delicious cooked on a barbecue.

1 For the marinade, combine the lemon juice, red wine, onion, olive oil, herbs and seasoning in a bowl. Stir the cubes of lamb into the marinade. Cover and chill in the refrigerator for 2–12 hours, stirring occasionally.

2 Remove the lamb pieces from the marinade and thread on six skewers with the onions, peppers, tomatoes and mushrooms. Preheat the grill (broiler).

3 Brush the kebabs with marinade and grill (broil) for 10–15 minutes, turning once. Arrange on cooked rice, with lemon and rosemary. Serve with crusty bread.

Per portion: Energy 259Kcal/1083kJ; Protein 23.6g; Carbohydrate 4g, of which sugars 3.4g; Fat 16.7g, of which saturates 6.5g; Cholesterol 86mg; Calcium 22mg; Fibre 1.9g; Sodium 104mg.

Jerusalem Barbecue Lamb Kebabs

In the early days of the modern state of Israel, the days of austerity, "lamb" kebabs would have been made with turkey and a little lamb fat, and "veal" kebabs with chicken and a small amount of veal. Turkey, chicken, beef and veal can all be cooked in this way.

SERVES FOUR TO SIX

INGREDIENTS

800g/1¾lb tender lamb, cubed
1.5ml/¼ tsp ground allspice
1.5ml/¼ tsp ground cinnamon
1.5ml/¼ tsp ground black pepper
1.5ml/¼ tsp ground cardamom
45–60ml/3–4 tbsp chopped
  fresh parsley
2 onions, chopped
5–8 garlic cloves, chopped
juice of ½ lemon or 45ml/3 tbsp dry
  white wine
45ml/3 tbsp extra virgin olive oil
sumac, for sprinkling (optional)
30ml/2 tbsp pine nuts
salt
For serving
  flat breads, such as pitta bread,
    tortillas or naan bread
  tahini
  crunchy vegetable salad

1 Put the lamb, allspice, cinnamon, black pepper, cardamom, half the parsley, half the onions, the garlic, lemon juice or wine and olive oil in a bowl and mix together. Season with salt now, if you like, or sprinkle on after cooking. Set aside and leave to marinate.

2 Meanwhile, light the barbecue and leave for about 40 minutes. When the coals are white and grey, the barbecue is ready for cooking. If using wooden skewers, soak them in water for about 30 minutes to prevent them from burning.

3 Thread the cubes of meat on to wooden or metal skewers, then cook on the barbecue for 2–3 minutes on each side, turning occasionally, until cooked evenly and browned.

4 Transfer the kebabs to a serving dish and sprinkle with the reserved onions, parsley, sumac, if using, pine nuts and salt, if you like. Serve the kebabs with warmed flat breads to wrap the kebabs in, a bowl of tahini for drizzling over and a vegetable salad.

COOK'S TIPS
• If sumac is available, its tangy flavour is fresh and invigorating, and its red colour is appealing.
• These kebabs can also be cooked under a hot grill (broiler).

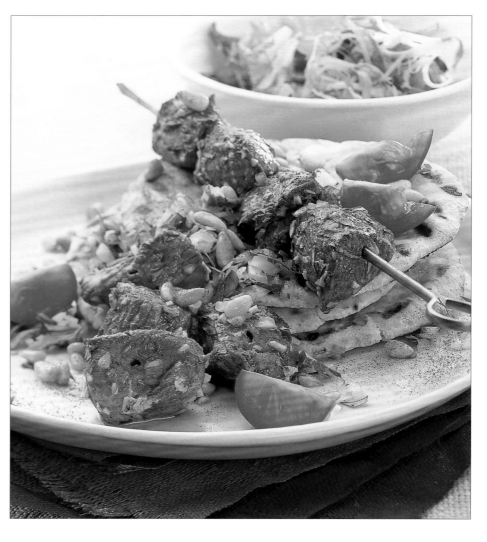

Per portion: Energy 513Kcal/2137kJ; Protein 41.4g; Carbohydrate 6.4g, of which sugars 4.7g; Fat 36g, of which saturates 11.9g; Cholesterol 152mg; Calcium 51mg; Fibre 1.6g; Sodium 177mg.

STEAK BÉARNAISE

BÉARNAISE, AFTER BÉARN IN SOUTH-WEST FRANCE, IS A CREAMY EGG AND BUTTER SAUCE FLAVOURED WITH FRESH TARRAGON. IT IS A CLASSIC COMPLEMENT TO GRIDDLED, GRILLED OR PAN-FRIED STEAK AND ALSO EXCELLENT WITH ROAST BEEF. ROASTED VEGETABLES MAKE A GOOD ACCOMPANIMENT.

SERVES FOUR

INGREDIENTS
4 sirloin steaks, each weighing about
  225g/8oz, trimmed
15ml/1 tbsp sunflower oil (optional)
salt and ground black pepper
For the Béarnaise sauce
90ml/6 tbsp white wine vinegar
12 black peppercorns
2 bay leaves
2 shallots, finely chopped
4 fresh tarragon sprigs
4 egg yolks
225g/8oz/1 cup unsalted (sweet)
  butter at room temperature, diced
30ml/2 tbsp chopped fresh tarragon
ground white pepper

1 Start by making the sauce. Put the vinegar, peppercorns, bay leaves, shallots and tarragon sprigs in a small pan and simmer until reduced to 30ml/2 tbsp. Strain the vinegar through a fine sieve.

2 Beat the egg yolks with salt and freshly ground white pepper in a small, heatproof bowl. Stand the bowl over a pan of very gently simmering water, then gradually beat the strained vinegar into the yolks.

3 Gradually beat in the butter, one piece at a time, allowing each addition to melt before adding the next. Do not allow the water to heat beyond a gentle simmer or the sauce will overheat and curdle.

4 While cooking the sauce, heat a griddle or grill until very hot.

COOK'S TIP
If you are confident about preparing egg and butter sauces, the best method is to reduce the flavoured vinegar before cooking the steak, then finish the sauce while the steak is cooking. This way, the sauce does not have to be kept hot and there is less risk of overheating it or allowing it to become too thick.

5 Beat the chopped fresh tarragon into the sauce and remove the pan from the heat. The sauce should be smooth, thick and glossy.

6 Cover the surface of the sauce with clear film (plastic wrap) or dampened greaseproof (waxed) paper to prevent a skin forming and leave over the pan of hot water, still off the heat, to keep hot while you cook the steak.

7 Season the steaks with salt and plenty freshly ground black pepper.

8 A pan is not usually oiled before cooking steak, but if it is essential to grease the pan, add only the minimum oil. Cook the steaks for 2–4 minutes on each side. The cooking time depends on the thickness of the steaks and the extent to which you want to cook them. As a guide, 2–4 minutes will give a medium-rare result.

9 Serve the steaks on warmed plates. Peel the clear film or dampened greaseproof paper off the sauce and stir it lightly, then spoon it over the steaks.

Per portion: Energy 796Kcal/3297kJ; Protein 51.1g; Carbohydrate 0.5g, of which sugars 0.4g; Fat 65.5g, of which saturates 37.2g; Cholesterol 459mg; Calcium 50mg; Fibre 0.2g; Sodium 450mg.

STUFFED BUTTERFLY OF BEEF WITH CHEESE AND CHILLI SAUCE

THIS RECIPE HAD ITS ORIGINS IN NORTHERN MEXICO OR IN NEW MEXICO, WHICH IS BEEF COUNTRY. IT IS A GOOD WAY TO COOK STEAKS, EITHER UNDER THE GRILL OR ON THE BARBECUE.

SERVES FOUR

INGREDIENTS

    4 fresh serrano chillies
    115g/4oz/½ cup full-fat soft cheese
    30ml/2 tbsp reposada tequila
    30ml/2 tbsp oil
    1 onion
    2 garlic cloves
    5ml/1 tsp dried oregano
    2.5ml/½ tsp salt
    2.5ml/½ tsp ground black pepper
    175g/6oz/1½ cups grated medium
       Cheddar cheese
    4 fillet steaks, at least 2.5cm/
       1in thick

1 Dry-roast the chillies in a griddle pan over a moderate heat, turning them frequently until the skins are blistered but not burnt. Put them in a strong plastic bag and tie the top to keep the steam in. Set aside for 20 minutes.

2 Remove the chillies from the bag, slit them and scrape out the seeds with a sharp knife. Cut the flesh into long narrow strips, then cut each strip into several shorter strips.

3 Put the full-fat soft cheese in a small heavy pan and stir over a very low heat until it has melted. Add the chilli strips and the tequila and stir to make a smooth sauce. Keep warm over a very low heat.

4 Heat the oil in a frying pan and cook the onion, garlic and oregano for about 5 minutes over a moderate heat, stirring frequently until the onion has browned. Season with the salt and pepper.

5 Remove the pan from the heat and add the grated Cheddar cheese, in two or three batches. Stir well so that it melts into the onion and garlic mixture without becoming rubbery.

6 Cut each steak almost but not quite in half across its width, so that it can be opened out, butterfly-fashion. Preheat the grill (broiler) to its highest setting.

7 Spoon a quarter of the cheese and onion filling on to one side of each steak and close the other side over it. Place the steaks in a grill pan and grill (broil) for 3–5 minutes on each side, depending on how you like your steak. Serve on heated plates with the vegetables of your choice, and with the cheese and chilli sauce poured over.

COOK'S TIP
One of the easiest ways of testing whether a steak is cooked is by touch. A steak that is very rare or "blue" will feel soft to the touch; the meat will be relaxed. A rare steak will feel like a sponge, and will spring back when lightly pressed. A medium-rare steak offers more resistance, while a well-cooked steak will feel very firm.

Per portion: Energy 580Kcal/2412kJ; Protein 51.1g; Carbohydrate 3g, of which sugars 2.2g; Fat 39.5g, of which saturates 20.6g; Cholesterol 175mg; Calcium 372mg; Fibre 0.5g; Sodium 735mg.

LONE STAR STEAK WITH POTATO DINNER

THIS TRADITIONAL AMERICAN MEAL IS USUALLY SERVED WITH CORN ON THE COB, BUT A CRISP, GREEN SALAD WOULD MAKE A LIGHTER ALTERNATIVE ACCOMPANIMENT.

SERVES FOUR

INGREDIENTS
    45ml/3 tbsp olive oil
    5 large garlic cloves, crushed
    5ml/1 tsp coarse black pepper
    2.5ml/½ tsp ground allspice
    5ml/1 tsp ground cumin
    2.5ml/½ tsp chilli powder
    10ml/2 tsp dried oregano
    15ml/1 tbsp cider vinegar
    4 boneless sirloin steaks, about
        2cm/¾ in thick
    salt
To serve
    tomato salsa
    freshly cooked corn on the
        cob (optional)
For the potatoes
    50ml/2fl oz/¼ cup vegetable oil
    1 onion, chopped
    5ml/1 tsp salt
    900g/2lb potatoes, boiled and diced
    30–75ml/2–5 tbsp chopped canned
        or bottled green chillies, according
        to taste

1 Heat the olive oil in a heavy frying pan. When hot, add the garlic and cook, stirring frequently, for about 3 minutes, until tender and just brown. Do not let the garlic burn, as it will become bitter.

2 Transfer the garlic and oil to a shallow dish large enough to hold the steaks in a single layer.

3 Add the pepper, allspice, cumin, chilli powder, oregano and vinegar to the garlic and stir to blend thoroughly. If necessary, add just enough water to obtain a fairly thick paste.

4 Add the steaks to the dish and turn to coat evenly on both sides with the spice mixture. Cover and leave to marinate for 2 hours or place in the refrigerator overnight. Bring the steaks to room temperature 30 minutes before cooking.

5 To make the potatoes, heat the oil in a large non-stick frying pan. Add the onion and salt. Cook over a medium heat for 5 minutes, until softened. Add the potatoes and chillies. Cook, stirring occasionally, for 15–20 minutes.

6 Season the steaks on both sides with salt to taste. Heat a ridged griddle pan. When hot, add the steaks and cook, turning once, until done to your taste. Allow about 1–2 minutes on each side for rare, 2–3 minutes for medium-rare, and 3–4 minutes for well done.

7 If necessary, briefly reheat the potatoes. Serve immediately, with the tomato salsa and corn, if using.

VARIATION
The steaks can also be cooked on a barbecue. Prepare the fire, and when the coals are glowing red and covered with grey ash, spread them in a single layer. Cook the steaks in the centre of an oiled grill rack set about 13cm/5in above the coals for 1 minute per side to sear them. Move them away from the centre and cook for 10–12 minutes, or longer for medium-rare, turning once.

Per portion: Energy 560Kcal/2346kJ; Protein 45.4g; Carbohydrate 39.2g, of which sugars 5g; Fat 25.6g, of which saturates 5.9g; Cholesterol 89mg; Calcium 32mg; Fibre 2.8g; Sodium 640mg.

ROASTS

Although far fewer families sit down to a regular roast dinner every weekend, the fact remains that this is one of the easiest ways of cooking a well-balanced meal — and one of the most delicious. The important thing to remember is that taste really does tell, so it is worth buying the best meat, game, poultry and fish you can afford. Cultivate a good butcher and fish supplier or buy from a recommended source specializing in free-range, additive-free or organic meat or fish. Regard dishes such as Marmalade-glazed Goose or Roast Rib of Beef as special treats and you'll enjoy them all the more.

ROASTED VEGETABLES WITH SALSA VERDE

THERE ARE ENDLESS VARIATIONS OF THE ITALIAN SALSA VERDE, WHICH MEANS "GREEN SAUCE". USUALLY A BLEND OF FRESH CHOPPED HERBS, GARLIC, OLIVE OIL, ANCHOVIES AND CAPERS, THIS IS A SIMPLIFIED VERSION. HERE, IT IS SERVED WITH VEGETABLES AND A RICE DISH FROM CYPRUS.

SERVES FOUR

INGREDIENTS

   3 courgettes (zucchini),
      sliced lengthways
   1 large fennel bulb, cut
      into wedges
   450g/1lb butternut squash, cut into
      2cm/¾in chunks
   12 shallots
   2 red (bell) peppers, seeded
      and cut lengthways into
      thick slices
   4 plum tomatoes, halved and seeded
   45ml/3 tbsp olive oil
   2 garlic cloves, crushed
   5ml/1 tsp balsamic vinegar
   salt and ground black pepper
For the salsa verde
   45ml/3 tbsp chopped fresh mint
   90ml/6 tbsp chopped fresh flat
      leaf parsley
   15ml/1 tbsp Dijon mustard
   juice of ½ lemon
   30ml/2 tbsp olive oil
For the rice
   15ml/1 tbsp vegetable or olive oil
   75g/3oz/¾ cup vermicelli, broken
      into short lengths
   225g/8oz/generous 1 cup long
      grain rice
   900ml/1½ pints/3¾ cups
      vegetable stock

1 To make the salsa verde, place all the ingredients, with the exception of the olive oil, in a food processor or blender. Blend to a coarse paste, then add the oil, a little at a time, until the mixture forms a smooth purée.

2 Transfer the salsa to a bowl, season to taste with salt and pepper, cover and set aside.

3 Preheat the oven to 220°C/425°F/ Gas 7.To roast the vegetables, toss the courgettes, fennel, squash, shallots, peppers and tomatoes in the olive oil, garlic and balsamic vinegar. Set aside for 10 minutes to allow all the flavours to combine.

4 Place all the vegetables – apart from the squash and tomatoes – on a large baking sheet, brush with half the oil and vinegar mixture and season.

5 Roast the vegetables for 25 minutes, then remove the baking sheet from the oven. Using a fork, turn all the vegetables over and brush with the rest of the oil and vinegar mixture. Add the butternut squash and plum tomatoes, return to the oven and cook for a further 20–25 minutes, until all the vegetables are tender and lightly charred around the edges.

VARIATIONS
• Substitute 45ml/3 tbsp watercress for half the parsley in the salsa.
• Use sherry vinegar instead of balsamic vinegar to flavour the vegetables.
• If you like, add a medium aubergine (eggplant), cut into chunks, to the mixture of roasted vegetables.

6 Meanwhile, prepare the rice. Heat the oil in a heavy pan. Add the vermicelli and cook for about 3 minutes, or until golden and crisp. Season to taste.

7 Rinse the rice under cold running water, then drain well and add it to the vermicelli. Cook for 1 minute, stirring to coat it in the oil.

8 Add the vegetable stock, then cover the pan and allow to cook for about 12 minutes, until all the liquid is absorbed. Stir the rice, then cover and leave to stand for 10 minutes. Serve the warm rice with the roasted vegetables and salsa verde.

COOK'S TIP
The salsa verde will keep for up to 1 week if stored in an airtight container in the refrigerator.

Per portion: Energy 519Kcal/2160kJ; Protein 12.1g; Carbohydrate 75.3g, of which sugars 14.7g; Fat 18.7g, of which saturates 2.8g; Cholesterol 0mg; Calcium 151mg; Fibre 6.9g; Sodium 27mg.

ROASTED COD WITH FRESH TOMATO SAUCE

REALLY FRESH COD HAS A SWEET, DELICATE FLAVOUR AND A PURE WHITE FLAKY FLESH. SERVED WITH AN AROMATIC TOMATO SAUCE, IT MAKES A DELICIOUS MEAL.

SERVES FOUR

INGREDIENTS
    350g/12oz ripe plum tomatoes
    75ml/5 tbsp olive oil
    2.5ml/½ tsp sugar
    2 strips of pared orange rind
    1 fresh thyme sprig
    6 fresh basil leaves
    900g/2lb fresh cod fillet, skin on
    salt and ground black pepper
    steamed green beans, to serve

COOK'S TIP
Cod is becoming increasingly rare and expensive. You can substitute any firm white fish fillets in this dish. Try haddock, pollock, or that excellent and underrated fish, coley. When raw, coley flesh looks grey, but it turns white on cooking.

1 Preheat the oven to 230°C/450°F/ Gas 8. Coarsely chop the tomatoes.

2 Heat 15ml/1 tbsp of the olive oil in a heavy pan, add the tomatoes, sugar, orange rind, thyme and basil, and simmer for about 5 minutes, until the tomatoes are soft.

3 Press the tomato mixture through a fine sieve, discarding the solids that remain in the sieve. Pour into a small pan and heat gently.

4 Scale the cod fillet and cut on the diagonal into four pieces. Season well.

5 Heat the remaining oil in a heavy frying pan and cook the cod, skin side down, until the skin is crisp. Place the fish on a greased baking sheet, skin side up, and roast in the oven for 8–10 minutes, until the fish is cooked through. Serve the fish on the steamed green beans with the tomato sauce.

Per portion: Energy 319Kcal/1330kJ; Protein 41.8g; Carbohydrate 2.7g, of which sugars 2.7g; Fat 15.6g, of which saturates 2.3g; Cholesterol 104mg; Calcium 27mg; Fibre 0.9g; Sodium 143mg.

ROAST MONKFISH WITH GARLIC

MONKFISH TIED UP AND COOKED IN THIS WAY IS KNOWN IN FRENCH AS A "GIGOT", BECAUSE IT RESEMBLES A LEG OF LAMB. THE COMBINATION OF MONKFISH AND GARLIC IS SUPERB. FOR A CONTRAST IN COLOUR, SERVE IT WITH VIBRANT GREEN BEANS.

SERVES FOUR TO SIX

INGREDIENTS
  1kg/2¼lb monkfish tail, skinned
  14 fat garlic cloves
  5ml/1 tsp fresh thyme leaves
  30ml/2 tbsp olive oil
  juice of 1 lemon
  2 bay leaves
  salt and ground black pepper

1 Preheat the oven to 220°C/425°F/ Gas 7. Remove any membrane from the monkfish tail and cut out the central bone. Peel two garlic cloves and cut them into thin slivers. Sprinkle a quarter of these and half the thyme leaves over the cut side of the fish, then close it up and use fine kitchen string to tie it into a neat shape, like a boned piece of meat. Pat dry with kitchen paper.

2 Make incisions on either side of the fish and push in the remaining garlic slivers. Heat half the olive oil in a frying pan which can safely be used in the oven. When the oil is hot, put in the monkfish and brown it all over for about 5 minutes, until evenly coloured. Season with salt and pepper, sprinkle with lemon juice and then sprinkle over the remaining thyme.

3 Tuck the bay leaves under the monkfish, arrange the remaining (unpeeled) garlic cloves around it and drizzle the remaining olive oil over the fish and the garlic. Transfer the frying pan to the oven and roast the monkfish for 20–25 minutes, until the flesh is cooked through.

4 Place on a warmed serving dish with the garlic and some green beans. To serve, remove the string and cut the monkfish into 2cm/¾in thick slices.

COOK'S TIPS
• The garlic heads can be used whole.
• When serving the monkfish, invite each guest to pop out the soft garlic pulp with a fork and spread it over the monkfish.
• Use two smaller monkfish tails.

Per portion: Energy 253Kcal/1065kJ; Protein 45.2g; Carbohydrate 3.1g, of which sugars 0.3g; Fat 6.6g, of which saturates 1.1g; Cholesterol 40mg; Calcium 26mg; Fibre 0.8g; Sodium 51mg.

ROASTED CHICKEN WITH GRAPES AND FRESH ROOT GINGER

THIS DISH, WITH ITS BLEND OF SPICES AND SWEET FRUIT, IS INSPIRED BY MOROCCAN FLAVOURS.
SERVE WITH COUSCOUS, MIXED WITH A HANDFUL OF COOKED CHICKPEAS.

SERVES FOUR

INGREDIENTS
1–1.6kg/2¼–3½lb chicken
115–130g/4–4½oz fresh root
  ginger, grated
6–8 garlic cloves, coarsely chopped
juice of 1 lemon
about 30ml/2 tbsp olive oil
2–3 large pinches of ground cinnamon
500g/1¼lb seeded red and
  green grapes
500g/1¼lb seedless green grapes
5–7 shallots, chopped
about 250ml/8fl oz/1 cup chicken stock
salt and ground black pepper

1 Rub the chicken with half of the ginger, the garlic, half of the lemon juice, the olive oil, cinnamon, salt and lots of pepper. Leave to marinate.

2 Meanwhile, cut the red and green seeded grapes in half, remove the seeds and set aside. Add the whole green seedless grapes to the halved ones.

3 Preheat the oven to 180°C/350°F/ Gas 4. Heat a heavy frying pan or flameproof casserole until hot.

4 Remove the chicken from the marinade, add to the pan and cook until browned on all sides. (There should be enough oil on the chicken to brown it but, if not, add a little extra.)

5 Put some of the shallots into the chicken cavity with the garlic and ginger from the marinade and as many of the red and green grapes that will fit inside. Roast in the oven for 40–60 minutes, or until the chicken is tender.

VARIATIONS

• This dish is good made with duck in place of the chicken. Marinate and roast as above, adding 15–30ml/1–2 tbsp honey to the pan sauce as it cooks.
• Use boneless chicken breast portions, with the skin still attached, instead of a whole chicken. Pan-fry the chicken portions, rather than roasting them.

6 Remove the chicken from the pan and keep warm. Pour off any oil from the pan, reserving any sediment in the base of the pan. Add the remaining shallots to the pan and cook for about 5 minutes until softened.

7 Add half the remaining red and green grapes, the remaining ginger, the stock and any juices from the roast chicken and cook over a medium-high heat until the grapes have cooked down to a thick sauce. Season with salt, ground black pepper and the remaining lemon juice to taste.

8 Serve the chicken on a warmed serving dish, surrounded by the sauce and the reserved grapes.

COOK'S TIP

Seeded Italia or muscat grapes have a delicious, sweet fragrance and are perfect for using in this recipe.

Per portion: Energy 454Kcal/1891kJ; Protein 31.6g; Carbohydrate 19.5g, of which sugars 19.5g; Fat 28.1g, of which saturates 7g; Cholesterol 165mg; Calcium 28mg; Fibre 1g; Sodium 116mg.

GALVESTON CHICKEN

A LIGHTLY SPICED MARINADE TURNS ORDINARY ROAST CHICKEN INTO A SPECIAL MEAL WITH SCARCELY ANY EXTRA EFFORT DEMANDED OF THE COOK. WHAT COULD BE BETTER?

2 Insert a skewer through the chicken, at the thighs, to keep it flat during cooking. Place the chicken in a shallow, non-metallic dish and pour over the lemon juice.

3 In a small bowl, combine the garlic, cayenne, paprika, oregano, pepper, and oil. Mix well. Rub the mixture evenly over the surface of the chicken.

4 Cover and set aside to marinate for 2–3 hours at room temperature or in the refrigerator overnight. Bring the chicken back to room temperature 30 minutes before roasting.

5 Season the chicken well with salt on both sides. Transfer it to a shallow roasting pan.

6 Put the roasting pan in a cold oven and set the temperature to 200°C/400°F/Gas 6. Roast until the chicken is done, about 1–1½ hours, turning occasionally and basting with the roasting juices. To test if it is cooked through, insert a skewer into the thickest part. If the juices that run out are clear, it is ready.

SERVES FOUR

INGREDIENTS
  1.5kg/3½ lb chicken
  juice of 1 lemon
  4 garlic cloves, crushed
  15ml/1 tbsp cayenne
  15ml/1 tbsp paprika
  15ml/1 tbsp dried oregano
  2.5ml/½ tsp coarse black pepper
  10ml/2 tsp olive oil
  5ml/1 tsp salt

COOK'S TIP
Roasting chicken in an oven that has not been preheated produces a particularly crispy skin.

1 With a sharp knife or poultry shears, remove the backbone from the chicken. Turn it breast side up. With the heel of your hand, press down to break the breastbone, and open the chicken flat like a book.

Per portion: Energy 407Kcal/1688kJ; Protein 37.2g; Carbohydrate 0g, of which sugars 0g; Fat 28.5g, of which saturates 7.7g; Cholesterol 198mg; Calcium 12mg; Fibre 0g; Sodium 626mg.

ROASTED DUCKLING
ON A BED OF HONEYED POTATOES

THE RICH FLAVOUR OF DUCK COMBINED WITH THESE SWEETENED POTATOES GLAZED WITH HONEY MAKES AN EXCELLENT TREAT FOR A DINNER PARTY OR SPECIAL OCCASION.

SERVES FOUR

INGREDIENTS

1 duckling, giblets removed
60ml/4 tbsp light soy sauce
150ml/¼ pint/⅔ cup fresh
   orange juice
3 large floury potatoes, cut
   into chunks
30ml/2 tbsp clear honey
15ml/1 tbsp sesame seeds
salt and ground black pepper

1 Preheat the oven to 200°C/400°F/ Gas 6. Place the duckling in a roasting pan. Prick the skin well.

2 Mix the soy sauce and orange juice together and pour over the duck. Cook for 20 minutes.

3 Place the potato chunks in a bowl, stir in the honey and toss to mix well. Remove the duckling from the oven and spoon the potatoes all around and under the duckling.

4 Roast for 35 minutes and remove from the oven. Toss the potatoes in the juices so the underside will be cooked and turn the duck over. Put back in the oven and cook for a further 30 minutes.

5 Remove the duckling from the oven and carefully scoop off the excess fat, leaving the juices behind.

6 Sprinkle the sesame seeds over the potatoes, season and turn the duckling back over, breast side up, and cook for a further 10 minutes. Remove the duckling and potatoes from the oven and keep warm, allowing the duck to stand for a few minutes.

7 Pour off the excess fat and simmer the juices on the hob (stovetop) for a few minutes. Serve the juices with the carved duckling and potatoes.

Per portion: Energy 806Kcal/3341kJ; Protein 20.8g; Carbohydrate 32.3g, of which sugars 6.4g; Fat 66.8g, of which saturates 17.9g; Cholesterol 0mg; Calcium 53mg; Fibre 2.1g; Sodium 403mg.

MARMALADE-GLAZED GOOSE

SUCCULENT ROAST GOOSE IS THE CLASSIC CENTREPIECE FOR A TRADITIONAL CHRISTMAS LUNCH.
RED CABBAGE COOKED WITH LEEKS, AND BRAISED FENNEL ARE TASTY ACCOMPANIMENTS.

SERVES EIGHT

INGREDIENTS
    4.5kg/10lb oven-ready goose
    1 cooking apple, peeled, cored and
      cut into eighths
    1 large onion, cut into eighths
    bunch of fresh sage, plus extra sprigs
      to garnish
    30ml/2 tbsp ginger
      marmalade, melted
    salt and ground black pepper
For the stuffing
    25g/1oz/2 tbsp butter
    1 onion, finely chopped
    15ml/1 tbsp ginger marmalade
    450g/1lb/2 cups ready-to-eat
      prunes, chopped
    45ml/3 tbsp Madeira
    225g/8oz/4 cups fresh
      white breadcrumbs
    30ml/2 tbsp chopped fresh sage
For the gravy
    1 onion, chopped
    15ml/1 tbsp plain (all-purpose) flour
    150ml/¼ pint/⅔ cup Madeira
    600ml/1 pint/2½ cups chicken stock

1 Preheat the oven to 200°C/400°F/
Gas 6. Prick the skin of the goose all
over with a fork and season the bird
generously, both inside and out.

COOK'S TIP
Red cabbage goes well with goose. Cook
1 small leek, sliced, in 75g/3oz/6 tbsp
butter, add 1kg/2¼lb/9 cups shredded
red cabbage, with the grated rind of
1 orange, and cook for 2 minutes. Add
30ml/2 tbsp Madeira and 15ml/1 tbsp
brown sugar and cook for 15 minutes.

2 Mix the apple, onion and sage leaves
and spoon the mixture into the rump
end of the goose.

3 To make the stuffing, melt the butter
in a large pan and cook the onion for
about 5 minutes, or until softened but
not coloured. Remove the pan from
the heat and stir in the marmalade,
chopped prunes, Madeira, breadcrumbs
and chopped sage.

4 Stuff the neck end of the goose with
some of the stuffing, and set the
remaining stuffing aside in the
refrigerator. Sew up the bird or secure it
with skewers to prevent the stuffing
from escaping during cooking.

5 Place the goose in a large roasting
pan. Butter a piece of foil and use to
cover the goose loosely, then place in
the oven for 2 hours.

6 Baste the goose frequently during
cooking and remove excess fat from the
pan as necessary, using a small ladle or
serving spoon. (Strain, cool and chill the
fat in a covered container: it is excellent
for roasting potatoes.)

7 Remove the foil from the goose and
brush the melted ginger marmalade
over the goose, then roast for
30–40 minutes more, or until cooked
through. To check if the goose is cooked,
pierce the thick part of the thigh with a
metal skewer; the juices will run clear
when the bird is cooked. Remove from
the oven and cover with foil, then leave
to stand for 15 minutes before carving.

8 While the goose is cooking, shape the
remaining stuffing into walnut-size balls
and place them in an ovenproof dish.
Spoon 30ml/2 tbsp of the goose fat over
the stuffing balls and bake for about
15 minutes before the goose is cooked.

9 To make the gravy, pour off all but
15ml/1 tbsp of fat from the roasting
pan, leaving the meat juices behind.
Add the onion and cook for about
3–5 minutes, or until softened but not
coloured. Sprinkle in the flour and then
gradually stir in the Madeira and stock.
Bring to the boil, stirring constantly,
then simmer for 3 minutes, or until
thickened and glossy. Strain the gravy
and serve it with the carved goose and
stuffing. Garnish with sage leaves.

Per portion: Energy 823Kcal/3443kJ; Protein 57.6g; Carbohydrate 47.1g, of which sugars 23.8g; Fat 43.3g, of which saturates 14g; Cholesterol 177mg; Calcium 106mg; Fibre 4.5g; Sodium 395mg.

SOMERSET CIDER-GLAZED HAM

WILLIAM THE CONQUEROR INTRODUCED CIDER MAKING TO ENGLAND FROM NORMANDY IN 1066. THIS WONDERFUL OLD WEST-COUNTRY HAM GLAZED WITH CIDER IS TRADITIONALLY SERVED WITH CRANBERRY SAUCE AND IS IDEAL FOR CHRISTMAS FEASTING.

SERVES EIGHT TO TEN

INGREDIENTS
 2kg/4½lb middle gammon
   (cured ham) in a single piece
 1.3 litres/2¼ pints/5⅔ cups medium-
   dry (hard) cider
 1 large or 2 small onions
 about 30 whole cloves
 3 bay leaves
 10 black peppercorns
 45ml/3 tbsp soft light brown sugar
 bunch of flat leaf parsley, to garnish
For the cranberry sauce
 2 clementines
 350g/12oz/3 cups cranberries
 175g/6oz/¾ cup soft light brown sugar
 30ml/2 tbsp port

1 Weigh the ham and calculate the cooking time at 20 minutes per 450g/1lb, then place it in a large casserole or pan. Stud the onion or onions with 5–10 of the cloves and add to the casserole or pan with the bay leaves and peppercorns.

2 Add 1.2 litres/2 pints/5 cups of the cider and enough water just to cover the ham. Heat until simmering and then carefully skim off the scum that rises to the surface using a large spoon or ladle. Start timing the cooking from the moment the stock begins to simmer.

VARIATION
Use honey in place of the soft brown sugar for the glaze and serve the ham with redcurrant sauce or jelly.

3 Cover with a lid or foil and simmer gently for the calculated time. Towards the end of the cooking time, preheat the oven to 220°C/425°F/Gas 7.

4 Heat the sugar and remaining cider in a pan; stir until the sugar has dissolved.

5 Simmer for 5 minutes to make a dark, sticky glaze. Remove the pan from the heat and leave to cool for 5 minutes.

6 Lift the ham out of the casserole or pan using a slotted spoon and a large fork. Carefully and evenly, cut the rind from the ham, then score the fat into a neat diamond pattern. Place the ham in a roasting pan or ovenproof dish.

7 Press a clove into the centre of each diamond, then carefully spoon over the glaze. Roast for 20–25 minutes, or until the fat is brown, glistening and crisp.

8 Grate the rind and squeeze the juice from the clementines. Simmer all the cranberry sauce ingredients in a heavy pan for 15–20 minutes, stirring frequently. Transfer the sauce to a jug (pitcher). Serve the ham hot or cold, garnished with parsley and with the cranberry sauce.

COOK'S TIPS
• A large stock pot or preserving pan can be used in place of the casserole or pan for cooking the ham.
• Leave the ham until it is just cool enough to handle before removing the rind. Snip off the string using a sharp knife or scissors, then carefully slice off the rind, leaving a thin, even layer of fat. Use a narrow-bladed, sharp knife for the best results – a filleting knife, or a long, slim ham knife would be ideal.

Per portion: Energy 409Kcal/1712kJ; Protein 44g; Carbohydrate 16.8g, of which sugars 16.8g; Fat 18.8g, of which saturates 6.3g; Cholesterol 58mg; Calcium 27mg; Fibre 0.7g; Sodium 2202mg.

ROAST PORK WITH SAGE AND ONION STUFFING

SAGE AND ONION MAKE A CLASSIC STUFFING FOR ROAST PORK, DUCK AND TURKEY, WITH THE SAGE COUNTERACTING THE FATTINESS OF THE RICH MEATS. SERVE WITH APPLE SAUCE AND ROAST POTATOES.

SERVES SIX TO EIGHT

INGREDIENTS
  1.3–1.6kg/3–3½lb boneless loin of pork
  60ml/4 tbsp fine, dry breadcrumbs
  10ml/2 tsp chopped fresh sage
  25ml/1½ tbsp plain (all-
    purpose) flour
  300ml/½ pint/1¼ cups (hard) cider
  150ml/¼ pint/⅔ cup water
  5–10ml/1–2 tsp crab apple or
    redcurrant jelly
  salt and ground black pepper
  fresh thyme sprigs, to garnish
For the stuffing
  25g/1oz/2 tbsp butter
  50g/2oz bacon, finely chopped
  2 large onions, finely chopped
  75g/3oz/1½ cups fresh
    white breadcrumbs
  30ml/2 tbsp chopped fresh sage
  5ml/1 tsp chopped fresh thyme
  10ml/2 tsp finely grated lemon rind
  1 small (US medium)
    egg, beaten

1 Preheat the oven to 220°C/425°F/ Gas 7. To make the stuffing, melt the butter in a pan and cook the bacon until it begins to brown, then add the onions and cook gently until softened. Mix with the breadcrumbs, sage, thyme, lemon rind and egg, then season well.

2 Cut the rind off the piece of pork in one piece and score it well. Cooking the rind separately makes crisper crackling than leaving it on the pork.

3 Place the pork fat side down, and season. Add a layer of stuffing, then roll up and tie neatly.

4 Lay the rind over the pork and rub in 5ml/1 tsp salt. Roast for 2–2½ hours, basting with the pork fat once or twice. Reduce the temperature to 190ºC/375ºF/ Gas 5 after 20 minutes. Shape the remaining stuffing into balls and add to the roasting pan for the last 30 minutes.

5 Remove the rind from the pork. Increase the oven temperature to 220°C/425°F/Gas 7 and roast the rind for a further 20–25 minutes, until crisp.

6 Mix the dry breadcrumbs and sage and press them into the fat. Cook the pork for 10 minutes, then cover and set aside in a warm place for 15–20 minutes.

7 Remove all but 30–45ml/2–3 tbsp of the fat from the roasting pan and place it on the hob (stovetop). Stir in the flour, followed by the cider and water. Bring to the boil and then cook gently for 10 minutes. Strain the gravy into a clean pan, add the crab apple or redcurrant jelly, and cook for another 5 minutes. Adjust the seasoning.

8 Serve the pork cut into thick slices and the crisp crackling cut into strips with the cider gravy, garnished with thyme.

Per portion: Energy 426Kcal/1789kJ; Protein 52.4g; Carbohydrate 23.7g, of which sugars 5.3g; Fat 14.1g, of which saturates 5.7g; Cholesterol 180mg; Calcium 67mg; Fibre 1.4g; Sodium 475mg.

ROASTED AND MARINATED PORK

YUAN, A SAUCE MADE FROM SAKE, SHOYU, MIRIN AND CITRUS FRUIT, IS OFTEN USED IN JAPAN TO MARINATE INGREDIENTS EITHER BEFORE OR AFTER COOKING. IN THIS RECIPE, THE SAUCE GIVES A DELICATE FLAVOUR TO PORK. IF POSSIBLE, LEAVE THE MEAT TO MARINATE OVERNIGHT.

SERVES FOUR

INGREDIENTS
    600g/1lb 5oz pork fillet (tenderloin)
    1 garlic clove, crushed
    generous pinch of salt
    4 spring onions (scallions), trimmed,
       white part only
    10g/¼oz dried wakame, soaked in
       water for 20 minutes and drained
    10cm/4in celery stick, trimmed and
       cut in half crossways
    1 carton salad cress
For the yuan sauce
    105ml/7 tbsp shoyu
    45ml/3 tbsp sake
    60ml/4 tbsp mirin
    1 lime, sliced into thin rings

4 Cut the white part of the spring onions in half crossways, then in half lengthways. Remove the round cores, then lay the spring onion quarters flat on a chopping board. Slice them very thinly lengthways to make fine shreds.

5 Soak the shreds in a bowl of ice-cold water. Repeat with the remaining parts of the spring onions. When the shreds curl up, drain and gather them into a loose ball.

6 Cut the drained wakame into 2.5cm/1in squares or narrow strips. Slice the celery very thinly lengthways. Soak in cold water, then drain and gather together as before.

7 Remove the pork from the marinade and wipe with kitchen paper. Slice it very thinly. Strain the marinade and keep it in a gravy boat or jug (pitcher). Arrange the sliced pork on a large serving plate with the vegetables around it. Serve cold with the yuan sauce.

1 Preheat the oven to 200°C/400°F/Gas 6. Rub the pork with crushed garlic and salt, and leave for 15 minutes.

2 Roast the pork for 20 minutes, then turn the meat over and reduce the oven temperature to 180°C/350°F/Gas 4. Cook for a further 20 minutes, or until the pork is cooked. Test by inserting a skewer or the point of a sharp knife into the meat. If the juices run clear, the meat is cooked. If there are any traces of pink in the juices, roast the pork for a little longer.

3 Meanwhile, mix the yuan sauce ingredients in a container that is big enough to hold the pork. When the meat is cooked, immediately put it in the sauce, and leave it to marinate for at least 2 hours, or overnight.

Per portion: Energy 188Kcal/787kJ; Protein 32.5g; Carbohydrate 0.7g, of which sugars 0.6g; Fat 6.1g, of which saturates 2.1g; Cholesterol 95mg; Calcium 18mg; Fibre 0.2g; Sodium 377mg.

ROAST LEG OF LAMB

WHEN YOUNG LAMB WAS SEASONAL TO SPRINGTIME, A ROAST LEG WAS AN EASTER SPECIALITY, SERVED WITH A SAUCE USING THE FIRST SPRIGS OF MINT OF THE YEAR AND EARLY NEW POTATOES. ROAST LAMB IS NOW WELL ESTABLISHED AS A YEAR-ROUND FAMILY FAVOURITE FOR SUNDAY LUNCH, OFTEN SERVED WITH CRISP ROAST POTATOES.

SERVES SIX

INGREDIENTS
  1.5kg/3¼lb leg of lamb
  4 garlic cloves, sliced
  2 fresh rosemary sprigs
  30ml/2 tbsp light olive oil
  300ml/½ pint/1¼ cups red wine
  5ml/1 tsp clear honey
  45ml/3 tbsp redcurrant jelly
  salt and ground black pepper
For the roast potatoes
  45ml/3 tbsp white vegetable fat
    or lard
  1.3kg/3lb potatoes, such as Desirée,
    cut into chunks
For the mint sauce
  about 15g/½oz fresh mint
  10ml/2 tsp caster (superfine) sugar
  15ml/1 tbsp boiling water
  30ml/2 tbsp white wine vinegar

1 Preheat the oven to 220°C/425°F/ Gas 7. Make small slits into the lamb all over the leg. Press a slice of garlic and a few rosemary leaves into each slit, then place the lamb in a roasting pan and season well. Drizzle the oil over the lamb and roast for about 1 hour.

COOK'S TIP
To make a quick and tasty gravy from the pan juices, add about 300ml/½ pint/ 1¼ cups red wine, stock or water and boil, stirring occasionally, until reduced and well-flavoured. Season to taste, then strain into a sauce boat to serve.

2 Meanwhile, mix the wine, honey and redcurrant jelly in a small pan and heat, stirring, until the jelly melts. Bring to the boil, then reduce the heat and simmer until reduced by half. Spoon this glaze over the lamb and return it to the oven for 30–45 minutes.

3 To make the potatoes, put the fat in a roasting pan on the oven shelf above the meat. Boil the potatoes for about 5–10 minutes, then drain them and fluff up the surface of each with a fork.

4 Add the prepared potatoes to the hot fat and baste well, then roast them for 40–50 minutes, or until they are crisp.

5 Meanwhile, make the mint sauce. Place the mint on a chopping board and sprinkle the sugar over the top. Chop the mint finely, then transfer the mint and sugar to a bowl.

6 Add the boiling water and stir until the sugar has dissolved. Add 15ml/ 1 tbsp vinegar and taste the sauce before adding the remaining vinegar. (You may want to add slightly less or more than the suggested quantity.) Leave the mint sauce to stand until you are ready to serve the meal.

7 Cover the lamb with foil and set it aside in a warm place to rest for 10–15 minutes before carving. Serve with the crisp roast potatoes, mint sauce and a selection of seasonal vegetables.

Per portion: Energy 732Kcal/3080kJ; Protein 78g; Carbohydrate 36.4g, of which sugars 4.2g; Fat 31.6g, of which saturates 12.7g; Cholesterol 257mg; Calcium 36mg; Fibre 2.2g; Sodium 182mg.

ROAST VEAL WITH PARSLEY STUFFING

COOKING THIS LOIN OF VEAL, WITH ITS FRAGRANT PARSLEY AND LEEK STUFFING, IN A ROASTING BAG MAKES SURE THAT IT IS SUCCULENT AND FULL FLAVOURED WHEN SERVED.

SERVES SIX

INGREDIENTS
    25g/1oz/2 tbsp butter
    15ml/1 tbsp sunflower oil
    1 leek, finely chopped
    1 celery stick, finely chopped
    50g/2oz/1 cup fresh
      white breadcrumbs
    50g/2oz/½ cup chopped fresh flat
      leaf parsley
    900g/2lb boned loin of veal
    salt and ground black pepper

VARIATION
Other mild herbs can be used in the stuffing instead of parsley. Try tarragon, chervil and chives, but avoid strong-flavoured herbs, such as marjoram, oregano and thyme, which tend to overpower the delicate flavour of veal.

1 Preheat the oven to 180°C/350°F/ Gas 4. Heat the butter and oil in a frying pan until foaming. Cook the leek and celery until they are just starting to colour, then remove the pan from the heat and stir in the breadcrumbs, parsley and seasoning.

2 Lay the loin of veal out flat. Spread the stuffing over the meat, then roll it up carefully and tie the roll at regular intervals to secure it in a neat shape.

3 Place the veal in a roasting bag and close the bag with an ovenproof tie, then place it in a roasting pan. Roast the veal for 1¼ hours.

4 Pierce the meat with a metal skewer to check whether it is cooked: when cooked the meat juices will run clear. Leave the veal to stand for about 10–15 minutes, then carve it into thick slices and serve with gravy, sautéed potatoes, asparagus and sugar snaps.

ESCALOPES OF VEAL WITH CREAM SAUCE

THIS QUICK, EASY DINNER-PARTY DISH IS DELICIOUS SERVED WITH BUTTERED TAGLIATELLE AND LIGHTLY STEAMED GREEN VEGETABLES.

SERVES FOUR

INGREDIENTS
    15ml/1 tbsp plain (all-purpose) flour
    4 veal escalopes (US scallops), each
      weighing about 75–115g/3–4oz
    30ml/2 tbsp sunflower oil
    1 shallot, chopped
    150g/5oz/2 cups oyster
      mushrooms, sliced
    30ml/2 tbsp Marsala or
      medium-dry sherry
    200ml/7fl oz/scant 1 cup
      crème fraîche
    30ml/2 tbsp chopped fresh tarragon
    salt and ground black pepper

COOK'S TIP
If the sauce seems to be too thick, add 30ml/2 tbsp water.

1 Season the flour and use to dust the veal escalopes, then set aside.

2 Heat the oil in a large frying pan and cook the shallot and mushrooms for 5 minutes. Add the escalopes and cook over a high heat for about 1½ minutes on each side. Pour in the Marsala or sherry and cook until reduced by half.

3 Use a spatula to remove the veal escalopes from the pan. Stir the crème fraîche, tarragon and seasoning into the juices remaining in the pan and simmer gently for 3–5 minutes, or until the sauce is thick and creamy.

4 Return the escalopes to the pan and heat through for 1 minute before serving.

Top per portion: Energy 233Kcal/981kJ; Protein 33.4g; Carbohydrate 7.6g, of which sugars 1.1g; Fat 7.9g, of which saturates 3.6g; Cholesterol 135mg; Calcium 49mg; Fibre 1.3g; Sodium 260mg.
Below per portion: Energy 376Kcal/1564kJ; Protein 25g; Carbohydrate 5.5g, of which sugars 1.5g; Fat 27.5g, of which saturates 14.9g; Cholesterol 108mg; Calcium 44mg; Fibre 0.6g; Sodium 73mg.

ROAST RIB OF BEEF

THIS ROAST LOOKS SPECTACULAR, AND SERVED IN TRADITIONAL STYLE, WITH YORKSHIRE PUDDINGS AND HORSERADISH SAUCE, IT MAKES A PERFECT CELEBRATION MEAL.

SERVES EIGHT TO TEN

INGREDIENTS
    45ml/3 tbsp mixed peppercorns
    15ml/1 tbsp juniper berries
    2.75kg/6lb rolled rib of beef
    30ml/2 tbsp Dijon mustard
    15ml/1 tbsp olive oil
For the Yorkshire puddings
    150ml/¼ pint/⅔ cup water
    150ml/¼ pint/⅔ cup milk
    115g/4oz/1 cup plain (all-
        purpose) flour
    pinch of salt
    2 eggs, beaten
    60ml/4 tbsp lard, melted, or
        sunflower oil (optional)
For the caramelized shallots
    20 shallots
    5 garlic cloves, peeled
    60ml/4 tbsp light olive oil
    15ml/1 tbsp caster (superfine) sugar
For the gravy
    150ml/¼ pint/⅔ cup red wine
    600ml/1 pint/2½ cups beef stock
    salt and ground black pepper

1 Preheat the oven to 230°C/450°F/ Gas 8. Coarsely crush the peppercorns and juniper berries. Sprinkle half the spices over the meat, then transfer to a roasting pan and roast for 30 minutes.

COOK'S TIP
If you prefer to cook beef on the bone, buy a 3.6kg/8lb forerib. Trim off the excess fat, sprinkle over the spices, then follow the instructions in steps 1 and 2. Roast at the lower temperature for 2 hours for rare beef, 2½ hours for medium rare, and 3 hours for well done.

2 Reduce the oven temperature to 180°C/350°F/Gas 4. Mix the mustard and oil into the remaining crushed spices and spread the resulting paste over the meat. Roast the meat for a further 1¼ hours if you like your meat rare, 1 hour 50 minutes for a medium-rare result or 2 hours 25 minutes for a roast that is medium to well done. Baste the beef frequently during cooking.

3 Make the Yorkshire puddings as soon as the beef is in the oven. Stir the water into the milk. Sift the flour and salt into a bowl. Make a well in the middle and gradually whisk in the eggs followed by the milk and water to make a smooth batter. Cover and leave to stand for about 1 hour. (The batter can be made well in advance and chilled overnight in the refrigerator if convenient.)

4 An hour before the beef is due to be ready, mix the shallots and garlic cloves with the light olive oil and spoon into the roasting pan around the beef. After 30 minutes, sprinkle the caster sugar over the shallots and garlic. Stir the shallots and garlic two or three times during cooking.

5 Transfer the meat to a large serving platter, cover tightly with foil and set aside in a warm place for 20–30 minutes. (This resting time makes carving easier.) Increase the oven temperature to 230°C/450°F/ Gas 8. Divide 60ml/4 tbsp dripping from the meat or the lard or oil, if using, among 10 individual Yorkshire pudding tins (muffin pans) and heat in the oven for 5 minutes.

6 Spoon the Yorkshire pudding batter into the hot fat in the tins and bake for 20–30 minutes, or until risen, firm and a golden brown colour. The time depends on the size of the tins: larger Yorkshire puddings will take longer than those in smaller tins.

7 Make the gravy while the Yorkshire puddings are cooking. Simmer the red wine and beef stock together in a pan for about 5 minutes to intensify the flavour of the gravy.

8 Skim the fat from the meat juices in the roasting pan, then pour in the wine mixture and simmer until the gravy is reduced and thickened slightly to a syrupy consistency. Stir frequently with a wooden spoon to remove all of the roasting residue from the roasting pan. Season to taste.

9 Serve the beef with the individual Yorkshire puddings, caramelized shallots and gravy. Offer roast potatoes or game chips as accompaniments, along with a selection of lightly cooked, seasonal vegetables.

Per portion: Energy 828Kcal/3444kJ; Protein 64.8g; Carbohydrate 14.2g, of which sugars 3.3g; Fat 55.7g, of which saturates 22.9g; Cholesterol 229mg; Calcium 74mg; Fibre 0.7g; Sodium 137mg.

BAKED DISHES

Baking is a very versatile cooking method, as this eclectic selection of recipes proves. Crunchy, golden toppings will prove a hit with everyone, and slow baking brings out the full flavour. For a family supper that is sure to please, choose Roasted Ratatouille Moussaka or a hearty Country Meat Loaf. Smoked Haddock and New Potato Pie is another excellent choice, and you can ring the changes by choosing whatever fish is readily available and therefore relatively inexpensive. Do try Fillets of Brill in Red Wine Sauce, which proves once and for all that red wine and fish can go beautifully together.

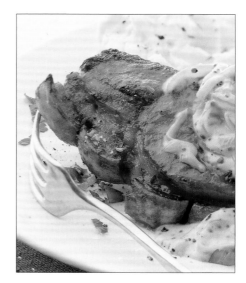

ROASTED RATATOUILLE MOUSSAKA

BASED ON THE CLASSIC GREEK DISH, THIS MOUSSAKA REALLY HAS A TASTE OF THE MEDITERRANEAN. ROASTING BRINGS OUT THE DEEP RICH FLAVOURS OF THE VEGETABLES, WHICH GIVE A COLOURFUL CONTRAST TO THE LIGHT AND MOUTHWATERING EGG-AND-CHEESE TOPPING. THIS DISH IS PERFECT AS A VEGETARIAN MAIN COURSE, ALTHOUGH IT MAY BE SERVED AS A HEARTY WINTER SIDE DISH, TOO.

SERVES FOUR TO SIX

INGREDIENTS
  2 red (bell) peppers, seeded and cut
    into large chunks
  2 yellow (bell) peppers, seeded and
    cut into large chunks
  2 aubergines (eggplant), cut into
    large chunks
  3 courgettes (zucchini), thickly sliced
  45ml/3 tbsp olive oil
  3 garlic cloves, crushed
  400g/14oz can chopped tomatoes
  30ml/2 tbsp sun-dried tomato paste
  45ml/3 tbsp chopped fresh basil or
    15ml/1 tbsp dried basil
  15ml/1 tbsp balsamic vinegar
  1.5ml/¼ tsp soft light brown sugar
  salt and ground black pepper
  basil leaves, to garnish
For the topping
  25g/1oz/2 tbsp butter
  25g/1oz/¼ cup plain (all-
    purpose) flour
  300ml/½ pint/1¼ cups milk
  1.5ml/¼ tsp freshly grated nutmeg
  250g/9oz ricotta cheese
  3 eggs, beaten
  25g/1oz/⅓ cup freshly grated
    Parmesan cheese

1 Preheat the oven to 230°C/450°F/ Gas 8. Arrange the chunks of red and yellow peppers, aubergines and courgettes in an even layer in a large roasting pan. Season well with salt and ground black pepper.

2 Mix together the oil and crushed garlic cloves and pour them over the vegetables. Shake the roasting pan to thoroughly coat the vegetables in the garlic mixture.

3 Roast in the oven for 15–20 minutes, until slightly charred, lightly tossing the vegetables once during the cooking time. Remove the pan from the oven and set aside. Reduce the oven temperature to 200°C/400°F/Gas 6.

4 Put the chopped tomatoes, sun-dried tomato paste, basil, balsamic vinegar and brown sugar in a large, heavy pan and gently heat to boiling point. Reduce the heat and simmer, uncovered, for about 10–15 minutes, until reduced and thickened, stirring occasionally. Season with salt and freshly ground black pepper to taste.

5 Carefully tip the roasted vegetables out of their pan and into the pan of tomato sauce. Mix well, coating the vegetables thoroughly in the tomato sauce. Spoon into an ovenproof dish.

6 To make the topping, melt the butter in a large, heavy pan over a gentle heat. Stir in the flour and cook for 1 minute. Pour in the milk, stirring constantly, then whisk until blended. Add the nutmeg and continue whisking over a gentle heat until thickened. Cook for a further 2 minutes, then remove from the heat and leave to cool slightly.

7 Mix in the ricotta cheese and beaten eggs thoroughly. Season with salt and plenty of freshly ground black pepper to taste.

8 Level the surface of the roasted vegetable mixture with the back of a spoon. Spoon the moussaka topping over the vegetables and sprinkle with the Parmesan cheese. Bake for 30–35 minutes, until the topping is golden brown. Serve immediately, garnished with basil leaves.

VARIATION
Rather than baking this recipe in one large dish, divide the roasted vegetables and topping among individual gratin dishes. Reduce the baking time to 25 minutes. Individual portions can also be frozen and, when needed, simply removed from the freezer, left to thaw and baked for 30–35 minutes – ideal for those with a solitary vegetarian in the family, or for unexpected guests.

Per portion: Energy 570Kcal/2367kJ; Protein 22.1g; Carbohydrate 27.5g, of which sugars 21.7g; Fat 42.1g, of which saturates 20.3g; Cholesterol 223mg; Calcium 339mg; Fibre 7.1g; Sodium 447mg.

COD, BASIL, TOMATO AND POTATO PIE

FRESH AND SMOKED FISH MAKE A GREAT COMBINATION, ESPECIALLY WITH THE HINT OF TOMATO AND BASIL. SERVED WITH A GREEN SALAD, THIS MAKES AN IDEAL DISH FOR LUNCH OR A FAMILY SUPPER.

2 Melt 75g/3oz/6 tbsp of the butter in a large pan, add the onion and cook for about 5 minutes, until softened and tender but not browned. Sprinkle over the flour and half the chopped basil. Gradually add the reserved fish cooking liquid, adding a little more milk if necessary to make a fairly thin sauce, stirring constantly to make a smooth consistency. Bring to the boil, season with salt and pepper, and add the remaining basil.

3 Remove the pan from the heat, then add the fish and tomatoes and stir gently to combine. Pour into an ovenproof dish.

SERVES EIGHT

INGREDIENTS

    1kg/2¼lb smoked cod fillets
    1kg/2¼lb fresh cod fillets
    900ml/1½ pint/3¾ cups milk
    1.2litres/2 pints/5 cups water
    2 fresh basil sprigs
    1 fresh lemon thyme sprig
    150g/5oz/⅔ cup butter
    1 onion, chopped
    75g/3oz/⅔ cup plain
     (all-purpose) flour
    30ml/2 tbsp chopped fresh basil
    4 firm plum tomatoes, peeled
     and chopped
    12 medium floury potatoes
    salt and ground black pepper
    crushed black pepper corns,
     to garnish
    lettuce leaves, to serve

1 Place both kinds of fish in a roasting pan with 600ml/1 pint/2½ cups of the milk, the water and the herb sprigs. Bring to a simmer and cook gently for about 3–4 minutes. Remove from the heat and leave the fish to cool in the liquid for about 20 minutes. Drain the fish, reserving the cooking liquid for use in the sauce. Flake the fish, removing the skin and any remaining bones.

4 Preheat the oven to 180°C/350°F/ Gas 4. Cook the potatoes in boiling water until tender. Drain then add the remaining butter and milk and mash. Season to taste and spoon over the fish mixture, using a fork to create a pattern. You can freeze the pie at this stage. Bake for 30 minutes until the top is golden. Sprinkle with the crushed pepper corns and serve hot with lettuce.

Per portion: Energy 474Kcal/1989kJ; Protein 49.6g; Carbohydrate 30.7g, of which sugars 4.6g; Fat 17.8g, of which saturates 10.2g; Cholesterol 155mg; Calcium 62mg; Fibre 2.5g; Sodium 1672mg.

FISH PIE

THIS DISH CAN BE VARIED TO SUIT YOUR TASTE AND POCKET. THIS IS A SIMPLE PIE, BUT YOU COULD ADD PRAWNS OR HARD-BOILED EGGS, OR MIX THE POTATO TOPPING WITH SPRING ONIONS.

SERVES FOUR

INGREDIENTS

   450g/1lb cod or haddock fillets
   225g/8oz smoked cod fillets
   300ml/½ pint/1¼ cups milk
   ½ lemon, sliced
   1 bay leaf
   1 fresh thyme sprig
   4–5 black peppercorns
   50g/2oz/¼ cup butter
   25g/1oz/¼ cup plain (all-
      purpose) flour
   30ml/2 tbsp chopped fresh parsley
   5ml/1 tsp anchovy essence (extract)
   150g/5oz/2 cups sliced mushrooms
   salt, ground black pepper and
      cayenne pepper
For the topping
   450g/1lb potatoes, cooked and
      mashed with milk
   50g/2oz/¼ cup butter
   2 tomatoes, sliced
   25g/1oz/¼ cup grated Cheddar
      cheese (optional)

1 Put the fish, skin side down, in a shallow pan. Add the milk, lemon slices, bay leaf, thyme and peppercorns. Bring to the boil, then lower the heat and poach gently for about 5 minutes, until just cooked. Strain off and reserve the milk. Remove the fish skin and flake the flesh, discarding any bones.

2 Melt half the butter in a small pan, stir in the flour and cook gently, stirring, for 1 minute. Add the milk and boil, whisking, until smooth and creamy. Stir in the parsley and anchovy essence and season to taste.

3 Heat the remaining butter in a frying pan, add the sliced mushrooms and sauté until tender. Season and add to the flaked fish. Mix the sauce into the fish and stir gently to combine. Transfer the mixture to an ovenproof dish.

4 Preheat the oven to 200°C/400°F/ Gas 6. Beat the mashed potato with the butter until very creamy. Season, then spread the topping evenly over the fish. Fork up the surface and arrange the sliced tomatoes around the edge. Sprinkle the exposed topping with the grated cheese, if using.

5 Bake for 20–25 minutes, until the topping is lightly browned. If you prefer, finish browning under a grill (broiler).

VARIATION
Instead of using plain mashed potatoes, try a mixture of mashed potato and mashed swede (rutabaga) or celeriac.

Per portion: Energy 382Kcal/1600kJ; Protein 34.8g; Carbohydrate 24.3g, of which sugars 3.1g; Fat 16.8g, of which saturates 9.9g; Cholesterol 118mg; Calcium 62mg; Fibre 2.7g; Sodium 859mg.

SMOKED HADDOCK AND NEW POTATO PIE

SMOKED HADDOCK HAS A SALTY FLAVOUR AND CAN BE BOUGHT EITHER DYED OR UNDYED. THE DYED FISH HAS A STRONG YELLOW COLOUR, WHILE THE OTHER IS ALMOST CREAMY IN COLOUR.

SERVES FOUR

INGREDIENTS
   450g/1lb smoked haddock fillet
   475ml/16fl oz/2 cups semi-skimmed
      (low-fat) milk
   2 bay leaves
   1 onion, quartered
   4 cloves
   450g/1lb new potatoes
   butter, for greasing
   30ml/2 tbsp cornflour (cornstarch)
   60ml/4 tbsp double (heavy) cream
   30ml/2 tbsp chopped fresh chervil
   salt and ground black pepper
   mixed vegetables, to serve

VARIATIONS
Instead of using all smoked haddock for this pie, use half smoked and half fresh. Cook the two types together, as described in Step 1. A handful of peeled prawns (shrimp) is a good addition to this pie if you want to make it even more filling.

COOK'S TIP
The fish gives out liquid as it cooks, so it is best to start with a slightly thicker sauce than you might think is necessary.

1 Preheat the oven to 200°C/400°F/ Gas 6. Place the haddock in a deep-sided frying pan. Pour the milk over and add the bay leaves.

2 Stud the onion with the cloves and place it in the pan with the fish and milk. Cover the top and simmer for about 10 minutes or until the fish starts to flake.

3 Remove the fish with a slotted spoon and set aside to cool. Strain the liquid from the pan into a separate pan and set aside.

4 To prepare the potatoes, cut them into thin slices, leaving the skins on.

5 Blanch the potatoes in a large pan of lightly salted, boiling water for about 5 minutes. Drain.

6 Grease the base and sides of a 1.2 litre/2 pint/5 cup ovenproof dish. Then using a knife and fork, carefully flake the fish.

7 Reheat the milk in the pan. Mix the cornflour with a little water to form a paste and stir in the cream and the chervil. Add to the milk in the pan and cook until thickened.

8 Arrange one-third of the potatoes over the base of the dish and season with pepper. Lay half of the fish over. Repeat layering, finishing with a layer of potatoes on top.

9 Pour the sauce over the top, making sure that it sinks down through the mixture. Cover with foil and cook for 30 minutes. Remove the foil and cook for a further 10 minutes to brown the surface. Serve immediately with a selection of mixed vegetables.

Per portion: Energy 300Kcal/1266kJ; Protein 23.9g; Carbohydrate 32.4g, of which sugars 1.9g; Fat 9.3g, of which saturates 5.3g; Cholesterol 61mg; Calcium 56mg; Fibre 1.5g; Sodium 881mg.

BAKED SEA BREAM WITH TOMATOES

John Dory, turbot or sea bass can all be cooked this way. If you prefer to use filleted fish, choose a chunky fillet, like cod, and bake it skin side up. Roasting the tomatoes brings out their sweetness, which contrasts beautifully with the flavour of the fish.

2 Meanwhile, cut the potatoes into 1cm/½in slices. Par-boil for 5 minutes. Drain and set aside.

3 Grease an ovenproof dish with oil. Arrange the potatoes in a single layer with the lemon slices over; sprinkle on the bay leaf, thyme and basil. Season and drizzle with half the remaining olive oil. Lay the fish on top, season; pour over the wine and the rest of the oil. Arrange the tomatoes around the fish.

SERVES FOUR TO SIX

INGREDIENTS
   8 ripe tomatoes
   10ml/2 tsp caster (superfine) sugar
   200ml/7fl oz/scant 1 cup olive oil
   450g/1lb new potatoes
   1 lemon, sliced
   1 bay leaf
   1 fresh thyme sprig
   8 fresh basil leaves
   1 sea bream, about 900g–1kg/
      2–2¼lb, cleaned and scaled
   150ml/¼ pint/⅔ cup dry white wine
   30ml/2 tbsp fresh white breadcrumbs
   2 garlic cloves, crushed
   15ml/1 tbsp finely chopped
      fresh parsley
   salt and ground black pepper
   fresh flat parsley or basil leaves,
      chopped, to garnish

1 Preheat the oven to 240°C/475°F/ Gas 9. Using a sharp knife, cut the tomatoes in half lengthways and arrange them in a single layer in a large, ovenproof dish, cut side up. Sprinkle with the caster sugar, season to taste with salt and pepper and drizzle over a little of the olive oil. Roast for 30–40 minutes, until the tomatoes are soft and lightly browned on top.

4 Mix together the breadcrumbs, garlic and parsley and sprinkle over the fish. Bake for 30 minutes, until the flesh comes away easily from the bone. Garnish with chopped parsley or basil.

Per portion: Energy 571Kcal/2383kJ; Protein 25.9g; Carbohydrate 29.4g, of which sugars 7.2g; Fat 37.1g, of which saturates 4.9g; Cholesterol 48mg; Calcium 82mg; Fibre 3g; Sodium 224mg.

FILLETS OF BRILL IN RED WINE SAUCE

FORGET THE OLD MAXIM THAT RED WINE AND FISH DO NOT GO WELL TOGETHER. THE ROBUST SAUCE ADDS COLOUR AND RICHNESS TO THIS EXCELLENT DISH. TURBOT, HALIBUT AND JOHN DORY ARE ALSO GOOD COOKED THIS WAY.

SERVES FOUR

INGREDIENTS

  4 brill fillets, about 175–200g/6–7oz
    each, skinned
  150g/5oz/⅔ cup chilled butter,
    diced, plus extra for greasing
  115g/4oz shallots, thinly sliced
  200ml/7fl oz/scant 1 cup robust
    red wine
  200ml/7fl oz/scant 1 cup fish stock
  salt and ground white pepper
  fresh chervil or flat leaf parsley
    leaves, to garnish

3 Using a fish slice or spatula, carefully lift the fish and shallots on to a serving dish, cover with foil and keep hot.

4 Transfer the dish to the hob (stovetop) and bring the cooking liquid to the boil over a high heat. Cook it until it has reduced by half. Lower the heat and whisk in the chilled butter, one piece at a time, to make a smooth, shiny sauce. Season with salt and ground white pepper, set aside and keep hot.

5 Divide the shallots among four warmed plates and lay the brill fillets on top. Pour the sauce over and around the fish and garnish with the chervil or flat leaf parsley.

1 Preheat the oven to 180°C/350°F/ Gas 4. Season the fish on both sides with salt and pepper. Generously butter a flameproof dish, which is large enough to take all the brill fillets in a single layer without overlapping. Spread the shallots over the base and lay the fish fillets on top. Season.

2 Pour in the red wine and fish stock, cover the dish and bring the liquid to just below boiling point. Transfer the dish to the oven and bake for 6–8 minutes, until just cooked.

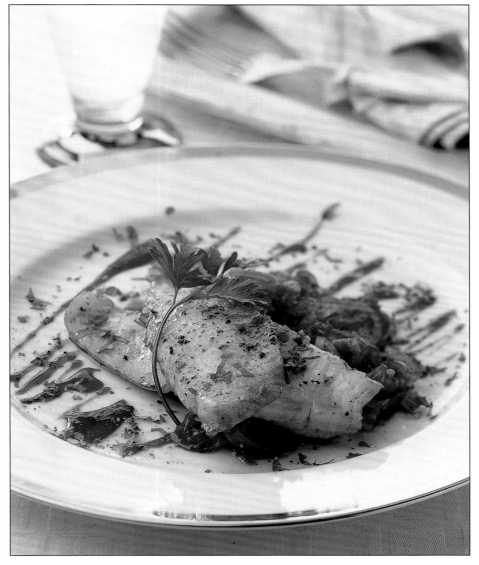

Per portion: Energy 511Kcal/2123kJ; Protein 35.7g; Carbohydrate 1.3g, of which sugars 1.3g; Fat 36.7g, of which saturates 19.5g; Cholesterol 156mg; Calcium 97mg; Fibre 0.4g; Sodium 454mg.

SINIYA

THE NAME OF THIS CLASSIC JEWISH SEPHARDI DISH SIMPLY MEANS FISH AND TAHINI SAUCE. IN THIS VERSION, THE FISH IS FIRST WRAPPED IN VINE LEAVES, THEN SPREAD WITH TAHINI AND BAKED. A FINAL SPRINKLING OF POMEGRANATE SEEDS ADDS A FRESH, INVIGORATING FLAVOUR.

SERVES FOUR

INGREDIENTS

4 small fish, such as trout, sea
   bream, red mullet or snapper, each
   weighing about 300g/11oz, cleaned
at least 5 garlic cloves, chopped
juice of 2 lemons
75ml/5 tbsp olive oil
about 20 brined vine (grape) leaves
tahini, for drizzling
1–2 pomegranates
fresh mint and coriander (cilantro)
   sprigs, to garnish

VARIATION
Instead of whole fish, use fish fillets or
steaks such as fresh tuna. Make a bed
of vine (grape) leaves and top with the
fish and marinade. Bake for about
5–10 minutes, until the fish is half
cooked, then top with the tahini as above
and grill (broil) until golden brown and
lightly crusted on top.

1 Preheat the oven to 180°C/350°F/
Gas 4. Put the fish in a shallow, ovenproof
dish, large enough to fit all the fish
without touching each other. In a bowl,
combine the garlic, lemon juice and oil;
spoon over the fish. Turn the fish to coat.

2 Rinse the vine leaves well under cold
water, then wrap the fish in the leaves.
Arrange the fish in the same dish and
spoon any marinade in the dish over
the top of each. Bake for 30 minutes.

3 Drizzle the tahini over the top of each
wrapped fish, making a ribbon so that
the tops and tails of the fish and some
of the vine leaf wrapping still show.
Return to the oven and bake for a
further 5–10 minutes, until the top is
golden and slightly crusted.

4 Meanwhile, cut the pomegranates in
half and scoop out the seeds. Sprinkle
the seeds over the fish, garnish with
mint and coriander, and serve.

Per portion: Energy 402Kcal/1681kJ; Protein 46.8g; Carbohydrate 2.6g, of which sugars 2.6g; Fat 22.8g, of which saturates 4.1g; Cholesterol 192mg; Calcium 86mg; Fibre 0.5g; Sodium 176mg.

BACON-WRAPPED TROUT WITH OATMEAL AND ONION STUFFING

THIS STUFFING IS BASED ON A SCOTTISH SPECIALITY, A MIXTURE OF OATMEAL AND ONION CALLED SKIRLIE. HERRING CAN BE COOKED IN THE SAME WAY. THIS IS VERY GOOD WITH SLICES OF COOKED POTATOES, BRUSHED WITH OLIVE OIL AND GRILLED UNTIL GOLDEN ON EACH SIDE.

SERVES FOUR

INGREDIENTS
10 dry-cured streaky (fatty) bacon
    rashers (strips)
40g/1½oz/3 tbsp butter
1 onion, finely chopped
115g/4oz/1 cup oatmeal
30ml/2 tbsp chopped fresh parsley
30ml/2 tbsp chopped fresh chives
4 trout, about 350g/12oz each,
    gutted and boned
juice of ½ lemon
salt and ground black pepper
watercress, cherry tomatoes and
    lemon wedges, to serve

For the herb mayonnaise
6 watercress sprigs
15ml/1 tbsp chopped fresh chives
30ml/2 tbsp coarsely
    chopped parsley
90ml/6 tbsp lemon mayonnaise
30ml/2 tbsp crème fraîche
2.5–5ml/½–1 tsp tarragon mustard

1 Preheat oven to 190°C/375°F/Gas 5. Chop two of the bacon rashers. Melt 25g/1oz/2 tbsp of the butter in a large frying pan and cook the bacon briefly. Add the finely chopped onion and cook gently, stirring occasionally, for 5–8 minutes, until softened.

2 Add the oatmeal and cook until the oatmeal darkens and absorbs the fat, but do not allow it to overbrown. Stir in the parsley, chives and seasoning. Cool.

3 Wash and dry the trout, then stuff with the oatmeal mixture. Wrap each fish in two bacon rashers and place in an ovenproof dish. Dot with the remaining butter and sprinkle with the lemon juice. Bake for 20–25 minutes, until the bacon browns and crisps.

4 Meanwhile, make the mayonnaise. Place the watercress, chives and parsley in a sieve and pour boiling water over them. Drain, rinse under cold water, and drain well on kitchen paper.

5 Purée the herbs in a mortar with a pestle. (This is easier than using a food processor for this small quantity.) Stir the puréed herbs into the lemon mayonnaise together with the crème fraîche. Add tarragon mustard to taste and stir to combine.

6 When cooked, transfer the trout to warmed serving plates and serve immediately with watercress, tomatoes and lemon wedges, accompanied by the herb mayonnaise.

Per portion: Energy 870Kcal/3625kJ; Protein 65.9g; Carbohydrate 24.5g, of which sugars 2.6g; Fat 57.1g, of which saturates 17.8g; Cholesterol 300mg; Calcium 115mg; Fibre 2.5g; Sodium 1245mg.

BAKED SALMON WITH WATERCRESS SAUCE

WHOLE BAKED SALMON IS A CLASSIC DISH SERVED AT WEDDING PARTIES AND JUST ABOUT ANY OTHER BIG OCCASION. BAKING THE SALMON IN FOIL PRODUCES A FLESH RATHER LIKE THAT OF A POACHED FISH BUT WITH THE EASE OF BAKING. DECORATING THE FISH WITH THIN SLICES OF CUCUMBER LOOKS PRETTY AND WILL CONCEAL ANY FLESH THAT MAY LOOK RAGGED AFTER SKINNING.

SERVES SIX TO EIGHT

INGREDIENTS
  2–3kg/4½–6¾lb salmon,
    cleaned, with head and tail
    left on
  3–5 spring onions (scallions),
    thinly sliced
  1 lemon, thinly sliced
  1 cucumber, thinly sliced
  fresh dill sprigs, to garnish
  lemon wedges, to serve
For the watercress sauce
  3 garlic cloves, chopped
  200g/7oz watercress leaves,
    finely chopped
  40g/1½oz fresh tarragon,
    finely chopped
  300g/11oz mayonnaise
  15–30ml/1–2 tbsp freshly squeezed
    lemon juice
  200g/7oz/scant 1 cup unsalted
    (sweet) butter
  salt and ground black pepper

1 Preheat the oven to 180°C/350°F/ Gas 4. Rinse the salmon and lay it on a large piece of foil. Stuff the fish cavity with the sliced spring onions and layer the lemon slices inside and around the fish, then sprinkle with plenty of salt and ground black pepper.

2 Loosely fold the foil around the fish and fold the edges over to seal. Bake for about 1 hour.

3 Remove the fish from the oven and leave to stand, still wrapped in the foil, for about 15 minutes, then unwrap the parcel and leave the fish to cool.

4 When the fish is cool, carefully lift it on to a large plate, still covered with lemon slices. Cover the fish tightly with clear film (plastic wrap) and chill for several hours.

5 Before serving, discard the lemon slices around the fish. Using a blunt knife to lift up the edge of the skin, carefully peel the skin away from the flesh, avoiding tearing the flesh, and pull out any fins at the same time.

6 Arrange the cucumber slices in overlapping rows along the length of the fish, to resemble large fish scales.

COOK'S TIP
Do not prepare the sauce more than a few hours ahead of serving as the watercress will discolour it.

7 To make the sauce, put the garlic, watercress, tarragon, mayonnaise and lemon juice in a food processor or blender or a bowl, and process or mix to combine.

8 Melt the butter, then add to the watercress mixture, a little at a time, processing or stirring, until the butter has been incorporated and the sauce is thick and smooth. Cover and chill before serving. Serve the fish, garnished with dill, with the sauce and lemon wedges.

VARIATION
Instead of cooking a whole fish, prepare 6–8 salmon steaks. Place each fish steak on an individual square of foil, then top with a slice of onion and a slice of lemon and season generously with salt and ground black pepper. Loosely wrap the foil up around the fish, fold the edges to seal and place the parcels on a baking sheet. Bake as above for 10–15 minutes, or until the flesh is opaque. Serve cold with watercress sauce, garnished with slices of cucumber.

Per portion: Energy 1044Kcal/4323kJ; Protein 51.6g; Carbohydrate 1.4g, of which sugars 1.2g; Fat 92.4g, of which saturates 28.5g; Cholesterol 231mg; Calcium 135mg; Fibre 0.7g; Sodium 558mg.

BRAISED PORK CHOPS WITH ONION AND MUSTARD SAUCE

THE PIQUANT SAUCE ADDS PUNCH AND EXTRA FLAVOUR TO THIS SIMPLE SUPPER DISH. SERVE IT WITH CELERIAC AND POTATO MASH AND A GREEN VEGETABLE, SUCH AS BROCCOLI OR CABBAGE.

SERVES FOUR

INGREDIENTS

4 pork loin chops, at least
  2cm/¾in thick
30ml/2 tbsp plain (all-purpose) flour
45ml/3 tbsp olive oil
2 Spanish (Bermuda) onions, sliced
2 garlic cloves, finely chopped
250ml/8fl oz/1 cup dry (hard) cider
150ml/¼ pint/⅔ cup chicken stock
generous pinch of brown sugar
2 fresh bay leaves
6 fresh thyme sprigs
2 strips lemon rind
120ml/4fl oz/½ cup double
  (heavy) cream
30–45ml/2–3 tbsp wholegrain
  mustard
30ml/2 tbsp chopped fresh parsley
salt and ground black pepper

1 Preheat the oven to 200°C/400°F/ Gas 6. Trim the chops of excess fat. Season the flour with salt and pepper and use to coat the chops. Heat 30ml/ 2 tbsp of the oil in a frying pan and brown the chops on both sides, then transfer them to an ovenproof dish.

2 Add the remaining oil to the pan and cook the onions over a fairly gentle heat until they soften and begin to brown at the edges. Add the garlic and cook for 2 minutes more.

3 Stir in any leftover flour, then gradually stir in the cider and stock. Season well with salt and pepper and add the brown sugar, bay leaves, thyme sprigs and lemon rind. Bring the sauce to the boil, stirring constantly, then pour over the chops.

4 Cover and cook in the oven for 20 minutes. Reduce the heat to 180°C/ 350°F/Gas 4 and continue cooking for another 30–40 minutes. Remove the foil for the last 10 minutes of the cooking time. Remove the chops from the dish and keep warm, covered with foil.

5 Tip the remaining contents of the dish into a pan or, if the dish is flameproof, place it over a direct heat. Discard the herbs and lemon rind, then bring to the boil.

6 Add the cream and continue to boil, stirring constantly. Taste for seasoning, adding a pinch more sugar if necessary. Finally, stir in the mustard to taste and pour the sauce over the braised chops. Sprinkle with the chopped parsley and serve immediately.

VARIATIONS
• For a less rich sauce, omit the cream and purée the sauce in a blender. Reheat, thinning with a little extra stock if necessary, then adjust the seasoning and add mustard to taste. This will produce a sharper tasting sauce that will need less mustard.
• If you prefer, you can use vegetable or pork stock instead of chicken.
• This recipe also works extremely well with veal chops.

Per portion: Energy 694Kcal/2881kJ; Protein 32g; Carbohydrate 19.8g, of which sugars 9.3g; Fat 53g, of which saturates 21.6g; Cholesterol 131mg; Calcium 80mg; Fibre 2.1g; Sodium 207mg.

PORK ESCALOPES BAKED WITH APPLE AND POTATO RÖSTI

THE JUICES FROM THE PORK COOK INTO THE APPLES AND POTATOES GIVING THEM A WONDERFUL FLAVOUR AS WELL AS MAKING A DELICIOUS SAUCE.

SERVES FOUR

INGREDIENTS

2 large potatoes, finely grated
1 medium cooking apple, grated
2 garlic cloves, crushed
1 egg, beaten
butter, for greasing
15ml/1 tbsp olive oil
4 large prosciutto slices
4 pork escalopes (US scallops), about 175g/6oz each
4 sage leaves
1 medium cooking apple, cut into thin wedges
25g/1oz/2 tbsp butter, diced
salt and ground black pepper
caramelized apple wedges, to serve

COOK'S TIPS
• Do not be tempted to overcook the pork as it will start to dry out.
• If you can't find cooking apples, use an all-purpose eating variety, such as Granny Smith.

1 Preheat the oven to 200°C/400°F/ Gas 6. Squeeze out all the excess liquid from the grated potatoes and apple. Mix the grated ingredients together with the garlic, egg and seasoning.

2 Divide the potatoes into four portions and spoon each quarter on to a baking sheet that has been lined with foil and greased. Form a round with the potatoes and flatten out slightly with the back of a spoon. Drizzle with a little olive oil. Cook for 10 minutes.

3 Meanwhile, lay the prosciutto on a clean surface and place a pork escalope on top. Lay a sage leaf and apple wedges over each escalope and top each piece with the butter. Wrap the prosciutto around each piece of meat, making sure it is covered completely.

4 Remove the potatoes from the oven, place each pork parcel on top and return to the oven for 20 minutes. Carefully lift the pork and potatoes off the foil and serve with caramelized wedges of apple and any cooking juices on the side.

Per portion: Energy 396Kcal/1659kJ; Protein 42.7g; Carbohydrate 19.2g, of which sugars 4.4g; Fat 16.9g, of which saturates 6.7g; Cholesterol 177mg; Calcium 29mg; Fibre 1.5g; Sodium 310mg.

MOUSSAKA

THIS IS A TRADITIONAL EASTERN MEDITERRANEAN DISH, POPULAR IN BOTH GREECE AND TURKEY.
LAYERS OF MINCED LAMB, AUBERGINES, TOMATOES AND ONIONS ARE TOPPED WITH A CREAMY YOGURT
AND CHEESE SAUCE IN THIS DELICIOUS, AUTHENTIC RECIPE.

SERVES FOUR

INGREDIENTS
  450g/1lb aubergines (eggplant)
  150ml/¼ pint/⅔ cup olive oil
  1 large onion, chopped
  2–3 garlic cloves, finely chopped
  675g/1½lb lean minced (ground) lamb
  15ml/1 tbsp plain (all-purpose) flour
  400g/14oz can chopped tomatoes
  30ml/2 tbsp chopped fresh herbs
  450g/1lb fresh tomatoes, sliced
  salt and ground black pepper
For the topping
  300ml/½ pint/1¼ cups yogurt
  2 eggs
  25g/1oz feta cheese, crumbled
  25g/1oz/⅓ cup freshly grated
    Parmesan cheese

1 Cut the aubergines into thin slices and layer them in a colander, sprinkling each layer with salt.

2 Cover the aubergines with a plate and a weight, then leave for about 30 minutes. Pat dry with kitchen paper.

3 Heat 45ml/3 tbsp of the oil in a large, heavy pan. Cook the onion and garlic until softened, but not coloured. Add the lamb and cook over a high heat, stirring frequently, until browned.

4 Stir in the flour until mixed, then stir in the canned tomatoes, herbs and seasoning. Bring to the boil, reduce the heat and simmer gently for 20 minutes.

5 Meanwhile, heat a little of the remaining oil in a large frying pan. Add as many aubergine slices as can be laid in the pan in a single layer, then cook until golden on both sides. Set the cooked aubergines aside. Heat more oil and continue cooking the aubergines, in batches, adding oil as necessary.

COOK'S TIP
Salting and drying the aubergines before cooking reduces the amount of fat that they absorb and helps them to brown more quickly.

6 Preheat the oven to 180°C/350°F/ Gas 4. Arrange half the aubergine slices in a large, shallow ovenproof dish, then add a layer of half the fresh tomatoes.

7 Top the slices with about half of the meat and tomato sauce mixture, then add a layer of the remaining aubergine slices, followed by the remaining tomato slices. Spread the remaining meat mixture over the aubergines and tomatoes.

8 Beat together the yogurt and eggs, then mix in the feta and Parmesan cheeses. Pour the mixture over the meat and spread it evenly.

9 Transfer the moussaka to the oven and bake for 35–40 minutes, or until golden and bubbling.

VARIATION
Use large courgettes (zucchini) instead of aubergines (eggplant), if you like. Cut them diagonally into fairly thick slices.

Per portion: Energy 753Kcal/3132kJ; Protein 46.2g; Carbohydrate 19.4g, of which sugars 17.6g; Fat 55.3g, of which saturates 17.6g; Cholesterol 237mg; Calcium 329mg; Fibre 4.9g; Sodium 425mg.

COUNTRY MEAT LOAF

THREE DIFFERENT KINDS OF MEAT ARE COMBINED WITH HERBS AND OTHER FLAVOURINGS TO MAKE THIS HEARTY AND APPETIZING TRADITIONAL MEAT LOAF.

SERVES SIX

INGREDIENTS

30ml/2 tbsp butter or margarine
115g/4oz/½ cup chopped onion
2 garlic cloves, crushed
50g/2oz/½ cup chopped celery
450g/1lb lean minced (ground) beef
225g/½lb minced (ground) veal
225g/½lb lean minced (ground) pork
2 eggs
50g/2oz/1 cup fine fresh
  bread crumbs
15g/½oz/½ cup chopped
  fresh parsley
30ml/2 tbsp chopped fresh basil
2.5ml/½ tsp fresh or dried
  thyme leaves
2.5ml/½ tsp salt
2.5ml/½ tsp pepper
30ml/2 tbsp Worcestershire sauce
60ml/4 tbsp chilli sauce or
  tomato ketchup
6 bacon rashers (strips)

1 Preheat the oven to 180°C/350°F/ Gas 4. Melt the butter or margarine in a small frying pan over a low heat. Add the onion, garlic and celery and cook, stirring occasionally, for 8–10 minutes, until softened. Remove from the heat and leave to cool slightly.

COOK'S TIP
To test if the meat loaf is cooked through, insert a skewer. If the juices run clear and skewer comes out fairly clean, then it is ready.

2 In a large mixing bowl combine the onion, garlic and celery with all the other ingredients except the bacon. Mix together lightly, using a fork or your fingers. Do not overwork or the meat loaf will be too compact.

3 Form the meat mixture into an oval loaf. Carefully transfer it to a shallow baking tin (pan).

4 Lay the bacon across the top of the meat loaf. Bake for 1¼ hours, basting occasionally with the juices and bacon fat in the tin.

5 Remove from the oven and drain off the fat. Leave the meat loaf to stand for 10 minutes before serving.

Per portion: Energy 285Kcal/1188kJ; Protein 18.6g; Carbohydrate 11.9g, of which sugars 5.1g; Fat 18.4g, of which saturates 8.3g; Cholesterol 119mg; Calcium 62mg; Fibre 1g; Sodium 572mg.

TAMALE PIE

THIS IS A TEXAN VERSION OF A TRADITIONAL MEXICAN RECIPE, ALTHOUGH SO MANY VARIATIONS EXIST THAT BOTH SIDES OF THE BORDER CAN CLAIM THE ORIGINAL.

SERVES EIGHT

INGREDIENTS
    115g/4oz bacon, chopped
    1 onion, finely chopped
    450g/1lb lean minced (ground) beef
    10–15ml/2–3 tsp chilli powder
    5ml/1 tsp salt
    400g/14oz can tomatoes
    40g/1½oz/⅓ cup chopped
      black olives
    175g/6oz/1 cup corn kernels, freshly
      cooked or thawed frozen
    120ml/4fl oz/½ cup sour cream
    115g/4oz/1 cup grated Cheddar or
      Monterey Jack cheese
For the tamale topping
    250–300ml/8–10fl oz/1–1¼ cups
      chicken stock
    175g/6oz/1½ cups masa harina
      or cornmeal
    90ml/6 tbsp margarine or
      vegetable shortening
    2.5ml/½ tsp baking powder
    50ml/2fl oz/¼ cup milk
    salt and ground black pepper

1 Preheat the oven to 190°C/375°F/ Gas 5. Cook the bacon in a large, heavy frying pan for 2–3 minutes, until the fat runs. Pour off any excess fat, leaving 15–30ml/1–2 tbsp. Add the onion and cook, over a medium heat, stirring occasionally, for about 5 minutes, until just softened.

2 Add the beef, chilli powder and salt and cook for 5 minutes, stirring to break up the meat. Stir in the tomatoes and cook for 5 minutes more, breaking them up with a spoon.

3 Add the olives, corn, and sour cream, and mix well. Transfer to a 38cm/15in long rectangular or oval ovenproof dish. Set aside.

4 To make the topping, bring the chicken stock to the boil in a pan over a medium heat and season it with salt and pepper if necessary.

5 In a food processor, combine the masa harina or cornmeal, margarine or shortening, baking powder and milk. Process until combined. With the machine still running, gradually pour in the hot stock until a smooth, thick batter is formed. If the batter is too thick to spread, add additional hot stock or water, a little at a time.

6 Pour the batter over the top of the beef mixture, spreading it evenly with a metal spatula.

7 Bake for about 20 minutes, until the top is just browned. Sprinkle the surface evenly with the grated cheese and continue baking for a further 10–15 minutes, until the cheese has melted. Serve immediately.

Per portion: Energy 492Kcal/2044kJ; Protein 23.3g; Carbohydrate 26.6g, of which sugars 6.1g; Fat 32.1g, of which saturates 17.4g; Cholesterol 96mg; Calcium 206mg; Fibre 1.6g; Sodium 827mg.

PIZZAS, TARTS AND PIES

Although pizzas are now commonplace, filling supermarket freezers and fast becoming the world's favourite takeaway food, the home-made variety is almost always superior. Making your own dough enables you to tailor the toppings to the tastes of your guests. We've supplied recipes for basics like Fiorentina Pizza and Hot Pepperoni Pizza, but you can add extra ingredients or invite diners to invent their own combinations. This chapter also includes delectable pastries like Cheese and Onion Flan, Filo-wrapped Fish and Rich Game Pie.

SUN-DRIED TOMATO CALZONE

CALZONE IS A TRADITIONAL FOLDED PIZZA. IN THIS TASTY VEGETARIAN VERSION, YOU CAN ADD MORE OR FEWER RED CHILLI FLAKES, DEPENDING ON PERSONAL TASTE.

SERVES TWO

INGREDIENTS
    4 baby aubergines (eggplant)
    3 shallots, chopped
    45ml/3 tbsp olive oil
    1 garlic clove, chopped
    50g/2oz/⅓ cup sun-dried tomatoes
       in oil, drained
    1.5ml/¼ tsp dried red chilli flakes,
       if using
    10ml/2 tsp chopped fresh thyme
    75g/3oz mozzarella cheese, cubed
    salt and ground black pepper
    15–30ml/1–2 tbsp freshly grated
       Parmesan cheese, plus extra to serve
For the dough
    225g/8oz/2 cups strong white
       bread flour
    5ml/1 tsp salt
    2.5ml/½ tsp easy-blend (rapid-rise)
       dried yeast
    15ml/1 tbsp olive oil
    150ml/¼ pint/⅔ cup warm water

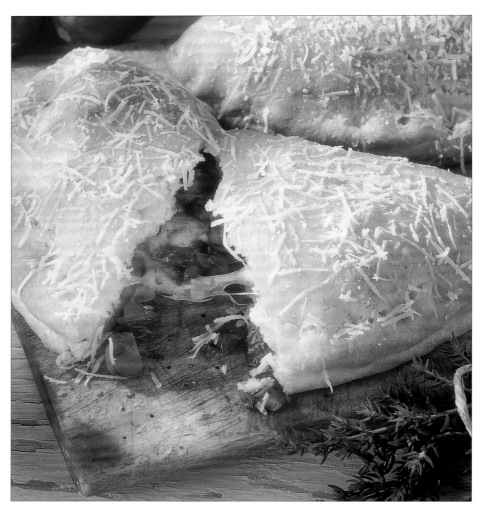

1 Make the dough. Place the dry ingredients in a bowl and mix to form a soft dough with the oil and water. Knead for 10 minutes. Put in an oiled bowl, cover and leave in a warm place until doubled in size.

2 Preheat the oven to 220°C/425°F/ Gas 7. Dice the aubergines. Cook the shallots in a little oil until soft. Add the aubergines, garlic, sun-dried tomatoes, chilli, if using, thyme and seasoning. Cook for 5 minutes. Divide the dough in half and roll out each piece on a lightly floured work surface to an 18cm/7in round.

3 Spread the aubergine mixture over half of each round, leaving a 2.5cm/1in border, then sprinkle on the mozzarella. Dampen the edges with water, then fold over the dough to enclose the filling. Press the edges firmly together to seal. Place on greased baking sheets.

4 Brush with half the remaining oil and make a small hole in the top of each calzone to allow steam to escape. Bake for 15–20 minutes, until golden. Remove from the oven and brush with the remaining oil. Sprinkle over the Parmesan and serve immediately.

Per portion: Energy 777Kcal/3259kJ; Protein 25.3g; Carbohydrate 92.2g, of which sugars 6.2g; Fat 36.7g, of which saturates 11.8g; Cholesterol 37mg; Calcium 494mg; Fibre 7g; Sodium 323mg.

CLASSIC MARINARA PIZZA

THE COMBINATION OF SIMPLE INGREDIENTS, FRESH GARLIC, GOOD QUALITY OLIVE OIL AND A TASTY TOMATO SAUCE GIVES THIS PIZZA AN UNMISTAKABLY ITALIAN FLAVOUR. ALTHOUGH PLAIN IN LOOKS, THE TASTE OF THE MARINARA IS UTTERLY DELICIOUS.

SERVES TWO

INGREDIENTS
  60ml/4 tbsp extra virgin olive oil or
    sunflower oil
  675g/1½lb plum tomatoes, peeled,
    seeded and chopped
  4 garlic cloves, cut into slivers
  15ml/1 tbsp chopped
    fresh oregano
  salt and ground black pepper
For the pizza base
  225g/8oz/2 cups plain (all-purpose)
    white flour
  pinch of salt
  10ml/2 tsp baking powder
  50g/2oz/4 tbsp margarine
  about 150ml/¼ pint/⅔ cup milk

1 Preheat the oven to 220°C/425°F/ Gas 7. Use non-stick baking parchment to line a baking sheet. Sift the flour, salt and baking powder in a bowl and rub the margarine lightly into the flour until it resembles breadcrumbs.

2 Pour in enough milk to form a soft dough and knead. Roll the dough out to a round about 25cm/10in in diameter.

3 Place the dough on the prepared baking sheet and make the edges slightly thicker than the centre.

4 Heat 30ml/2 tbsp of the oil in a pan. Add the seeded and chopped plum tomatoes and cook, stirring frequently for about 5 minutes, until soft.

5 Place the tomatoes in a sieve over a bowl and leave to drain for about 5 minutes.

6 Empty the juice from the bowl and force the tomatoes through the sieve into the bowl with the back of a spoon. You may also use a food processor or blender and process until smooth.

7 Brush the pizza base with half the remaining oil. Spoon over the tomatoes and sprinkle with garlic and oregano. Drizzle over the remaining oil and season with salt and pepper.

8 Bake for 15–20 minutes, until the pizza is crisp and golden. Serve immediately, while piping hot.

Per portion: Energy 858Kcal/3597kJ; Protein 15.6g; Carbohydrate 101.7g, of which sugars 16g; Fat 46.2g, of which saturates 4.5g; Cholesterol 4mg; Calcium 272mg; Fibre 6.9g; Sodium 266mg.

FIORENTINA PIZZA

AN EGG ADDS THE FINISHING TOUCH TO THIS SPINACH PIZZA; TRY NOT TO OVERCOOK IT THOUGH, AS IT'S BEST WHEN THE YOLK IS STILL SLIGHTLY SOFT IN THE MIDDLE.

SERVES TWO TO THREE

INGREDIENTS
  45ml/3 tbsp olive oil
  1 small red onion, thinly sliced
  175g/6oz fresh spinach,
   stalks removed
  1 pizza base, about
   25–30cm/10–12in diameter
  1 small jar pizza sauce
  freshly grated nutmeg
  150g/5oz mozzarella cheese
  1 egg
  25g/1oz/¼ cup grated Gruyère cheese

1 Heat 15ml/1 tbsp of the oil and cook the onion until soft. Add the spinach and cook until wilted. Drain any liquid.

2 Preheat the oven to 220°C/425°F/ Gas 7. Brush the pizza base with half the remaining olive oil. Spread the pizza sauce evenly over the base, using the back of a spoon, then top with the spinach mixture. Sprinkle over a little freshly grated nutmeg.

3 Thinly slice the mozzarella and arrange over the spinach. Drizzle over the remaining oil. Bake for 10 minutes, then remove from the oven.

4 Make a small well in the centre of the pizza topping and carefully break the egg into the hole.

5 Sprinkle over the grated Gruyère cheese and return to the oven for a further 5–10 minutes, until crisp and golden. Serve immediately.

VARIATION
Italians make a folded pizza called calzone. It is made in the same way as a pizza but is folded in half to conceal the filling. Add the egg with the rest of the pizza topping, fold over the dough, seal the edges and bake for 20 minutes.

Per portion: Energy 808Kcal/3377kJ; Protein 33.1g; Carbohydrate 72g, of which sugars 10.3g; Fat 44.8g, of which saturates 16.3g; Cholesterol 151mg; Calcium 640mg; Fibre 5.3g; Sodium 911mg.

PEPPERY TOMATO PIZZA

PUNGENT ROCKET AND AROMATIC FRESH BASIL ADD COLOUR AND FLAVOUR TO THIS CRISP PIZZA,
A PERFECT ADDITION TO ANY PICNIC, BUFFET OR OUTDOOR MEAL.

SERVES TWO

INGREDIENTS
  10ml/2 tsp olive oil
  1 garlic clove, crushed
  150g/5oz can chopped tomatoes
  2.5ml/½ tsp caster (superfine) sugar
  30ml/2 tbsp torn fresh basil leaves
  2 tomatoes, seeded and chopped
  150g/5oz mozzarella cheese, sliced
  20g/¾oz rocket (arugula) leaves
For the pizza base
  225g/8oz/2 cups strong white
    bread flour
  5ml/1 tsp salt
  2.5ml/½ tsp easy-blend (rapid-rise)
    dried yeast
  30ml/2 tbsp olive oil

1 To make the pizza base, place the dry ingredients in a bowl. Add the oil and 150ml/¼ pint/⅔ cup warm water. Mix to form a soft dough.

2 Turn out the dough and knead until it is smooth and elastic. Place in an oiled bowl and cover. Leave in a warm place for 45 minutes, or until doubled in bulk.

3 Preheat the oven to 220°C/425°F/ Gas 7. Make the topping. Heat the oil in a frying pan and cook the garlic for 1 minute. Add the canned tomatoes and sugar and cook for 10 minutes.

4 Knead the risen dough lightly, then roll out to form a rough 30cm/12in round. Place on a lightly oiled baking sheet and push up the edges of the dough to form a shallow, even rim.

5 Season the tomato mixture and stir in the basil. Spoon it over the pizza base, then top with the chopped fresh tomatoes. Arrange the mozzarella slices on top of the tomato mixture. Season with sea salt and pepper and drizzle with a little olive oil.

6 Bake for 10–12 minutes, until crisp and golden. Scatter the rocket leaves over the pizza just before serving.

Per portion: Energy 735Kcal/3087kJ; Protein 26.1g; Carbohydrate 93g, of which sugars 7.3g; Fat 31.3g, of which saturates 12.7g; Cholesterol 44mg; Calcium 459mg; Fibre 5.5g; Sodium 330mg.

PISSALADIÈRE

THIS FAMOUS ONION AND ANCHOVY DISH IS A TRADITIONAL MARKET FOOD OF NICE IN SOUTHERN FRANCE. IT CAN BE MADE USING EITHER SHORTCRUST PASTRY OR, AS HERE, YEASTED DOUGH, SIMILAR TO A PIZZA BASE. EITHER WAY, IT IS MOST DELICIOUS EATEN LUKEWARM RATHER THAN PIPING HOT.

SERVES SIX

INGREDIENTS
    250g/9oz/2¼ cups strong white bread
        flour, plus extra for dusting
    50g/2oz/⅓ cup fine polenta
        or semolina
    5ml/1 tsp salt
    175ml/6fl oz/¾ cup lukewarm water
    5ml/1 tsp dried yeast
    5ml/1 tsp caster (superfine) sugar
    30ml/2 tbsp extra virgin olive oil
For the topping
    60–75ml/4–5 tbsp extra virgin
        olive oil
    6 large sweet Spanish (Bermuda)
        onions, thinly sliced
    2 large garlic cloves, thinly sliced
    5ml/1 tsp chopped fresh thyme, plus
        several sprigs
    1 fresh rosemary sprig
    1–2 × 50g/2oz cans anchovies in
        olive oil
    50–75g/2–3oz small black olives,
        preferably small Niçoise olives
    salt and ground black pepper

1 Mix the flour, polenta or semolina and salt in a large mixing bowl. Pour half the water into a bowl. Add the yeast and sugar, then leave in a warm place for 10 minutes, until frothy. Pour the yeast mixture into the flour mixture with the remaining water and the olive oil.

2 Using your hands, mix all the ingredients together to form a dough, then turn out and knead for 5 minutes, until smooth, springy and elastic.

3 Return the dough to the clean, floured bowl and place it in a plastic bag or cover with oiled clear film (plastic wrap), then set the dough aside at room temperature for 30–60 minutes to rise and double in bulk.

4 Meanwhile, start to prepare the topping. Heat 45ml/3 tbsp of the olive oil in a large, heavy pan and add the sliced onions. Stir well to coat the onions in the oil, then cover the pan and cook over a very low heat, stirring occasionally, for 20-30 minutes. (Use a heat-diffuser mat to keep the heat low, if possible.)

5 Add a little salt to taste and the garlic, chopped thyme and rosemary sprig. Stir well and continue cooking for another 15–25 minutes, or until the onions are soft and deep golden yellow but not browned at all. Uncover the pan for the last 5–10 minutes' cooking if the onions seem very wet. Remove and discard the rosemary. Set the onions aside to cool.

6 Preheat the oven to 220°C/425°F/ Gas 7. Roll out the dough thinly and use to line a large baking sheet, about 30 × 23–25cm/12 × 9–10in. Taste the onions for seasoning before spreading them over the dough.

7 Drain the anchovies, cut them in half lengthways and arrange them in a lattice pattern over the onions. Sprinkle the olives and thyme sprigs over the top of the pissaladière and drizzle with the remaining olive oil. Bake for about 20–25 minutes, or until the dough is browned and cooked. Season with pepper and serve warm, cut into slices.

VARIATIONS
• Shortcrust pastry can be used instead of yeast dough as a base: bake it blind for 10–15 minutes before adding the filling.
• If you enjoy anchovies, try spreading about 60ml/4 tbsp anchovy purée (paste) – *anchoïade* – over the base before adding the onions. Alternatively, spread black olive paste over the base.

Per portion: Energy 431Kcal/1797kJ; Protein 9.9g; Carbohydrate 51.6g, of which sugars 10g; Fat 21.7g, of which saturates 3.1g; Cholesterol 8mg; Calcium 138mg; Fibre 3.8g; Sodium 825mg.

BRESAOLA AND ROCKET PIZZA

ALTHOUGH THE ARMENIANS ORIGINATED THE IDEA OF TOPPING FLATTENED DOUGH WITH SAVOURY INGREDIENTS BEFORE BAKING IT, IT WAS THE ITALIANS — THE NEAPOLITANS IN PARTICULAR — WHO DEVELOPED THE PIZZA IN THE 1830s.

SERVES FOUR

INGREDIENTS
- 150g/5oz packet pizza base mix
- 120ml/4fl oz/½ cup lukewarm water
- 225g/8oz/3¼ cups mixed wild mushrooms
- 25g/1oz/2 tbsp butter
- 2 garlic cloves, coarsely chopped
- 60ml/4 tbsp pesto
- 8 slices bresaola
- 4 tomatoes, sliced
- 75g/3oz/⅓ cup cream cheese
- 25g/1oz rocket (arugula)

1 Preheat the oven to 200°C/400°F/Gas 6. Tip the packet of pizza base mix into a large mixing bowl and pour in enough of the water to mix to a soft, not sticky, dough, following the instructions on the packet.

2 Turn out the dough on to a lightly floured surface and knead for about 5 minutes, or until smooth and elastic. Divide the dough into two equal pieces, knead lightly to form two balls, then pat out the balls of dough into flat rounds with your hands.

3 Roll out each piece of dough on a lightly floured surface to a 23cm/9in round and transfer to baking sheets.

4 Slice the wild mushrooms. Melt the butter in a frying pan and cook the garlic for 2 minutes. Add the mushrooms and cook over a high heat for about 5 minutes, or until the mushrooms have softened but are not overcooked.

5 Spread pesto on the pizza bases, to within 2cm/¾in of the edge of each one. Arrange the bresaola and tomato slices around the rims of the pizzas, then spoon the cooked mushrooms into the middle.

6 Dot the cream cheese on top of the pizzas and bake for 15–18 minutes, or until the bases are crisp and the cheese just melted. Top each pizza with a handful of rocket leaves just before serving. Serve immediately.

COOK'S TIP
If you are in a hurry, buy two ready-made pizza bases instead of the pizza mix and bake for 10 minutes.

Per portion: Energy 448Kcal/1873kJ; Protein 16.6g; Carbohydrate 34.7g, of which sugars 6g; Fat 28g, of which saturates 12.8g; Cholesterol 56mg; Calcium 179mg; Fibre 3.5g; Sodium 213mg.

HOT PEPPERONI PIZZA

THERE IS NOTHING MORE MOUTHWATERING THAN A FRESHLY BAKED PIZZA, ESPECIALLY WHEN THE TOPPING INCLUDES TOMATOES, MOZZARELLA CHEESE, PEPPERONI AND RED CHILLIES.

SERVES FOUR

INGREDIENTS
  225g/8oz/2 cups strong white
    bread flour
  10ml/2 tsp easy-blend (rapid-rise)
    dried yeast
  5ml/1 tsp granulated sugar
  2.5ml/½ tsp salt
  15ml/1 tbsp olive oil
  175ml/6fl oz/¾ cup mixed lukewarm
    milk and water
For the topping
  400g/14oz can chopped
    tomatoes, strained
  2 garlic cloves, crushed
  5ml/1 tsp dried oregano
  225g/8oz mozzarella cheese, grated
  2 dried red chillies, crumbled
  225g/8oz pepperoni, sliced
  30ml/2 tbsp drained capers
  fresh oregano, to garnish

1 Sift the flour, stir in the yeast, sugar and salt and make a well in the centre. Stir the oil into the milk and water, then stir into the flour. Mix to a soft dough.

2 Knead the dough on a lightly floured surface for 10 minutes until it is smooth and elastic. Cover and leave in a warm place for about 30 minutes, or until the dough has doubled in bulk.

3 Preheat the oven to 220°C/425°F/ Gas 7. Turn the dough out on to a lightly floured surface and knead lightly for 1 minute. Divide it in half and roll each piece out to a 25cm/10in round. Place on lightly oiled pizza trays or baking sheets. To make the topping, mix the strained tomatoes, garlic and dried oregano in a bowl.

4 Spread half the tomato mixture over each base, leaving a border around the edge. Set half the mozzarella aside. Divide the rest between the pizzas, sprinkling it over evenly. Bake for 7–10 minutes, until the dough rim on each pizza is pale golden.

5 Sprinkle the crumbled chillies over the pizzas, then arrange the pepperoni slices and capers on top. Sprinkle with the remaining mozzarella. Return the pizzas to the oven and bake for 7–10 minutes more. Sprinkle over the fresh oregano and serve immediately.

Per portion: Energy 631Kcal/2638kJ; Protein 28.8g; Carbohydrate 47.6g, of which sugars 4.7g; Fat 37.5g, of which saturates 16.8g; Cholesterol 80mg; Calcium 317mg; Fibre 2.7g; Sodium 1498mg.

CHEESE AND ONION FLAN

THE USE OF YEAST DOUGHS FOR TARTS AND FLANS IS POPULAR IN VARIOUS REGIONS OF FRANCE. CHOOSE A STRONG CHEESE SUCH AS LIVAROT, MUNSTER OR PORT SALUT IN THIS RECIPE.

SERVES FOUR

INGREDIENTS
    15g/½oz/1 tbsp butter
    1 onion, halved and sliced
    2 eggs
    250ml/8fl oz/1 cup single
      (light) cream
    225g/8oz strong semi-soft
      cheese, sliced
    salt and ground black pepper
    salad leaves, to serve
For the yeast dough
    10ml/2 tsp dried yeast
    120ml/4fl oz/½ cup milk
    5ml/1 tsp sugar
    1 egg yolk
    225g/8oz/2 cups plain (all-purpose)
      flour, plus extra for kneading
    2.5ml/½ tsp salt
    50g/2oz/4 tbsp butter, softened

1 To make the dough, place the yeast in a bowl. Warm the milk in a small pan until it is at body temperature and stir into the yeast with the sugar. Continue stirring until the yeast has dissolved completely. Leave the yeast mixture to stand for about 3 minutes, then beat in the egg yolk.

COOK'S TIP
If you prefer to use easy-blend (rapid-rise) yeast, omit step 1. Beat the egg yolk and milk together in a jug (pitcher). Add the dry yeast to the flour and salt in the food processor and pulse to combine. Pour in the egg and milk mixture and proceed with the recipe as normal.

2 Put the flour and salt in a food processor fitted with a metal blade and pulse to combine. With the machine running, slowly pour in the yeast mixture. Scrape down the sides and continue processing for 2–3 minutes. Add the softened butter and process for another 30 seconds.

3 Transfer the dough to a lightly greased bowl. Cover the bowl with a dishtowel and leave to rise in a warm place for about 1 hour, until the dough has doubled in bulk.

4 Remove the dough from the bowl and place on a lightly floured surface. Knock back (punch down) the dough by hitting it with your fist. Sprinkle a little more flour on the work surface and roll out the dough to a 30cm/12in round.

5 Line a 23cm/9in flan tin (quiche pan) with the dough. Gently press it into the tin and trim off any overhanging pieces, leaving a 3mm/⅛in rim around the flan case (pie shell). Cover with a dishtowel, set aside in a warm place and leave the dough to rise again for about 30 minutes, or until puffy.

6 Meanwhile, melt the butter in a heavy pan and add the onion. Cover the pan and cook over a medium-low heat, stirring occasionally, for about 15 minutes, until softened and lightly coloured. Remove the lid and continue cooking, stirring frequently, until the onion is very soft and caramelized.

7 Preheat the oven to 180°C/350°F/ Gas 4. Beat together the eggs and cream. Season and stir in the cooked onion.

8 Arrange the cheese on the base of the flan case. Pour over the egg mixture and bake for 30–35 minutes, until the base is golden and the centre is just set. Cool slightly on a wire rack and serve warm with salad leaves.

Per portion: Energy 747Kcal/3113kJ; Protein 27.1g; Carbohydrate 49.6g, of which sugars 5.9g; Fat 49.2g, of which saturates 29.9g; Cholesterol 271mg; Calcium 619mg; Fibre 2.3g; Sodium 576mg.

TUNA AND EGG GALETTE

THIS FLAKY PASTRY TART COMBINES SOFT-CENTRED EGGS AND A SLIGHTLY PIQUANT FISH FILLING.
IT MAKES A WONDERFUL DISH FOR A SUMMER SUPPER AND IS ALSO A GREAT BUFFET-TABLE STANDBY.

SERVES FOUR

INGREDIENTS
2 sheets of ready-rolled puff pastry
plain (all-purpose) flour, for dusting
beaten egg, to glaze
60ml/4 tbsp olive oil
175g/6oz tuna steak
2 onions, sliced
1 red (bell) pepper, seeded
 and chopped
2 garlic cloves, crushed
45ml/3 tbsp capers, drained
5ml/1 tsp grated lemon rind
30ml/2 tbsp lemon juice
5 eggs
salt and ground black pepper
chopped flat leaf parsley, to garnish

1 Preheat the oven to 190°C/375°F/
Gas 5. Lay a sheet of pastry on a lightly
floured baking sheet and cut to a
28 × 18cm/11 × 7in rectangle. Brush
the whole sheet with beaten egg.

2 Cut the second sheet of pastry to the
same size. Cut out a rectangle from
the centre and discard, leaving a
2.5cm/1in border. Lift the border on to
the first sheet. Brush the border with
beaten egg and prick the base.

3 Bake the pastry case (pie shell) for
about 15 minutes until golden.

COOK'S TIP
If you are using fresh, unfrozen pastry,
the remaining rectangle of pastry can
be wrapped in clear film (plastic wrap)
and frozen. Allow to thaw at room
temperature for 1 hour before using.

4 Heat 30ml/2 tbsp of the oil in a frying
pan and cook the tuna steak for
2–3 minutes on each side, until golden
but still pale pink in the middle. Transfer
to a plate and flake into small pieces.

5 Add the remaining oil to the pan and
cook the onions, red pepper and garlic
for 6–8 minutes, until softened, stirring
occasionally. Remove the pan from the
heat and stir in the tuna, capers and
lemon rind and juice. Season well.

6 Spoon the filling into the pastry case
and level the surface with the back of a
spoon. Break the eggs into the filling
and return the galette to the oven for
about 10 minutes, or until the eggs
have just cooked through. Garnish with
chopped parsley and serve immediately.

COOK'S TIP
To make sure the eggs do not become
hard on top during baking, cover the tart
with lightly oiled foil.

Per portion: Energy 544Kcal/2263kJ; Protein 21.7g; Carbohydrate 27.7g, of which sugars 4.7g; Fat 39.5g, of which saturates 10.1g; Cholesterol 260mg; Calcium 102mg; Fibre 1.9g; Sodium 320mg.

FILO-WRAPPED FISH

THIS DELICIOUS DISH COMES FROM JERUSALEM, WHERE WHOLE FISH ARE WRAPPED IN FILO PASTRY AND SERVED WITH A ZESTY TOMATO SAUCE. THE CHOICE OF FISH CAN BE VARIED ACCORDING TO WHAT IS IN SEASON AND WHAT IS FRESHEST ON THE DAY OF PURCHASE.

SERVES THREE TO FOUR

INGREDIENTS
  450g/1lb salmon or cod steaks
    or fillets
  1 lemon
  30ml/2 tbsp olive oil, plus extra
    for brushing
  1 onion, chopped
  2 celery sticks, chopped
  1 green (bell) pepper, diced
  5 garlic cloves, chopped
  400g/14oz fresh or canned
    tomatoes, chopped
  120ml/4fl oz/½ cup passata
    (bottled strained tomatoes)
  30ml/2 tbsp chopped fresh flat
    leaf parsley
  2–3 pinches of ground allspice or
    ground cloves
  cayenne pepper, to taste
  pinch of sugar
  about 130g/4½ oz filo pastry
    (6–8 large sheets)
  salt and ground black pepper

1 Sprinkle the salmon or cod steaks or fillets with salt and black pepper and a squeeze of lemon juice. Set aside while you prepare the sauce.

2 Heat the olive oil in a pan, add the chopped onion, celery and pepper and cook for about 5 minutes, until the vegetables are softened. Add the garlic and cook for a further 1 minute, then add the tomatoes and passata and cook until the tomatoes have softened and the mixture is of a sauce consistency.

3 Stir the parsley into the sauce, then season with allspice or cloves, cayenne pepper, sugar and salt and pepper.

4 Preheat the oven to 200°C/400°F/Gas 6. Take a sheet of filo pastry, brush with a little olive oil and cover with a second sheet. Place a piece of fish on top of the pastry, towards the bottom edge, then top with 1–2 spoonfuls of the sauce, spreading it evenly.

5 Roll the fish in the pastry, taking care to enclose the filling completely. Arrange on a baking sheet and repeat with the remaining fish and pastry. You should have about half the sauce remaining, to serve with the fish.

6 Bake for 10–15 minutes, or until golden. Meanwhile, reheat the remaining sauce if necessary. Serve immediately with the remaining sauce.

Per portion: Energy 509Kcal/2135kJ; Protein 36.2g; Carbohydrate 37.2g, of which sugars 10.4g; Fat 25.1g, of which saturates 4.2g; Cholesterol 75mg; Calcium 137mg; Fibre 5g; Sodium 192mg.

SALMON IN PUFF PASTRY

THIS IS AN ELEGANT PARTY DISH, MADE WITH RICE, EGGS AND SALMON ENCLOSED IN PUFF PASTRY.

SERVES SIX

INGREDIENTS
    450g/1lb puff pastry, thawed
      if frozen
    1 egg, beaten
    3 hard-boiled eggs
    90ml/6 tbsp single (light) cream
    200g/7oz/1¾ cups cooked long
      grain rice
    30ml/2 tbsp finely chopped
      fresh parsley
    10ml/2 tsp chopped fresh tarragon
    675g/1½lb salmon fillets
    40g/1½oz/3 tbsp butter
    juice of ½ lemon
    salt and ground black pepper

2 In a bowl, mash the hard-boiled eggs with the cream, then stir in the cooked rice. Add the parsley and tarragon and season well. Spoon this mixture on to the prepared pastry.

5 Roll out the remaining pastry and cut out a semi-circular piece to cover the head portion and a tail shape to cover the tail. Brush both pieces of pastry with a little beaten egg and place on top of the fish, pressing down firmly to secure. Score a criss-cross pattern on the tail.

1 Preheat the oven to 190°C/375°F/ Gas 5. Roll out two-thirds of the pastry into a large oval, measuring about 35cm/14in in length. Cut into a curved fish shape and place on a lightly greased baking sheet. Use the trimmings to make narrow strips. Brush one side of each strip with a little beaten egg and secure in place around the rim of the pastry to make a raised edge. Prick the base all over with a fork, then bake for 8–10 minutes until the sides are well risen and the pastry is lightly golden. Leave to cool.

COOK'S TIP
If the pastry seems to be browning too quickly, cover it with foil during cooking and remove from the oven for the last 5 minutes. It is important that the "fish" cooks for the recommended time, so that the salmon is sufficiently cooked through.

3 Cut the salmon into 2cm/¾in chunks. Melt the butter until it starts to sizzle, then add the salmon. Turn the pieces over in the butter so that they begin to colour but do not cook through.

4 Remove from the heat and arrange the salmon pieces on top of the rice, piled in the centre. Stir the lemon juice into the butter in the pan, then spoon the mixture over the salmon pieces.

6 Cut the remaining pastry into small rounds and, starting from the tail end, arrange the rounds in overlapping lines to represent scales. Add an extra one for an eye. Brush the whole fish shape with the remaining beaten egg.

7 Bake for 10 minutes, then reduce the temperature to 160°C/325°F/Gas 3 and cook for a further 15–20 minutes, until the pastry is evenly golden. Slide the fish on to a serving plate and serve.

VARIATION
If time is short you may prefer to use this simplified method. Roll out the pastry into a rectangle, then make pastry edges to contain the filling. Part bake the pastry, add the filling, top with plain, rolled out pastry and return it to the oven.

Per portion: Energy 668Kcal/2782kJ; Protein 31g; Carbohydrate 36.6g, of which sugars 0.7g; Fat 45.3g, of which saturates 14g; Cholesterol 209mg; Calcium 98mg; Fibre 1.1g; Sodium 389mg.

CHICKEN-MUSHROOM PIE

THIS IS A GREAT FAMILY FAVOURITE, ESPECIALLY POPULAR ON A COLD WINTER'S EVENING. IT'S ALSO A GOOD WAY TO USE UP LEFTOVER ROAST CHICKEN.

SERVES SIX

INGREDIENTS

15g/½oz dried porcini mushrooms
50g/2oz/¼ cup butter
30ml/2 tbsp flour
250ml/8fl oz/1 cup simmering
   chicken stock
50ml/2fl oz/¼ cup whipping cream
   or milk
1 onion, coarsely chopped
2 carrots, sliced
2 celery sticks, coarsely chopped
50g/2oz fresh mushrooms, quartered
450g/1lb cooked chicken
   meat, cubed
50g/2oz/½ cup shelled fresh or
   frozen peas
beaten egg, for glazing
salt and ground black pepper
For the pastry
225g/8oz/2 cups plain (all-
   purpose) flour
1.5ml/¼ tsp salt
115g/4oz/½ cup cold butter, cut
   into pieces
75g/3oz/⅓ cup shortening
60–120ml/4–8 tbsp iced water

1 For the pastry, sift the flour and salt into a bowl. With a pastry blender or two knives, cut in the butter and shortening until the mixture resembles coarse breadcrumbs. Sprinkle with 90ml/6 tbsp iced water and mix until the dough holds together. If the dough is too crumbly, add a little more water, 15ml/1 tbsp at a time. Gather the dough into a ball and flatten into a round. Wrap in greaseproof (waxed) paper and chill for at least 30 minutes.

2 Place the dried porcini mushrooms in a small bowl. Add hot water to cover and leave to soak for about 30 minutes until softened. Lift out of the water with a slotted spoon, leaving any grit behind, and drain. Discard the soaking water.

3 Preheat the oven to 190°C/375°F/ Gas 5. Melt 30ml/2 tbsp of the butter in a heavy pan. Stir in the flour and cook, whisking constantly, for about 1 minute, until bubbling. Gradually, add the warm stock and cook over a medium heat, whisking constantly, until the mixture comes to the boil. Cook, still whisking, for 2–3 minutes more. Whisk in the cream or milk and season to taste with salt and pepper. Remove the pan from the heat and set aside.

4 Heat the remaining butter in a large, non-stick frying pan until foaming. Add the onion and carrots and cook over a medium heat, stirring occasionally, for about 5 minutes, until softened. Add the celery and fresh mushrooms and cook, stirring occasionally, for a further 5 minutes. Stir in the cubed chicken meat, fresh or frozen peas, and drained porcini mushrooms.

5 Add the chicken mixture to the cream sauce and stir to mix. Taste for seasoning. Transfer to a 2 litre/4 pint/ 10 cup rectangular ovenproof dish.

6 Roll out the dough on a lightly floured surface to about 3mm/⅛in thickness. Cut out a rectangle about 2.5cm/1in larger all around than the dish. Lay the rectangle of dough over the filling. Make a decorative edge, crimping the dough by pushing the index finger of one hand between the thumb and index finger of the other hand.

7 Cut several vents in the top of the pie to allow steam to escape. Brush the dough with the egg glaze.

8 Press together the dough trimmings, then roll out again. Cut into strips and lay them over the top of the pie. Glaze again. If you like, roll small balls of dough and set them in the "windows" in the lattice.

9 Bake for about 30 minutes, until the top of the pie is browned and the filling is piping hot. Serve the pie hot, straight from the dish.

Per portion: Energy 600Kcal/2501kJ; Protein 23.7g; Carbohydrate 38.8g, of which sugars 3.7g; Fat 40g, of which saturates 21.8g; Cholesterol 132mg; Calcium 92mg; Fibre 2.7g; Sodium 226mg.

RICH GAME PIE

TERRIFIC FOR STYLISH PICNICS OR JUST AS SMART FOR A FORMAL WEDDING BUFFET, THIS PIE LOOKS SPECTACULAR WHEN BAKED IN A FLUTED RAISED PIE MOULD. SOME SPECIALIST KITCHEN STORES HIRE THE MOULDS SO THAT YOU CAN AVOID THE EXPENSE OF PURCHASING THEM; ALTERNATIVELY A 20CM/8IN ROUND SPRINGFORM TIN CAN BE USED.

SERVES TEN

INGREDIENTS
  25g/1oz/2 tbsp butter
  1 onion, finely chopped
  2 garlic cloves, finely chopped
  900g/2lb mixed boneless game
    meat, such as skinless pheasant
    and/or pigeon (US squab) breast,
    venison and rabbit, diced
  30ml/2 tbsp chopped mixed fresh
    herbs such as parsley, thyme
    and marjoram
  salt and ground black pepper
For the pâté
  50g/2oz/¼ cup butter
  2 garlic cloves, finely chopped
  450g/1lb chicken livers, rinsed,
    trimmed and chopped
  60ml/4 tbsp brandy
  5ml/1 tsp ground mace
For the hot water crust pastry
  675g/1½lb/6 cups strong white
    bread flour
  5ml/1 tsp salt
  115ml/3½fl oz/scant ½ cup milk
  115ml/3½fl oz/scant ½ cup water
  115g/4oz/½ cup lard, diced
  115g/4oz/½ cup butter, diced
  beaten egg, to glaze
For the jelly
  300ml/½ pint/1¼ cups game or
    beef consommé
  2.5ml/½ tsp powdered gelatine

1 Melt the butter in a small pan, then add the onion and garlic and cook until softened but not coloured. Remove from the heat and mix with the diced game meat and the chopped mixed herbs. Season well, cover and chill.

2 To make the pâté, melt the butter in a pan until foaming. Add the garlic and chicken livers and cook until the livers are just browned. Remove the pan from the heat and stir in the brandy and mace. Process the mixture in a blender or food processor to a smooth purée, then set aside and leave to cool.

3 To make the pastry, sift the flour and salt into a bowl and make a well in the centre. Place the milk and water in a pan. Add the lard and butter and heat gently until melted, then bring to the boil and remove from the heat as soon as the mixture begins to bubble. Pour the hot liquid into the well in the flour and beat until smooth. Cover and leave until cool enough to handle.

4 Preheat the oven to 200°C/400°F/ Gas 6. Roll out two-thirds of the pastry and use to line a 23cm/9in raised pie mould. Spoon in half the game mixture and press it down evenly. Add the pâté and then top with the remaining game.

5 Roll out the remaining pastry to form a lid. Brush the edge of the pastry lining the mould with a little water and cover the pie with the pastry lid. Trim off excess pastry from around the edge. Pinch the edges together to seal in the filling. Make two holes in the centre of the lid and glaze with egg. Use pastry trimmings to roll out leaves to garnish the pie. Brush with egg.

6 Bake the pie for 20 minutes, then cover it with foil and cook for a further 10 minutes. Reduce the oven temperature to 150°C/300°F/Gas 2. Glaze the pie again with beaten egg and cook for a further 1½hours, keeping the top covered loosely with foil.

7 Remove the pie from the oven and leave it to stand for 15 minutes. Increase the oven temperature to 200°C/400°F/Gas 6. Stand the mould on a baking sheet and remove the sides. Quickly glaze the sides of the pie with beaten egg and cover the top with foil, then cook for a final 15 minutes to brown the sides. Leave to cool completely, then chill the pie overnight.

8 To make the jelly, heat the game or beef consommé in a small pan until just beginning to bubble, whisk in the gelatine until dissolved and leave to cool until just setting. Using a small funnel, carefully pour the jellied consommé into the holes in the pie. Chill until set. This pie will keep in the refrigerator for up to 3 days.

Per portion: Energy 731Kcal/3058kJ; Protein 44g; Carbohydrate 54.3g, of which sugars 2.5g; Fat 32g, of which saturates 17.9g; Cholesterol 223mg; Calcium 163mg; Fibre 2.3g; Sodium 444mg.

STEAK, MUSHROOM AND ALE PIE

THIS ANGLO-IRISH DISH IS A FIRM FAVOURITE ON MENUS AT RESTAURANTS SPECIALIZING IN TRADITIONAL FARE. PIPING HOT, CREAMY MASHED POTATOES OR PARSLEY-DRESSED BOILED POTATOES AND SLIGHTLY CRUNCHY CARROTS AND GREEN BEANS OR CABBAGE ARE PERFECT ACCOMPANIMENTS; FOR A BAR-STYLE MEAL, CHIPS OR BAKED POTATOES AND A SIDE SALAD CAN BE SERVED WITH THE PIE.

SERVES FOUR

INGREDIENTS

25g/1oz/2 tbsp butter
1 large onion, finely chopped
115g/4oz/1½ cups chestnut or button (white) mushrooms, halved
900g/2lb lean beef in one piece, such as braising steak
30ml/2 tbsp plain (all-purpose) flour
45ml/3 tbsp sunflower oil
300ml/½ pint/1¼ cups stout or brown ale
300ml/½ pint/1¼ cups beef stock or consommé
500g/1¼lb puff pastry, thawed if frozen
beaten egg, to glaze
salt and ground black pepper

1 Melt the butter in a large, flameproof casserole, add the onion and cook gently, stirring occasionally, for about 5 minutes, or until it is softened but not coloured. Add the halved mushrooms and continue cooking for a further 5 minutes, stirring occasionally.

2 Meanwhile, trim the meat and cut it into 2.5cm/1in cubes. Season the flour and toss the meat in it.

COOK'S TIP
To make individual pies, divide the filling among four individual pie dishes. Cut the pastry into quarters and cover as above. If the dishes do not have rims, press a narrow strip of pastry around the edge of each dish to seal the lid in place. Cook as above, reducing the cooking time slightly.

3 Use a slotted spoon to remove the onion mixture from the casserole and set aside. Add and heat the oil, then brown the steak, in batches, over a high heat to seal in the juices.

4 Replace the vegetables, then stir in the stout or ale and stock or consommé. Bring to the boil, reduce the heat and simmer for about 1 hour, stirring occasionally, or until the meat is tender. Season to taste and transfer to a 1.5 litre/2½ pint/6¼ cup pie dish. Cover and leave to cool. If possible, chill the meat filling overnight as this allows the flavour to develop. Preheat the oven to 230°C/450°F/Gas 8.

5 Roll out the pastry in the shape of the dish and about 4cm/1½in larger all around. Cut a 2.5cm/1in strip from the edge of the pastry. Brush the rim of the dish with water and press the pastry strip on it. Brush the pastry rim with beaten egg and cover the pie with the pastry lid. Press the lid firmly in place and then trim the excess from around the edge.

6 Use the blunt edge of a knife to tap the outside edge of the pastry, pressing it down with your finger as you seal in the filling. (This technique is known as knocking up.)

7 Pinch the pastry between your fingers to flute the edge. Roll out any remaining pastry trimmings and cut out shapes to garnish the pie, brushing the shapes with a little beaten egg before pressing them lightly in place.

8 Make a hole in the middle of the pie to allow steam to escape, brush the top carefully with beaten egg and chill for 10 minutes to rest the pastry.

9 Bake the pie for 15 minutes, then reduce the oven temperature to 200°C/400°F/Gas 6 and bake for a further 15–20 minutes, or until the pastry is risen and golden.

Per portion: Energy 1061Kcal/4423kJ; Protein 58.8g; Carbohydrate 59.3g, of which sugars 7.6g; Fat 65.3g, of which saturates 24g; Cholesterol 164mg; Calcium 129mg; Fibre 3.2g; Sodium 622mg.

INDEX